Collective Entrepreneurship in the Contemporary European Services Industries

FRONTIERS OF MANAGEMENT HISTORY

Edited by: Dr Kevin D. Tennent, University of York, UK; Dr Alex G. Gillett, University of York, UK

Frontiers of Management History focuses on new and emerging scholarship on management history, presenting innovative methodological approaches to study history, and new or disruptive ways of thinking about and theorizing management and business history. The books within the series combine the craft of the business historian with the methodology of the social scientist, to offer interdisciplinary perspectives on the management history field, alongside theories, frameworks, critiques, and applications for practice. Featuring a wide range of theoretical, empirical, and historiographical contributions concerned with organizations from various sectors, the series creates a new space in which to engage a new generation of historians and social scientists, to contribute to the future direction of business, organizational, and management history.

Previous volumes:

London Transport: A Hybrid in History 1905–1948
By James Fowler

The Red Taylorist: The Life and Times of Walter Nicholas Polakov
By Diana Kelly

The Emergence of Modern Hospital Management and Organisation in the World 1880s–1930s
By Paloma Fernández Pérez

Strategy and Managed Decline: London Transport 1948–87
By James Fowler

Collective Entrepreneurship in the Contemporary European Services Industries: A Long Term Approach

EDITED BY

PALOMA FERNÁNDEZ PÉREZ

Universitat de Barcelona, Spain

AND

ELENA SAN ROMÁN

Universidad Complutense de Madrid, Spain

United Kingdom – North America – Japan – India – Malaysia – China

Emerald Publishing Limited
Howard House, Wagon Lane, Bingley BD16 1WA, UK

First edition 2023

Reprints and permissions service
Contact: permissions@emeraldinsight.com

British Library Cataloguing in Publication Data
A catalogue record for this book is available from the British Library

ISBN: 978-1-80117-951-5 (Print)
ISBN: 978-1-80117-950-8 (Online)
ISBN: 978-1-80117-952-2 (Epub)

Printed and bound by CPI Group (UK) Ltd, Croydon, CR0 4YY

ISOQAR certified
Management System,
awarded to Emerald
for adherence to
Environmental
standard
ISO 14001:2004.

ISOQAR
REGISTERED
Certificate Number 1985
ISO 14001

INVESTOR IN PEOPLE

Contents

List of Tables and Figures

Tables

Figures

About the Authors

Fariza Achcaoucaou is an Associate Professor of International Business and Strategy at the Universitat de Barcelona, where she is also the Director of the MSc in International Business. Her research interests fall at the intersection of international business and innovation, focusing on foreign subsidiaries of multinational corporations. Her scientific publications are particularly related to international innovation networks, subsidiary's R&D role evolution, and HQ-subsidiary relationships.

Lizbeth Arroyo is a Project Manager and a Researcher at the University of Barcelona (UB). Her doctoral research is focused on the influence of the context on entrepreneurship practices. Particularly, in the entrepreneurial identity construction and the legitimacy process. She takes a sociological approach that encompasses the fields of theory of ideology, entrepreneurial identity, and organizational values. She participates in European and regional development projects focused on entrepreneurship and innovation, such as HEI-TRUE Project, GEM or GUESSS projects.

Felix Barahona Márquez holds a PhD in Business, Master of Research in Business, and Bachelor in Economics from the Universitat de Barcelona. Also, he graduated in Business Sciences from the Universitat de Barcelona. He is an Associate Professor and the Coordinator of the Business Logistics degree at EU Mediterrani (Barcelona). Also, he is an Adjunct Professor in Strategic Management at Universitat de Barcelona. His main research interests deal with: multinational firms from emerging economies; cultural adaptation to host countries; analysis of business sectors; cooperative relationships between firms.

Susana Domingo Pérez holds a PhD in Business Administration and Management from the Universitat Politècnica de Catalunya. She graduated in Business Administration from the Universitat de Barcelona. She is the Director of the Department of Business & Management Strategy at UPF Barcelona School of Management, the Director of the Executive and the Full Time MBAs and the Director of the StartLab of this School. She is an Adjunct Professor at Universitat Pompeu Fabra. She promoted and led the Business Shuttle, an entrepreneurship promotion unit at Universitat Pompeu Fabra (2011–2021).

Pierre-Yves Donzé is a Professor of Business History at Osaka University (Japan) and a Visiting Professor at the University of Fribourg (Switzerland) and EM Normandie Business School (France). He is a Member of the Council of the European Business History Association and a Co-editor of Business History. His research focuses on the history of the dynamics of global competition in a broad range of industries, from luxury goods and fashion to healthcare and food. He has published numerous articles in international journals of business history, international business, and history.

Paloma Fernández Pérez, Ph.D., in History by the University of California at Berkeley. Professor of Economic and Business History at the Universitat de Barcelona in Spain. She is an expert in the history of entrepreneurship and innovation of families in business in past and present times. Past council member of the EBHA Council, the Spanish Association of Economic Historians and the *Business History Conference*. Past coeditor of the journal *Business History*. Founder and coeditor in chief of the *Journal of Evolutionary Studies in Business*. She received twice the ICREA Academia Award for excellence in research in Humanities.

Águeda Gil-López is an Assistant Professor of Economic History at Complutense University of Madrid (Spain). In 2018, she was awarded with the Complutense Extraordinary PhD Prize of Economics. Her research interests include business history, tourism, entrepreneurship, and family business. Her most recent publications include the articles 'Bricolage and Innovation in the Emergence and Development of the Spanish Tourism Industry', in *Enterprise & Society* (2022); and 'Driving Through Change at Speed. Opportunity Conditions and Entrepreneurial Responses in the History of the Express Industry', in *Revista de Historia Industrial* (2021).

Alex G. Gillett is a Senior Lecturer (Associate Professor) at the School for Business & Society, University of York, United Kingdom. Much of his work has focused on organizational networks, relationships and interaction across sectors. Alex has a keen interest in management history and is a Founding Committee Member of the Management and Business History Special Interest Group of the British Academy of Management.

Jorge Hernández-Barahona is a Graduate Teaching Assistant at the Complutense University of Madrid (Spain), where he is a PhD candidate. He holds a Master's Degree in Economics. He was awarded the Extraordinary Prize of the Degree in Economics (2016–2020) and the UCM Excellence Prize in the Branch of Social and Legal Sciences. His research interests include economic history, business history, and entrepreneurship.

Sarah L. Jack is the Jacob and Marcus Wallenberg Professor of Innovative and Sustainable Business Development at the Stockholm School of Economics (SSE),

Sweden. She is also Professor of Entrepreneurship at Lancaster University Management School (LUMS), UK. She is primarily interested in extending understanding about the relationship between entrepreneurship and the social context using social network theory and social capital theory and qualitative methods.

Teresa Mateo is a Graduate Teaching Assistant at the Complutense University of Madrid (Spain), where she is a PhD candidate. She studied Law and Business Administration at the Universidad Carlos III de Madrid (Spain). During 2013, she was a Research Assistant at IESE Business School (Madrid). Her research interests include business history, entrepreneurship, and family business.

Paloma Miravitlles is an Associate Professor in International Business and Strategy at the Department of Business, University of Barcelona. She is currently the responsible of the Business Section in the Department and has participated in several competitive research projects and published several academic articles on the presence of foreign multinationals in Spain. Her research interests are framed on strategic roles of subsidiaries, location factors to attract foreign direct investment and internationalization of innovation.

Elena San Román is a Professor of History at the Complutense University of Madrid (Spain) and an Associate Member of the Royal Academy of History (Spain). Her research interests are focused on business history, tourism, entrepreneurship, and family business. Her latest publications include the articles 'Contextualizing Corporate Entrepreneurship Theory: The Historical Case of the Spanish Engineering Consulting Firm TYPSA (1966–2000)', in *Management & Organizational History* (2021); 'German Capital and the Development of the Spanish Hotel Industry (1950s–1990s): A Tale of Two Strategic Alliances' in *Business History* (2020).

Ernest Solé Udina holds a PhD in Business from the Universitat de Barcelona, Master of Research in Business, Finance and Insurance, and Bachelor in Business Administration. He is a Senior Lecturer in the Operations and Technology Area at UPF Barcelona School of Management. He is an Adjunct Professor in Operations Management at Universitat Pompeu Fabra. His area of research is the financing of high-tech companies, with the presence of a high degree of information asymmetry. His specialties at UPF Barcelona School of Management are: the elaboration of teaching materials for in-company courses (Finance-Banking) and related tutoring activities, and the teaching in Finance, Operations and Supply Chain.

Tim Laurin Spieth is a Graduate of the University of Barcelona in MSc in International Business. He is currently working in the purchasing department of a German multinational corporation. He combines his professional expertise with academic interest in topics related to the strategic behaviour of multinational corporations, pricing and purchasing strategies, and the differences between the manufacturing and the service sector.

Espen Storli is a Professor of History at the Department of Modern History and Society, NTNU Norwegian University of Science and Technology. He has published widely on topics such as international cartels, multinational companies and on international trade in natural resources. His most recent book (co-edited with Andreas Sanders and Pål Thonstad Sandvik) is *The Political Economy of Resource Regulation: An International and Comparative History*, 1850–2015, published by University of British Columbia Press (2019).

Kevin D. Tennent is a Reader in Management at the School for Business and Society, University of York, UK. His research focuses around the development of strategy, purpose, and governance in public and private organisations, especially the interaction of stakeholders within the organization of large sporting events, the hybridization of the transport industry and the development of historic consciousness in management students.

Jaume Valls-Pasola is a Professor of Management at the University of Barcelona (Business Department). Within UB he has been appointed for different positions: Director of the Business Department, Coordinator of the Business PhD program and responsible of the UB 'Business and Management Research Group'. His research interests are in the fields of innovation management, creativity, and entrepreneurship. Since November 2021, he is the Director of the Catalan University Quality Assurance Agency, Agència de Qualitat Universitària de Catalunya (AQU) Catalunya.

Javier Vidal Olivares, PhD Universidad de Valencia, Full Professor of Economic and Business History at Universidad de Alicante, Spain. He has been visiting professor at Institute of Historical Research, University of London; European University Institute at Florence and he has also been Visiting Professor in some Latin American Universities, including Buenos Aires, Los Andes (Bogotá) and Universidad Nacional Autónoma de México. He has published widely about economic and business history in Spain, Europe and Latin America, especially in transport history, entrepreneurship, and family firms.

Ricardo Zózimo is an Assistant Professor in Entrepreneurship at Nova School of Business and Economics. Prior to joining Nova SBE, he was an Assistant Professor at Lancaster University Management School (United Kingdom) where he obtained his PhD focusing on the processes of entrepreneurial learning. His research interests lie on understanding further the processes of entrepreneurial learning within their social, historical, and cultural contexts.

Preface

Collective Entrepreneurship and Services Industries in the Long Term
Paloma Fernández Pérez and Elena San Román

1. Service Industries

Over the last decades, the EU has become a 'service economy' as far as service sectors have developed faster than manufacturing. This means that the performance of the EU economy will largely rest on the performance of the service sector. As the EUROSTAT highlighted, in 2020 services accounted for 73% of the EU's total gross value added, followed by industry and construction (25%) and agriculture (2%). In terms of employment, services represent an equal share of about 70% of total employment.[1]

Service industry is an old and broad concept that includes a myriad of sectors. During the last decades, this industry has evolved including new activities, such as those called business services, consisting of a range of professional and support services to settled companies. These emerging activities coexist along with and complement other more traditional services, with a long historical trajectory that makes them especially suitable to be analyzed from an economic and business long-term perspective.

This book focuses on five of the traditional activities within the services industries: tourism, healthcare, trading, transport, and the sports industries. All these sectors constitute a heterogeneous set of activities that draws on very different scientific and organizational complexity. Yet, they all share some relevant tendencies which justify the interest and convenience of embracing an aggregate and comparative study from a business history perspective.

First, until the COVID-19 pandemic, the five activities had experienced a fast growth for decades and had constituted some of the most dynamic sub-sectors in the world economy. These are also sectors largely impacted by the pandemic although in a different direction. Health services have become one of the most important economic sectors, both to cope with the increase in the number of sick people and the need to find a vaccine for the virus. Trade and transport,

---

[1] https://ec.europa.eu/eurostat (access 11/20/2022).

which draw on sophisticated networks that connect business and people globally, witnessed strong growth due to the new consumer and business needs associated with the global lockdown and the reduction of people's mobility. On the contrary, the lockdown triggered the biggest tourism crisis in the sector's history and also slowed down the development of sport and leisure businesses.

Second, the five sectors are highly labour-intensive and therefore fundamental for the employment of millions of people. This is particularly relevant considering the weakness and difficulties experienced by the Western labour markets in the last years and especially to build back the economy after the pandemic.

Third, they are activities with a long history, with origins dating back to the late nineteenth and first half of the twentieth centuries. Over the last decades, these activities have innovated and renewed themselves to meet the challenges that novel consumption patterns, and changes in the welfare state, in different expansive and recessive economic situations, have raised.

In this book, the chapters aim to provide a historical account, nurtured by existent theories of entrepreneurship, on how companies in the tourism, healthcare, trade, sports and transport activities have grown, innovated and become international along the course of the twentieth century. The book helps identify the set of intra- and extra-organizational drivers that have explained their past growth and might also support their future competitiveness and expansion. All the chapters specifically build on understanding entrepreneurship as the result of actions undertaken by groups of individuals connected by formal and/or informal ties, the so called collective entrepreneurship approach.

2. Entrepreneurship as a Social, Collective Process

Entrepreneurship research, once mainly focused on the individual actor, is increasingly interested in the influences of socially embedded ties, entrepreneurial groups, and collective entrepreneurial action (Aldrich, 2005; Ruef, Aldrich, & Carter, 2003; Steyaert & Katz, 2004; Swedberg, 2000). Hence, instead of focusing on the cognitive and creative capabilities of single individuals, or examining just the process of creating new ventures, which were main concerns in previous research, the academic attention has shifted towards the interactions among a group of individuals engaged in an entrepreneurial project. This shift has a revolutionary character as it establishes a 'new' unit of analysis in the interdisciplinary field: the entrepreneurial group, its dynamics and its influence on how the venture develops over time.

This emerging trend, which highlights the social nature of the entrepreneurial process, is largely influenced by a tradition of network thinking in entrepreneurship research (Acs & Audretsch, 2010; Ferreira, Fernandes, & Kraus, 2017). Generally, entrepreneurial networks are understood as two or more individuals who jointly establish a business and are linked by formal or informal ties. Conceived in this way, entrepreneurship is therefore a process that relies on a social structure and the activation of socially embedded ties to make things happen (Baker & Nelson, 2005; Garud & Karnøe, 2003; Jack & Anderson, 2002; Kim & Aldrich, 2005).

Literature focused on entrepreneurial groups or networks is wide as debates have grown extensively over the last decades. Management scholars have played a profound role in developing a powerful theoretical and empirical background that has been mainly focused on studying the influence of network structure and size as well as the type and strength of relationships being immersed in the performance and results of the entrepreneurial venture. Yet, what is now generally accepted is that we still do not know enough about how a network is actually formed, and how it develops and changes because few studies have addressed entrepreneurial networks as an evolutionary, historical, process (Anderson, Dodd, & Jack, 2010; Slotte-Kock & Coviello, 2010). Literature also acknowledges the scarcity of studies exploring the relationship between networks and business results beyond the start-up phase (Renzulli & Aldrich, 2005), as well as the content and nature of the relationships rooted within a network (Rodan & Galunic, 2004). Regarding the strength of ties, discussion on the role and importance of strong ties not only in the establishment but also in the subsequent development of an organization remains (Newbert, Tornikoski, & Quigley, 2013).

Another important debate related to the role played by networks in the entrepreneurship process is the role played by networks in driving business innovation and internationalization (Fernández Pérez, 2021). Particularly interesting in this sense is the contribution made by Cantwell (2016) and his ideas on the importance of knowledge exchanges on innovation and internationalization. He emphasized how in those exchanges, networks and entrepreneurial groups are critical. However, we still do not know enough about the specific role played by collective entrepreneurship in innovation and internationalization.

In sum, one of the major challenges facing collective entrepreneurship research is to explore how entrepreneurs create groups and activate social networks, how they evolve over time and how the development of networks informs the performance of the business, in terms of its innovative capacity and its internationalization process. To explore this question, this book points to two key avenues: (i) qualitative historical perspectives that take into account the evolutionary character of the entrepreneurial process; and (ii) multidisciplinary approaches that bring together empirical results with the mainstreams in collective entrepreneurship theory, especially those regarding the role played by this collective entrepreneurship in innovation and internationalization. Historical case studies, of long tradition for business historians, are thus necessarily called to contribute, given their capacity to provide detailed descriptions of specific cases of enterprises and entrepreneurs, to recognize the influence of the past on present events, to provide an understanding of the space-time contexts surrounding entrepreneurship and to work with a wide range of both oral and written sources. The book combines this necessary traditional research focused on case studies with entrepreneurship theories on collective entrepreneurship in order to dig deeper into the study of the growth, innovation and internationalization of the services activities and businesses in the Western world.

3. An Approach to the Content

The different chapters show how collective entrepreneurship has played an important role in driving growth, innovation, and internationalization of public and private companies in the service industries in a variety of countries such as Switzerland, the United Kingdom, or Spain. Indeed, some chapters show how entrepreneurs within both the domestic and international network act as gate-keepers providing other entrepreneurs with knowledge, reputation and experience which help identifying and exploiting opportunities. The book also suggests the importance of socially embedded ties and entrepreneurial groups as critical resources for sustaining an organization over time so that market constraints can be overcome and economic outcomes achieved.

'The Role of Business Services in the Development of European Commodity Trading Companies in the 20th Century', by Espen Storli, from NTNU in Norway, explores the apparent paradox of Switzerland's becoming the centre for international commodity trading in the Western world despite its lack of natural resources or maritime ports from the 1960s to the end of the 1980s. The collective nature of entrepreneurship appears in the dynamic interrelationship between the actors involved in international commodity trading.

The chapter 'Collective Entrepreneurship in the Spanish Hotel Industry: The Internationalization of a Domestic Cluster' by Jorge Hernández-Barahona, Teresa Mateo, Águeda Gil-López and Elena San Román, all from Universidad Complutense de Madrid, studies the tourism cluster of Majorca (Spain) and its connection with collective entrepreneurship. The authors explore the history of four world leading Spanish hotel companies, from their beginnings, in Majorca, in the 1950s, to their internationalization, in the 1980s and 1990s: Barceló, Meliá, Riu, and Iberostar. The chapter identifies common patterns of behaviour among the four companies over time, which in turn illustrate the dynamics of the tourism cluster and the role played by its context. The authors support the identification of Majorca as a tourism cluster and highlight several important characteristics of the island which reinforced and strengthened the cluster and boosted collective entrepreneurship through an intense flow of information between the companies.

The complexities of health systems in which collective entrepreneurship played different roles in the public and the private sector are also analyzed in the chapter 'Collective Entrepreneurship and the Development of Private Clinics in Geneva, 1860–2020'. Pierre-Yves Donzé, professor at Osaka University in Japan, analyses the long-term development of private clinics in Geneva to emphasize the nature of collective entrepreneurship carried out by medical doctors. As Donzé strongly demonstrates, over the long run doctors in Geneva were strongly attached to individual practice, but engaged in collective actions when it had become necessary to defend or promote their business.

Following in the health service, 'The Transfer of the North American Ideas of Hospital Management to Europe in the 20th Century: The Case of Spain' by Paloma Fernández Pérez, from Universitat de Barcelona in Spain, contributes to a better knowledge of the role played by collective entrepreneurship of scientists and doctors who transferred and adapted management ideas and technology from Western Europe and the United States to Spanish modern hospitals. Informal networks of doctors were key in this process. Some of them occupied official positions in the key public health administrations and were crucial to introducing the hospital accreditation systems, and the US ideas in Spain.

Gillet and Tennent's chapter offers a singular vision on collective entrepreneurship both because of the sector, leisure centres and specifically football clubs, and the analysis perspective chosen by the authors, focused on the interactions between the public sector and elite sports organizations working together in a remarkable collective entrepreneurial activity. The chapter analyses the entrepreneurship activity and the evolving policies of public services in leisure centre provision in England during the late the twentieth century. The authors, from the University of York, build on Houlihan (1991) to identify the central role played by local authorities in sport provision. This was complimented and reinforced by an increasing cadre of leisure sector professionals (Torkildsen, 2005, pp. 562–569) together with increasing architectural interest in the provision of leisure during the post-war reconstruction movement (Saumarez Smith, 2019).

Another interesting case on collective entrepreneurship is provided in the chapter 'Alliances as a Coopetitive Strategy of the Airlines: The Case of Iberia (1980–2020)', by Javier Vidal Olivares, from Universidad de Alicante. The end of market regulations initiated in 1978 by the United States gradually put an end to the previous system of bilateral agreements between airlines and paved the way for a wave of institutional changes at the international level. The new rules of the market regulation produced important changes in competition and the implementation of a new system of alliances, initially collaborative in nature but becoming more strategic as uncertainty increased since the beginning of the twenty-first century. As the chapter highlights, the use of a combination of strategies based on cooperation and competition, the so-called coopetition, were the response of important companies such as Air France or Qatar Airways to the market uncertainty (Chiambaretto & Fernandez, 2016; Chiambaretto & Wassmer, 2019). It was also the case of Iberia, the Spanish flag carrier that succeeded using both, collaborative and competitive strategies, to merge into the IAG conglomerate (British Airways and Iberia) with other airlines.

The chapter 'Building an Enterprise for the Future Through Network Bricolage and Memories of the Past' by Águeda Gil-López (Universidad Complutense de Madrid, Spain), Elena San Román (Universidad Complutense de Madrid, Spain), Sarah L. Jack (Stockholm School of Economics, Sweden) and Ricardo Zózimo (Nova University, Portugal) explores how network bricolage, as a form of collective entrepreneurship, develops over time and influences the shape and form of an organization. The authors build on Levi-Strauss' (1966) idea of bricolage associated with creating something from nothing by making do with the resources at hand to grasp opportunities and solve problems (Baker & Nelson, 2005; Desa & Basu, 2013; Kwong, Cheung, Mauzoor, & Rashid, 2019). Thus, network bricolage describes how pre-existing networks are considered as a resource at hand for the entrepreneur (Baker, Miner, & Eesley, 2003, p. 265). Using a historical organization study of SEUR, a Spanish courier company founded in 1942, this chapter shows how network bricolage is implemented as a dynamic process of collaborative efforts between bricoleurs who draw on their historical experience to build and develop an organization.

In 'The Asymmetry of Expectations on the Outcomes of Strategic Alliances Between Biotechnology Start-Ups and Pharmaceutical Corporations',

Felix Barahona Márquez (EU Mediterrani/Universitat de Barcelona), Susana Domingo Pérez (UPF Barcelona School of Management), Ernest Solé Udina (UPF Barcelona School of Management) focus on the relationship between biotechnology start-ups and larger pharmaceutical corporations when acting as partners in innovative strategic alliances. For three decades, these companies have become major players of innovation in the health sector and the development of many products is the result of the developed cooperation. However, the great differences between companies frequently lead to problems. The chapter reveals the concrete facts that can prevent reaching the proposed goals of these partners as well as the crucial importance of the human aspect to mitigate these potential problems.

The existence of internal and external factors that have an impact in organizations, with networks playing different roles inside or outside them, is analyzed in the chapter ' Effects of the Subsidiaries' Networks on the Service Multinationals Innovation Activity', in which the professors of Universitat de Barcelona, Paloma Miravitlles, Fariza Achcaoucaou and Tim Laurin Spieth, study how subsidiary embeddedness in internal and external networks to firms contributes to the innovative activities that generate creating competence and exploiting competence skills in the context of the service industry. The analysis of 137 foreign-owned subsidiaries in the service sector that perform innovation activities in contemporary Spain shows the positive impact of networks of the firm, inside and outside the firm, on the innovation of subsidiaries of multinational corporations.

In 'The Collective Entrepreneurial Process: From Public Entrepreneurship to Collective Action for the Common Good', by Lizbeth Arroyo and Jaume Valls-Pasola (Universitat de Barcelona) the authors analyze how public entrepreneurship boosts collective action, toward a common good. In this chapter a public entrepreneur triggered a collective action that led to the creation of the innovation community: The Coronavirus makers. This collaborative network groups together more than 20,000 researchers, developers, and engineers. They altruistically put their knowledge and resources at the service of the community to provide solutions for one of the healthcare system's main problems at that time: the shortage of medical supplies to cope with the increasing number of COVID-19 cases. The collective action of the Coronavirus makers has impacted the health and wellbeing fields, the community and the values that should define social change and allow the construction of a more open, equitable and sustainable society. Potentially, these findings confirm that collective entrepreneurship may, especially in services for citizens, derive from a function of collective action.

In summary, this book highlights the importance of a new vision on entrepreneurship focused on processes and collaboration rather than on the individuals. Through the lens of collective entrepreneurship, processes can be also explored over time, and this allows us to better understand the creative activity that underlies the envisioning and the pursuing of opportunities. This approach also offers the opportunity to examine not only how actors are situated, but also how they navigate within the context and how they relate to it and to the networks in which their activity is embedded.

Acknowledgement

Research has benefitted from public research project Spanish Project PGC201S8-093971-B-I00 granted by the Ministry of Science and Innovation Programme for Knowledge Generation, funded by MCIU/AEI/FEDER, UE

References

Acs, Z. J., & Audretsch, D. B. (1990). *Innovation and small firms.* Cambridge, MA: MIT Press.

Aldrich, H. E. (2005). Entrepreneurship. In N. J. Smelser & R. Swedberg (Eds.), *The handbook of economic sociology* (pp. 451–477). Princeton, NJ: Princeton University Press.

Anderson, A. R., Dodd, S. D., & Jack, S. (2010). Network practices and entrepreneurial growth. *Scandinavian Journal of Management, 26*(2), 121–133.

Baker, T., Miner, A. S., & Eesley, D. T. (2003). Improvising firms: Bricolage, account giving and improvisational competencies in the founding process. *Research Policy, 32*(2), 255–276.

Baker, T., & Nelson, R. E. (2005). Creating something from nothing: Resource construction through entrepreneurial bricolage. *Administrative Science Quarterly, 50*(3), 329–366.

Cantwell, J. (2016). Innovation and international business. *Industry and Innovation, 24*(1), 41–60.

Chiambaretto, P., & Fernandez, A. S. (2016). The evolution of coopetive and collaborative alliances in an alliance portfolio: The Air France case. *Industrial Marketing Management, 57*, 75–85. doi:10.1016/j.indmarman.2016.05.005

Chiambaretto, P., & Wassmer, U. (2019). Resource utilization as an internal driver of alliance portfolio evolution: The Qatar Airways case (1993–2010). *Long Range Planning, 52*(1), 51–71. doi:10.1016/j.lrp.2018.02.004

Desa, G, & Basu, S. (2013). Optimization or bricolage? Overcoming resource constraints in global social entrepreneurship: Optimization versus bricolage in global social entrepreneurship. *Strategic Entrepreneurship Journal, 7*(1), 26–49.

Fernández Pérez, P. (2021). *The emergence of modern hospital management and organisation in the world 1880s–1930s.* Bingley: Emerald Publishers.

Ferreira, J. J. M., Fernandes, C. I., & Kraus, S. (2017). Entrepreneurship research: Mapping intellectual structures and research trends. *Review of Managerial Science, 13*(1), 181–205.

Garud, R., & Karnøe, P. (2003). Bricolage versus breakthrough: Distributed and embedded agency in technology entrepreneurship. *Research Policy, 32*(2), 277–300.

Houlihan, B. (1991). *The government and politics of sport/Barrie Houlihan.* London: Routledge.

Jack, S., & Anderson, A. (2002). The effects of embeddedness on the entrepreneurial process. *Journal of Business Venturing, 17*, 467–487.

Kim, P. H., & Aldrich, H. E. (2005). Social capital and entrepreneurship. *Foundations and Trends in Entrepreneurship, 1*(2), 55–104.

Kwong, C. B., Cheung, C., Mauzoor, H., & Rashid, M. U. (2019). Entrepreneurship through Bricolage: A study of displaced entrepreneurs at times of war and conflict. *Entrepreneurship and Regional Development, 31*, 435–455.

Levi-Strauss, C. (1966). *The savage mind. The nature of human society series.* Chicago, IL: Univ. of Chicago Press.

Newbert, S., Tornikoski, E., & Quigley, N. (2013). Exploring the evolution of supporter networks in the creation of new organizations. *Journal of Business Venturing, 28,* 281–298.

Renzulli, L. A., & Aldrich, H. (2005). Who can you turn to? Tie activation within core business discussion networks. *Social Forces, 84*(1), 323–341.

Rodan, S., & Galunic, C. (2004). More than network structure: How knowledge heterogeneity influences managerial performance and innovativeness. *Strategic Management Journal, 25*(6), 541–562.

Ruef, M., Aldrich, H. E., & Carter, N. M. (2003). The structure of founding teams: Homophily, strong ties, and isolation among U.S. Entrepreneurs. *American Sociological Review, 68*(2), 195–222.

Saumarez Smith, O. (2019). The lost world of the British leisure centre. *History Workshop Journal, 88,* 180–203.

Slotte-Kock, S., & Coviello, N. (2010). Entrepreneurship research on network processes: A review and ways forward. *Entrepreneurship Theory and Practice, 34*(1), 31–57.

Steyaert, C., & Katz, J. (2004). Reclaiming the space of entrepreneurship in society: Geographical, discursive and social dimensions. *Entrepreneurship & Regional Development, 16*(3), 179–196.

Swedberg, R. (2000). *Entrepreneurship: the social science view.* New York: Oxford University Press.

Torkildsen, G. (2005). *Leisure and recreation management.* London: Routledge.

Acknowledgements

We thank the Spanish Ministerio de Ciencia, Innovación y Universidades (MCIU), Agencia Estatal de Investigación (AEI), and Fondo Europeo de Desarrollo Regional (FEDER), for funding through project PGC2018-093971-B-I00.

Chapter 1

The Role of Business Services in the Development of European Commodity Trading Companies in the 20th Century

Espen Storli

Abstract

After the end of World War II, Switzerland became a key hub for international commodity traders, even though most of the commodities they were dealing in were sourced from outside of Switzerland and were not meant for Swiss producers, refiners or consumers. The main aim of this chapter is to analyze why Switzerland became the centre for international commodity trading in the Western world. The chapter will especially focus on the period from the 1950s to the end of the 1980s. Given that commodity trading companies throughout history have been notoriously closed to external scrutiny, the chapter by need is mainly based on publicly available material. The chapter utilizes the concept of collective entrepreneurship as an analytical framework to situate the development.

Keywords: Commodity traders; Switzerland; collective entrepreneurship; global business; natural resources; business services

1. Introduction

Even in a modern service economy, access to natural resources is indispensable. Although Europe is rich in resources, modern European economic development has been, and continues to be, dependent on imports of a wide range of raw materials from countries outside of the region. This import dependence is not likely

Collective Entrepreneurship in the Contemporary European Services Industries:
A Long Term Approach, 1–10
doi:10.1108/978-1-80117-950-820231001

to decrease in the coming decades, and the European Commission has identified a number of critical raw materials where EU industry is largely dependent on imports (European Commission, 2020). As the EU example illustrates, the uneven global spread of natural resources means that they are seldom found in the same place that they are consumed. Raw materials have therefore throughout history been a primary driver of international trade.

Since the last decades of the nineteenth century, a significant part of the international trade in natural resources has been organized in global value chains by multinational companies (Hesse & Neveling, 2020). Frequently, the chains are established by vertically integrated firms that control the different stages of the production process from natural resource to consumer product. However, these stages can also be linked through arm's length market transactions with producers specializing in just one stage. This opens opportunities for middlemen to become involved. In the process of transforming natural resources into industrial commodities, specialized commodity trading companies have become important. These companies seldom mine, grow, refine, or smelt the commodities needed in production processes; their business model is to buy the output from one stage in the production chain, transport it to another geographical place, and then sell it on to a producer involved in the next stage of the value chain. By doing this, the commodity trading companies physically link the different stages of production together (Pirrong, 2014).

Historically, commodity trading companies were mainly based in either the main commodity producing regions of the world (such as large grain traders from the US Midwest or Argentina), or in the dominant centres of manufacturing or consumption (such as the large metal and mineral traders in the industrial heartland of Germany). After World War II, New York became the centre for international commodity trading. However, from the 1960s and after, the large commodity trading companies of the Western World have increasingly relocated to Europe, and they are now especially domiciled in Switzerland (Storli, 2020).

Although Switzerland is a highly industrialized society with a manufacturing industry reliant on access to a number of commodities, it is a country which has comparatively few natural resources, the main exception being hydro power (Breiding, 2012). Still, from the 1960s, the country became a key hub for international commodity traders, even though most of the commodities they were dealing in were sourced from outside of Switzerland and were not meant for Swiss producers, refiners or consumers. The main aim of this chapter is to analyze why Switzerland became the centre for international commodity trading in the Western world. The chapter will especially focus on the period from the 1960s to the end of the 1980s. Given that commodity trading companies throughout history have been notoriously closed to external scrutiny and – in the words of a recent investigation into the industry – 'have gone to great lengths to avoid giving out any information about themselves' (Blas & Farchy, 2021, p. 10), the chapter by need will mainly be based on publicly available material. The chapter will utilize the concept of collective entrepreneurship as an analytical framework to situate the development.

2. The Role and Functions of International Commodity Trading Companies

Commodity trading companies do not ordinarily fall within the category of service industries. According to the textbook definition, a service company is a business that generates income by providing services instead of selling physical products (see, for instance, Daniels, 1985). The main business model of a commodity trader is to engage in the trade of physical commodities. They buy a commodity from one producer and sell it on to a different producer typically in the next stage of a value chain, in the process physically linking the different stages of a production chain together. In a pure form, commodity traders do not usually plant, grow, mine, smelt or refine the commodities they trade in; however, to secure access to supplies, they might also take ownership of one or more stages of the manufacturing process. In their operations, commodity trading companies fulfil the roles of risk takers, information gatherers and arbitrageurs and not only shape global value chains, but also contribute to the integration of markets and the convergence of prices (Boon & Storli, 2023).

Hugo van Driel (2003) in an influential article proposed a multidimensional framework for understanding the role of middlemen such as commodity trading companies. He argues that there are four dimensions of conditions of supply and demand: place, time, quantity, and quality. Large gaps in these conditions will create relatively high uncertainty for buyers and sellers, but traders are especially suited to reduce this uncertainty by bridging the gaps. In van Driel's framework, middlemen reduce transaction costs by managing transport (transforming in place), by storing the commodities for sale at a convenient time (transforming in time), by collecting and distributing raw materials (transforming in quantity) and by processing, sorting, assorting and screening commodities (transforming in quality). Building on van Driel, Craig Pirrong (2014) has suggested that commodity trading companies fulfil important functions in the international economy because of their ability to transform commodities in space (through logistics), in time (through storage) and in form (through processing commodities). To be successful, commodity trading companies will try to identify the most valuable transformations, undertake the transactions necessary to carry out these transformations, and engage in the physical operations and actions necessary to carry them out.

However, to be able to transform commodities, the traders need to have access to raw materials. Historical analysis of the operations of commodity trading companies shows that the ability to supply business services to producers has often been a comparative advantage and a way to secure access to the important commodities. Pirrong (2014) identifies a number of business services that the commodity traders might offer to their customers. Chief among them are financial services. Commodity trading is highly capital intensive, and traders need access to liquidity to fund its activities. Usually, a company will have bilateral credit lines with several banks, and trading firms have often utilized the situation to provide trade credit to their buyers. Commodity trading companies have traditionally had better insight into the situation of the buyer and the market conditions for the commodities, and they will therefore be better placed than a bank to evaluate the creditworthiness of a customer and to monitor the operations. Credit can also be supplied to sellers, most commonly through off-take agreements, where a commodity trader agrees to purchase the future production of a seller (for instance, a mine or an agricultural producer) and help fund the operations through prepayment or a loan to the producer.

A different business service that can be offered is through a tolling arrangement. A trader that owns raw materials that need to be processed before being sold to a consumer can enter into an agreement with a processing company to have the materials refined for a specified fee (toll). In this way, the trader can find a market for the commodities, while the refiner can get income to help pay for the upkeep of costly industrial plants. Especially in periods where demand is low and the refiner might otherwise have to reduce capacity, tolling agreements can be attractive. Tolling agreements will often be combined with some form of financial service.

Throughout the twentieth century, a significant part of the extraction and production of natural resources have occurred within the bounds of vertically integrated multinational companies controlling the production from the natural resources, stage into consumption. However, commodity traders have provided an alternative for companies that are too small or unable to establish their own vertically integrated value chains. Commodity trading companies are specialists in marketing, logistics, and risk management, and these are services they will often offer to smaller producers. By outsourcing these specialized activities, a mining company, a refiner, or an agricultural producer can reduce the need to build a larger organization and to concentrate on their main activity.

Finally, there are a number of examples of commodity trading companies being willing and able to operate around political restrictions to trade in raw materials, both at a national and an international level and in this way offering business services to regimes or producers. Prominent examples are the involvement of commodity traders in breaking the UN embargo against South Africa in the 1980s (see, for instance, Ammann, 2009) or in the UN Oil for Food scandal involving Iraq in the early 2000s (see, for instance, Soussan, 2008). These services can also include offering help in more uncontroversial matters.

3. Collective Entrepreneurship and the Development of Commodity Trading Companies in Switzerland

Although having a history going back until the early twentieth century, the academic study of entrepreneurship has especially emerged as an important topic since the 1980s among management scholars and social scientists. The field has been dominated by approaches using large datasets to understand aspects such as new business formation, but with little focus on the temporal or geographical context. Business historians, on the other hand, have focussed on understanding the role of innovative entrepreneurship in driving changes in the historical context of business, industry, and the economy (Jones & Wadhwani, 2008). In recent decades, the importance of institutions and cultural and social factors for entrepreneurship has increasingly been highlighted also within the management literature (Casson, Yeung, Basu, & Wadeson, 2006, p. 28).

While there are different ways of understanding the concept of collective entrepreneurship, in its most prevalent form, it can be understood to refer to interactions inside and between networks and businesses. Ivar Jonsson has argued that collective entrepreneurship depends on societal factors such as culture and the infrastructure of human capital, and that collective entrepreneurship is territorially and socially embedded. Thus, collective entrepreneurship is determined by both local and country specific constraints. However, it is also affected by the structural development of international trade and the world market. Overall, the collective nature of entrepreneurship appears in the dynamic interrelationship between the actors involved in the entrepreneurial activity (Jonsson, 1995, pp. 52–56).

The history of global commodity trading companies illustrates the way that collective entrepreneurship can influence the development of an industry. When large, specialized international commodity trading firms first started to appear in the second half of the nineteenth century, they tended to group together in a few selected cities or regions of the world. Partially, this had to do with the shift in trading practices that followed the introduction of the new technology of the telegraph. Trading companies now progressively had to trade on their own account and not based on advances granted by purchasers. This meant that the need for short-term credit from merchant banks grew, and the traders increasingly clustered in the financial centres to be better able to secure credit lines (Dejung, 2013). When the new futures markets for globally traded commodities also started to emerge in the 1860s and 1870s, they were situated in the same financial centres (Engel, 2015). In metals and minerals, the financial hubs of Frankfurt, Hamburg, and London became the key centres of commodity trade, while in agriculture, the trade in some commodities was dominated by companies based close to the production (with grain as the most conspicuous example) or from traders that were based close to urban centres that combined both a large financial sector and large consumer markets (for instance, cotton and rubber). After 1945, US companies started to dominate trade in many commodities, and New York, the financial capital of the United States, now also became a key centre of global commodity trading companies. However, starting already in the 1950s, the large commodity traders increasingly started to shift their international operations away from the United States, and Switzerland grew to become the new global centre for commodity trading (Storli, 2020, pp. 459–461).

Switzerland's new status did not appear out of nowhere. Already in the second half of the nineteenth century, Swiss trading companies had become important international actors in commodity trading. Although landlocked on the European continent, Swiss firms very early started to employ representatives and travellers to gather information and to survey markets and, in the process, penetrating faraway international markets. A company such as Volkart Brothers was able to build up a thriving business trading cotton from British India starting in the 1850s and later also branched into coffee, tea, oil, cacao, and spices and expanded into new regions, such as Japan (Dejung, 2018). Other companies such as André &

Cie (in grain) and UTC (rubber, palm oil, and cacao) also became important global commodity traders during the twentieth century. By the time that foreign multinational commodity traders started to set up shop in Switzerland, the country was already a powerhouse in the global trade of raw materials (Guex, 1998).

The development that led Cargill, one of the world's largest grain traders, to set up their international trading arm in Geneva, is instructive for understanding the arguments for Switzerland becoming a commodity trading centre. Cargill, a US company established in 1865 to trade grain from the Midwest, has operated internationally since the 1920s with foreign offices and through contacts with foreign business agents. However, the success of these international operations had been limited. In the early 1950s, the company management started to discuss the need to reorganize the company's international business. The first impetus was based on the wish to reduce corporate and personal taxation, and it was also apparent that the company's main competitors, based in Europe and in Argentine, had much lower costs because of lower tax policies in their home countries. However, when the Cargill management started to look into the matter, it also became clear that to be successful in international trading, the company needed people with a special background and training to overcome language problems, currency problems, and to deal with local trade customs. In late 1951, after having considered places such as Nassau, Lichtenstein, Monaco, Tangiers, Liberia and Macao, Cargill decided to establish a new international company in Panama. The new company, called Cargill Internacional, although sharing owners with Cargill, was set up to be absolutely separate from the US operations for tax reasons (Broehl, 1992, pp. 769–772).

However, the directors of the company soon realized that Panama was not a convenient location for doing the actual trading, not the least because of the less than fully developed communication links with the rest of the world. Cargill therefore first set up a trading office in Winnipeg, Canada, but quickly moved the office to Montreal, when the traders realized that this was the grain trading centre of Canada. Cargill also established a European trading office in Antwerp. After having operated for a year with Montreal as the main international trading office, it had become clear that Europe was the centre for internationally based grain trade. The owners of Cargill considered Antwerp as a new headquarter for the international organization, but in the end decided on Geneva. In February 1956, Cargill reached an agreement with Swiss federal and cantonal tax authorities, and the new head office for international operations was set up in Geneva. The new office, organized as an independent company under the name Tradax, secured lines of credit from Swiss and German banks, and the traders in the office were soon immersed in what the business historian Wayne Broehl, the company chronicler, described as a '"fast track" business environment, one that begged for aggressive risk-taking and wide-ranging business contacts' (Broehl, 1992, p. 797). The semiautonomous Tradax swiftly became a huge success, with very high earnings, and the Cargill owners even contemplated moving most or even all of Cargill to Switzerland. Though not going that far, in 1966, the Geneva company became the administrative centre for Cargill's operations in all of the world except for North and Central America and five countries in South America (Broehl, 1998, pp. 91–92).

It was not only grain traders who built up their international operations in Switzerland in the 1950s and 1960s. In this period, the New York-based Philipp Brothers developed to become the world's dominant commodity trading company focussing on metals and minerals, and central to this growth was the office that the company set up in Zug, Switzerland. The New York company was established by émigré German Jews, and while it had originally focussed on the US market, in the years after World War II the old continent of Europe became more and more central to its business expansion. To rebuild Europe after the war, enormous stocks of commodities were needed, and that was just what commodity traders could supply. In 1950, Philipp Brothers established an office in Amsterdam, but while business quickly grew, access to credit lines in the Netherlands was a challenge in the first years. In the second half of the 1950s, the company established several new subsidiary offices in Europe, most significantly in Zug, Switzerland, in 1956 (Waszkis, 1992).

The Philipp Brothers management chose Zug as a location first and foremost for taxation reasons. The personal income tax rates were higher in the Netherlands than in Switzerland, and the small town of Zug, in the canton of Zug, was known to have the most advantageous tax rates in the country. In addition, Zug was also very close to the financial centre of Zurich, so the access to expertise in international tax, legal, and financial matters was also attractive to a company that was expanding its international business. Originally, Sigmund Jeselsohn, a banker, was put in charge of the Zug office, and the focus was on the financial and legal aspects of the company's business. However, the directors soon realized Zug was also an ideal location for doing actual trading, partially due to its geographical location in the centre of Europe, but also because of the financial strength, competence, and credit lines of the nearby Zurich banks. By 1958, Zug had become an important trading hub for Philipp Brothers, and when the United States the same year eased post-war restrictions for US subsidiaries on doing business with Communist countries, the office became a centre for trade with Hungary, Romania, Bulgaria, and Czechoslovakia. The Zug office grew rapidly, and in the 1960s, Philipp Brothers decided to use Zug as its European headquarters responsible for all of the company's European business. Soon, the Swiss office was also used as the headquarters for much of the world-wide business of Philipp Brothers (Waszkis, 1992, pp. 154–156).

In the 1970s, Philipp Brothers dominance of the global metal trade started to be challenged by a new entity set up by an ex-employee of the company. Marc Rich had worked for Philipp Brothers for twenty years when he in 1974 struck out on his own to set up Marc Rich + Co. AG. During the 1980s, this new company would become the most important metals and mineral trader in the world, while Philipp Brothers disappeared by 1990. In 1993, Marc Rich was forced out of his own company by his employees, and it was renamed Glencore. After several decades of growth and acquisitions, it is today one of the world's largest globally diversified natural resource companies and the largest company in Switzerland. Marc Rich in 1974 set up his headquarters in Zug, close to the offices of his former employer. The Swiss journalist Daniel Ammann, Marc Rich's biographer, has argued that there were three main reasons why Rich decided to make Zug his base.

First of all, Switzerland's status as politically neutral meant that Swiss companies could trade in most states. Second, Zug was close to Zurich, which was a global financial centre known for its discretion but also home to an international airport and also had renowned international schools, which were important to recruit international experts. Finally, Zug was a tax paradise which by international standards had very low income and corporate tax. Marc Rich + Co. and Philipp Brothers were not the only international companies to make Zug their home: a host of American companies arrived in the 1950s and 1960s, German and British companies came in the 1970s and 1980s, while after 1990, Russian companies did the same (Ammann, 2009, p. 77).

As Sébastian Guex has noted, even though Switzerland historically had no colonies, no outlet to the sea, and no major tradable natural resources, the country by 1985 had become, after Great Britain, the second centre in Europe for the trade of raw materials (Guex, 1998, p. 150). A key factor in this development was the arrival of a number of global trading companies to Switzerland in the years after 1945. In his analysis of why the companies were attracted to the country, Guex has proposed five explanatory factors. First, Switzerland's geographical location means that it already from the medieval times was a major crossroad in both the north-south and east-west commercial channels of Europe. The long history, tradition, and know-how in international trade meant that the country was well set to take advantage of new trading possibilities. Second, Switzerland's political neutrality meant that the country was able to stay out of both World Wars and also that in the post-World War II years, it could maintain commercial connections which might be closed to companies based in countries more caught up in the Cold War. Political neutrality meant that Swiss-based companies could act as middlemen between the East and the West. Third, Switzerland had well-developed and strong financial centres in cities like Zurich and Geneva. After 1945, Swiss bank, compared to other European banks, could offer abundant credit at an interest rate which was usually several points below that of foreign competitors. The Swiss franc was also one of the most stable and reliable currencies throughout the period. For international commodity trading companies, access to cheap(er) credit and stable currencies was a major draw. Fourth, the Swiss income and corporate tax were generally lower than in other European countries. Fifth, and finally, in what was in many parts of the world a politically unstable period, Switzerland was seen as a haven of stability when it came to economic policies and security (Guex, 1998, p. 169).

These factors must be seen as mutually reinforcing, but not of equal importance. The historical experiences of Cargill and Philipp Brothers illustrate how the Swiss taxation regime was the key factor for attracting the companies to set up subsidiaries in the country in the 1950s. However, low taxes are not sufficient to explain why the Swiss offices of these companies in just a few years became their centres for European and international trade. In both cases, the companies' traders found that the Swiss environment was very conducive to carrying out international trade and this meant that the importance of the offices within the corporate organizations grew and, as a consequence, also their sizes. Three factors were especially important. First, Swiss banks were very competitive and willing to supply credit lines, which was, and is, essential to commodity trading. Second, the 'fast-track' international business environments of Geneva described by Broehl (and also applicable for Zug/Zurich) were inspirational for the traders and also meant that it was possible to attract new talents. Third, the political neutrality meant that in a period of international tensions between the Eastern bloc and the West, and between the old colonial powers and the newly independent former colonies, Swiss-based traders often had more leeway to manoeuvre. These three factors taken together were especially important for the business services that the traders could supply to their customers from their Swiss bases. The combination of the availability of credit, the international outlook of the trading communities, and the reduced political hurdles are central to understanding the rise of the Geneva and Zug/Zurich trading hubs. Since the quality of the business services that could be supplied from Switzerland was difficult to replicate in other areas of the world, the place rapidly grew in importance.

4. Conclusions

Starting in the 1950s, Switzerland became increasingly important as a global centre for commodity trading. The importance has continued into the recent era, and at the time of writing, not only the world's largest commodity trader Glencore, is headquartered in the country, but other leading global commodity traders such as Vitol, Trafigura, Gunvor, and Mercuria have their main trading offices in Switzerland (all of them in Geneva). To understand this development, it is fruitful to frame it within the concept of collective entrepreneurship. Following Jonsson's prominent definition, the collective nature of entrepreneurship appears in the dynamic interrelationship between the actors involved in the entrepreneurial activity. In the cases of Cargill and Philipp Brothers in Geneva and Zug/Zurich, respectively, it was the combination of the existing Swiss financial expertise with the international outlook and contacts of the incoming American companies that made possible the innovation which formed the basis of the rapid growth of the companies. This expertise was territorially embedded and developed not the least because of a lack of political and economic constraints which could be found in other potential places to set up the business. Switzerland was not unique in having a low tax regime, nor in having a vibrant financial community, or a geographically advantageous position or being politically neutral, but the communities in Geneva and Zug/Zurich were unique in that all of these factors were present at the same time and place. Both Cargill and Philipp Brothers, as well as other global trading companies, went through search processes where they set up offices in different international locations before they settled on Switzerland as a main place to do their global business. This process was not given from the outset, but gradually developed during the post-World War II era, and the development of the commodity traders fits well with Jonsson's argument that the collective nature of the entrepreneurship can be witnessed in the dynamic interrelationship between the actors involved in the entrepreneurial activity.

References

Ammann, D. (2009). *The king of oil. The secret lives of Marc Rich*. New York, NY: St. Martin´s Griffin.

Blas, J., & Farchy, J. (2021). *The world for sale. Money, power and the traders who barter the earth´s resources*. London: Penguin Random House Business.

Boon, M. & Storli, E. (2023). Creating global capitalism: An introduction to commodity trading companies and the first global economy, *Business History*. doi: 10.1080/00076791.2023.2172163

Breiding, R. (2012). *Swiss made: The untold story behind Switzerland´s success*. London: Profile Books.

Broehl, W. (1992). *Cargill. Trading the world´s grain*. Hanover, New Hampshire: University Press of New England.

Broehl, W. (1998). *Cargill. Going global*. Hanover, New Hampshire: University Press of New England.

Casson, M., Yeung, B., Basu, A., & Wadeson, N. (2006). Introduction. In M. Casson, B. Yeung, A. Basu, & N. Wadeson (Eds.), *The Oxford handbook of entrepreneurship* (pp. 1–30). Oxford: Oxford University Press.

Daniels, P.W. (1985). *Service industries: A geographical appraisal*. London: Routledge.

Dejung, C. (2013). Worldwide ties: The role of family business in global trade in the nineteenth and twentieth centuries. *Business History*, *55*(6), 1001–1018.

Dejung, C. (2018). *Commodity trading, globalization and the colonial world*. London: Routledge.

Engel, A. (2015). Buying time: Futures trading and telegraphy in nineteenth-century global commodity markets. *Journal of Global History*, *10*(2), 284–306.

European Commission. (2020). *Critical raw materials for strategic technologies and sectors in the EU. A foresight study*. Luxembourg: Publications of the European Union.

Guex, S. (1998). Development of swiss trading companies. In G. Jones (Eds.), *The multinational traders* (pp. 178–201). London: Routledge.

Hesse, J.-O., & Neveling, P. (2020). Global value chains. In T. da Silva Lopes, C. Lubinski, & H. Tworek (Eds.), *The routledge companion to the makers of global business* (pp. 277–292). London: Routledge.

Jones, G., & Wadhwani, D. (2008). Entrepreneurship. In G. Jones & J. Zeitlin (Eds.), *The Oxford handbook of business history* (pp. 501–528). Oxford: Oxford University Press.

Jonsson, I. (1995). *West-nordic countries in crisis. Neo-structuralism, collective entrepreneurship and microsocieties facing global systems of innovation*. Copenhagen: New Social Science Monographs.

Pirrong, C. (2014). *The economics of commodity trading firms*. White paper commissioned by Trafigura. Retrieved from https://www.trafigura.com/media/1192/2014_trafigura_economics_of_commodity_trading_firms_en.pdf

Storli, E. (2020). Global commodity traders. In T. da Silva Lopes, C. Lubinski, & H. Tworek (Eds.), *The routledge companion to the makers of global business* (pp. 452–464). London: Routledge.

Soussan, M. (2008). *Backstabbing for beginners. My crash course in international diplomacy*. New York: Nation Books.

van Driel, H. (2003). The role of middlemen in the international coffee trade since 1870: The Dutch case. *Business History*, *45*(2), 77–101.

Waszkis, H. (1992). *Philipp brothers. The rise and fall of a trading giant, 1901–1990* (2nd ed.). London: Metal Bulletin Books Limited.

Chapter 2

Collective Entrepreneurship in the Spanish Hotel Industry: The Internationalization of a Domestic Cluster

Jorge Hernández-Barahona, Teresa Mateo, Águeda Gil-López and Elena San Román

Abstract

This chapter studies the tourism cluster of Majorca and its connection with collective entrepreneurship. To this end, the authors review the history of four world leading Spanish hotel companies, from their beginnings, in Majorca, in the 1950s, to their internationalization, in the 1980s and 1990s: Barceló, Meliá, Riu, and Iberostar. This allows us to identify common patterns of behaviour among them over time, which in turn illustrate the dynamics of the tourism cluster and the role played by its context. This qualitative and historical research allows us to make the following contributions: first, in line with other studies in the economic history of Spanish tourism, the four cases support the identification of Majorca as a tourism cluster. Second, the authors highlight several important characteristics of the island which reinforced and strengthened the cluster and boosted collective entrepreneurship, through an intense flow of information between the companies. Third, the authors illustrate coopetition as the key nature of the relationship between the clustered companies in a simultaneous process of competition and cooperation. Finally, the authors show how the strength of the tourism cluster, in Majorca, drove the companies to replicate the same dynamics and structures abroad.

Keywords: Collective entrepreneurship; cluster; coopetition; tourism; Majorca; internationalization

Collective Entrepreneurship in the Contemporary European Services Industries:
A Long Term Approach, 11–28
doi:10.1108/978-1-80117-950-820231002

1. Introduction

There is a general agreement on Business History and Organizational research that entrepreneurship is the result of a collective action. In attempting to debunk the myth of the isolated entrepreneurial hero, recent approaches went beyond the focus on the cognitive and creative capabilities of sole individuals. Hence, it was suggested that entrepreneurs are agents who drive change through the identification and exploitation of opportunities in a continuous interaction with other agents (Shane, 2003). The shift from the individual to the collective as the unit of analysis has a revolutionary character as it establishes a 'new' unit of analysis, the entrepreneurial group, as well as its dynamics and its influence on how organizations develop over time. Moreover, as agents of change, collective entrepreneurs' actions are assumed not to be determined or constrained by external forces, but embedded in context.

Insofar, as rooted in socially embedded ties, collective entrepreneurship is largely influenced by a tradition of network research in the fields of Entrepreneurship and Business History (Acs & Audretsch, 2010; Casson, 2010; Fernández Pérez & Rose, 2009; Ferreira, Fernandes, & Kraus, 2019). Generally, entrepreneurial networks are understood as the patterns of interpersonal formal or informal relations, which emerge from entrepreneurial activities. Conceived in this way, entrepreneurship is a process which relies on a social structure and the activation of socially embedded ties to make things happen (Jack & Anderson, 2002). From a historical perspective, important topics for study on networks have been, for example, the emergence of guilds and other trade associations in different historical contexts, the way these associations facilitated the spread of knowledge (Casson, 2003; Wilson & Popp, 2003), and the role of family ties for business development (Colli, Fernández Pérez, & Rose, 2003; Colli & Rose, 1999, 2003; Fernández Pérez & Colli, 2013). Likewise, several studies have looked at the role played by religious ties in business and industry growth (Trivellato, Halevi, & Antunes, 2014).

One of the ways in which Business History has approached the study of networks is through associations within clusters or industrial districts. While traditionally clusters have been understood as geographic concentrations of organizations (Porter, 1990), recent scholarship suggested that they can be seen as 'organizations of organizations' (Gadille, Tremblay, & Vion, 2013; Lupova-Henry, Blili, & Dal Zotto, 2021b). Indeed, some scholars have challenged the conventional notion of geographical proximity, i.e. the interpretation of cluster as districts. They suggested that knowledge and resource sharing are enacted through networks, often taking place in various industrial districts (Buchnea, 2016). Indeed, cluster is defined by the network itself and not the proximity.

Following this network approach, clusters constitute an inter-organizational network and therefore a powerful collective actor which drives innovation and entrepreneurship in many industries. There is a perceived insight that entrepreneurship is embedded within clusters and networks. For that reason, scholars noted that the collaborative action between clusters and networks generate dynamics of collaborative learning and knowledge spill over (Depret & Hamdouch, 2009; Moulaert, 2013). Therefore, clusters can be critical, particularly, in constrained contexts where lack of resources and institutional barriers can limit innovation and entrepreneurship (Lehmann & Benner, 2015; Lupova-Henry, Blili, & Dal Zotto, 2021a; Schrammel, 2013).

The study of clusters, as industrial districts, has a long tradition in Economic and Business History research. Research on clusters connects back to the so-called Marshallian economics (Becattini, 1990). Moreover, historical approaches to clusters have paid great attention to their influence on innovation and economic growth, greatly inspired by the work of Porter (1990) (Wilson & Popp, 2003). Indeed, the association of similar businesses allows for knowledge-sharing, as well as collaboration and competition, which encourages innovation and development. The geographic and territorial dimension of clusters has been central to the discussion and, therefore, historians attempted to explain the economic advantages that the geographic concentration of collaborating and competing firms have. For instance, the work edited by Wilson and Popp (2003) offers interesting insight on the historical development of industrial districts in Great Britain from the eighteenth to the twentieth centuries. There has also been an increased focus on the creation of industrial districts in tourism and specific holiday destinations (Cirer-Costa, 2014a, 2014b). An inspiring theoretical framework and conceptualizations for business history have been provided by Popp, Toms, and Wilson (2006) and Casson (2003), while Buchnea (2016) presented a comprehensive state of the art on the topic of clusters and networks, in business history research.

An important idea that transcends the above-mentioned historical studies is that we cannot generalize on the performance and characteristics of clusters. More in-depth research is needed, particularly, examining how networks and clusters emerge and evolve over time (Wilson & Popp, 2003). Indeed, detailed longitudinal perspectives in the network research field are limited (Gil-López, Zozimo, San Román, & Jack, 2016; Hollow, 2020). Moreover, since most of the networks and clusters literature have been applied to the manufacturing and technology-based industries, additional work is needed. More specifically, the network research field would benefit from work on the service sector where competitive advantages very often rely on the access to knowledge through interacting – either collaborative or competitive – with other businesses.

This chapter explores the formation process of a cluster, how it develops over time, and how a cluster, ultimately, drives collective entrepreneurship. Thus, we focus on the emergence and the development of the tourism cluster in Majorca (Cirer-Costa, 2014a, 2014b), by investigating how four major tourism companies developed and internationalized their businesses. We draw on these companies' trajectories, especially on how they took advantages of their increasingly dense domestic network. The four firms analyzed – Meliá, Barceló, Riu and Iberostar are all, currently, among the top 50 hotel chains in the world, either by revenue or number of rooms managed. They occupy competitive positions in major destinations such as, the Caribbean. These four companies are family firms, deeply embedded in the island of Majorca, which started their tourism business in the mid-twentieth century when Spain, and particularly the Islands, became competitive destinations for mass tourism (San Román, Puig, & Gil-López, 2020). Yet, the economic and institutional context was constraining with limited financial means, interventionist policies and lack of democracy.

The dynamics of what is known as Majorca's cluster had a powerful impact, driving collective entrepreneurship, enhancing the emergence, diversification, and growth of the companies. The Majorca's cluster dynamics also shaped the internationalization of the companies and the transformation of the sector, making Majorca the Spain's tourist emporium (Vallejo, 2019). Moreover, collective entrepreneurship fostered the expansion of the cluster and the growth of its actors, so that a kind of virtuous circle emerged. Besides, the cluster formed in the companies' home market became strong enough to influence their internationalization, in trying to replicate abroad the same home-based structure. In this chapter, we share the view of clusters as 'context-embedded' organizations (King et al., 2010; Lupova-Henry et al., 2021b), suggesting that through taking deliberate actions, the clustered entrepreneurs are influenced by their environment, but they also have the capacity to transform it.

The current research is qualitative, historical and follows the case study method. Data includes an extensive collection of written and oral sources gathered between 2013 and 2021. Oral sources include interviews with the companies' chairmen (Iberostar, Barceló and RIU) and with descendants of the founders (Meliá). In addition, in order to limit potential bias, we also interviewed outsiders (Eisenhardt & Graebner, 2007), including entrepreneurs, senior managers and employees who have had, or continue to have, connections with the four companies Moreover, to mitigate retrospective bias, we have collected companies' archival documents, external primary sources (historic press), and secondary sources – published books and articles about the companies (Eisenhardt & Graebner, 2007). The combination of oral and written sources, internal and external to the companies, provided different perspectives to guide our interpretations, supporting the overall credibility of the sources and the validity of our findings (Kipping, Wadhwani, & Bucheli, 2014).

2. The Development of Majorca's Tourism Cluster

Since the end of the First World War, the tourism in the Balearic Islands, and more specifically, in Majorca had increased considerably. The post-war boom of the 1920s along with improvements of communications between the islands and the mainland brought prosperity to the tourism industry which became the region's principal source of income.

Tourism expansion attracted entrepreneurs who lead the development of hotels and auxiliary firms of all kinds: shipping agencies, tourist guides, taxi services, and firms providing excursions (Cirer-Costa, 2014b). As a result, by the mid-1930s, Majorca had already become an extensive industrial district devoted to tourism (Cirer-Costa, 2014a). Majorca's tourism growth was interrupted by the Spanish Civil War and its recovery in the afterwar period was limited by Spain's isolated position. As a consequence, the port of Palma was left out of the newly re-established cruise routes. It was not until the 1950s, due to the growth of the European economy, and the progressive openness of Spain, that the Balearic Islands managed to restate their leading position.

Although Spain was still a closed economy, local firms deployed a deep local embeddedness. Majorca's tourism business developed as an increasingly dense local network, relying on other companies supplies of contacts, information, services and clients. The Balearics grew in popularity as its market saturation increased, during the 1970s, which led to a growing level of competitiveness. This was observed, especially, between hotel firms that started to absorb the activities formerly subcontracted to the auxiliary firms. Although no formal collaboration existed between the largest hotel firms, they worked close enough to keep track of the innovations introduced by competitors. This is something typical in hospitality where no patents can protect innovations.

Below we review the origins and the development of the four hotel companies – Barceló, Meliá, Riu and Iberostar – in Majorca and Spain. Table 1 summarizes their main characteristics.

2.1. Barceló: From Transport to Tourism

In 1931, Simón Barceló (1902–1958) created the 'Autocares Barceló' transport company in Felanitx (Majorca) whose activity was interrupted during the Spanish Civil War. In 1954, the company ventured, for the first time, into the travel agency sector offering tourist excursions around the island, in an attempt of increasing the business of the transport company.[1] For many years, the travel business operated as the affiliate of Ultramar Express, an agency based in Barcelona (Barceló Group, 2016). When Simón Barceló died in 1958, the company went into the hands of his sons, Gabriel and Sebastián. In 1960, the travel agency of Barceló split from Ultramar Express and became an independent company called Viajes Barceló (Pla, 1993).

By the early 1960s, the flow of tourists arriving in Majorca evidenced the scarcity of hotels. That was an opportunity to set up a hotel company (Pla, 1993): by 1972, Barceló had nine hotels in the Islands: six in Majorca, two in Ibiza and one in Menorca. It was also present in Costa Blanca and Costa del Sol and, in 1975, the company pioneered the expansion of the hotel business to the Canary Islands (Barceló Group, 2016).

The growth of Barceló in Majorca was nurtured by two key elements. First, the parallel expansion of Viajes Barceló that supplied customers to the hotels. Second, Gabriel Barceló supported the business from an institutional perspective. He developed the so-called 'Embajadas de Mallorca por España' (*Embassies of Majorca around Spain*) which helped enhance the touristic interest of Majorca in Spain. Gabriel Barceló also promoted the creation of the first 'Confederación de Asociaciones Empresariales de Baleares' (The Confederation of Business Associations of the Balearic Islands), which is now the most representative organization in defending the general interests of the businessmen in the region (Pla, 1993).

---

[1]Interview with Gabriel Barceló (6-9-2013).

Table 1.   Basic Data of the Four Companies.

Name	Start of Tourism Activity	Starting Point of Tourism Activity	Founder	Entrepreneurial Origins	First Hotel in Spain	First International Hotel	No. Hotels International 2019[a]	No. Rooms 2019[a]	Worldwide (by Numbers of Rooms)
Meliá	1956	Majorca	Gabriel Escarrer	Tourism	1956, Majorca	1985, Bali 1988, Dominican Republic	325	82,011	19th
Riu	1953	Majorca	Juan Riu	Fruit Trade	1953, Majorca	1991, Dominican Republic	99	47,982	32nd
Barceló	1954	Majorca	Simón Barceló	Bus Transport	1962, Majorca	1985, Dominican Republic	251	57,493	29th
Iberostar	1956	Majorca	Antonio Fluxá	Shoemaker	1962, Majorca	1993, Dominican Republic	104	35,700	47th

Source: Own elaboration based on the interviews.

[a]Data from *Hotels Magazine* 2019 (We use 2019 data because, due to the COVID-19, 2020 data are non-representative).

2.2. Meliá Hotels International (MHI): The Fastest and the Biggest

The expansion of MHI, formerly known as Sol Group, dates back to Gabriel Escarrer's business in Spain which, unlike Barceló, specialized only in the hotel segment to propel a fast expansion in the domestic market. His entrepreneurial career in the hotel industry started in 1956. In the early 1960s, he worked in partnership with Lorenzo Fluxà, whose son Miguel would launch the Iberostar Group 20 years later. Both entrepreneurs, Gabriel Escarrer and Lorenzo Fluxá, created in 1961 a joint venture 'Financiera Balear' that run a small group of lower category hotels in Majorca. Despite their fruitful collaboration, Gabriel Escarrer and Lorenzo Fluxà split in the mid-sixties.

During the subsequent years, Escarrer took advantage of the island's increasing popularity as a tourism destination for package holidaymakers, adding further properties to the portfolio of his company, Hoteles Mallorquines. The company expanded geographically in the 1960s and 1970s, acquiring hotels in the Canaries as well as in other Balearic Islands. After the decline of Franco's dictatorship, the tourism business in Spain developed rapidly, so that the Hoteles Mallorquines moved onto the Spanish mainland. By the early 1980s, the company gained presence in much of the country. In the mid-1980s, the company renamed itself Hoteles Sol (*Sun Hotels*), and became the largest hotel group in Spain through the purchase of 32 hotels from the HOTASA hotel chain. In 1987, Gabriel Escarrer acquired the Meliá hotels chain and renamed his company Sol Meliá, which in 2011 became MHI.

2.3. Riu: The Transformation of a Fruit Trader

Juan Riu (1908–1996) was a mechanic, a truck driver and a fruit trader before becoming a hotelier.[2] In 1950, he sold his fruit shop and emigrated searching for a better future. In Venezuela, he was offered the opportunity to manage a small hotel, with his wife María Bertrán and his son Luis Riu Bertrán (Pla, 1993). Three years later, he returned to Spain and bought the San Francisco Hotel in Majorca. This marked the beginning of a successful career in association with the German tour operator TUI (Touristik Union International) and shaped an expansion strategy based on the specialization in hotels alongside a steady equity partnership with the tour operator (San Román et al., 2020). The professional relationship with TUI dates to 1954, when Luis Riu established contact in Germany with a small travel agency, called Dr Tigges, with which he signed a contract to sell their rooms. Years later, Dr Tigges expanded and merged with other agencies to set TUI – the biggest German tour operator.[3]

During the 1960s and 1970s, RIU experienced a significant expansion in the Balearic Islands, consolidating its business partnership. By the early 1970s, RIU had already opened two other hotels in Majorca, and one campsite. In 1976, RIU

---

[2]Interview with Carmen Riu (26-2-2016).
[3]A sample of the contracts signed between Riu and TUI can be found in the Riu Archive, 26-30, 'Contracts and clearing documents between Riu and TUI' 1963–1966.

Hotels S.A. was established as a joint venture between RIU (60%) and TUI (40%) in order to build new hotels.[4] In the 1980s, RIU expanded into other destinations, particularly in the Canary Islands, where they opened their first hotel in 1985, in the island of Gran Canaria.

2.4. Iberostar: From Shoes to Tourism

In 1877, Antoni Fluxá (1853–1918) started to work as a shoemaker, opening a small artisanal workshop, in the town of Inca (Majorca). In the 1950s, his son Lorenzó Fluxá decided to diversify his business activity and moved into the tourism sector. Later on, in 1956, Lorenzo acquired a travel company known as Viajes Iberia.[5] Yet, soon Lorenzo Fluxá expanded his business in the business of hotel management, operating his own hotels and also some other rented hotels in venture with Gabriel Escarrer.

The Fluxá family's venture into the tourism sector took off under the leadership of Miguel Fluxá, Lorenzo Fluxá's second son. Miguel has joined the family business, in 1962, and developed the three areas of the tourism business – outbound, inbound and hospitality.[6] Up until the late 1970s, inbound activity was the principal and fastest growing area within Iberostar Group (San Román, 2017; San Román, Gil-López, Díez-Vial, & Jack, 2021). This inbound activity also launched the company onto the international scene with the creation of inbound companies in England (Iberotravel) and the United States (Visit Us). In the outbound sector, Iberostar established its own tour operator, Iberojet, in 1973.

In 1979, Iberostar Group's inbound business took a major step forward signing an exclusive contract with the German tour operator Neckermann to manage its incoming business in Spain and beginning to finance hotels owned by Iberostar Group (San Román, 2017; San Román et al., 2020).

In terms of the hospitality activity, expansion first happened in Spain – essentially in Majorca – involving years of intense building activity: eight hotels were built in only six years. Between 1984 and 1990, Iberostar built seven hotels in Majorca and one more in the Canary Islands (San Román, 2017).

2.5. Main Characteristics of the Majorca's Tourism Cluster: A Summary

The study of the emergence and growth of the four companies in the island of Majorca allows us to identify common patterns of behaviour, which in turn illustrate the dynamics of the cluster and the role played by context.

The entrepreneurs, except Escarrer, began their professional careers in tourism. However, the context of scarcity in Spain during the 1950s drove them to reinvent

---

[4]Riu Archive, 'Joint Venture Project describing the plan and next steps', 1971.
[5]Interview with Lorenzo Fluxá (2-10-2013).
[6]Interview with Miguel Fluxá (20-3-2013).

themselves. As different authors have pointed out, the emerging tourism cluster of Majorca allowed entrepreneurs to overcome a restricted context (Lehmann & Benner, 2015; Lupova-Henry et al., 2021a; Schrammel, 2013). In the four cases investigated, two different paths were found when initiating tourism: Barceló and Fluxá established travel agency businesses, while Escarrer and Riu took their first steps in hotel management – Riu still in Venezuela. Both activities, travel agencies and hotel management, share a common feature: they require low investment. Once the entrepreneurs had accumulated enough experience, the insufficient supply of accommodation in Majorca encouraged them to build their first hotels in the island. Thus, in the 1960s, the four entrepreneurs had already entered the hotel business, building their own facilities. The next step for the four companies to consolidate their position in the hotel market was to sign agreements with foreign tour operators, key players in the development of Majorca as a leading tourist destination (Cirer-Costa, 2009; Manera, Molina, Montiel, & Manera-Salom, 2020). These tour operators provided commercial and financial support, as well as key knowledge to grow nationally and internationally, to Spanish hotel companies. However, the relationship with foreign tour operators was different in each case (San Román et al., 2020). Meliá and Barceló limited this link to the promotion and distribution of their hotel rooms, while Iberostar signed financial and commercial agreements with Neckermann, without sharing stake of the hotels. Riu, on the other hand, developed a joint venture with TUI. In the 1970s, the saturation of the accommodation market in the island led the companies to build hotels in other national destinations, notably in the Mediterranean coast and in the Canary Islands.

These common patterns of behaviour show how the tourism business in Majorca developed through a local cluster that over time became stronger and in which networks and information sharing became key factors, not only for the individual companies but also for the island as a whole.

3. The Landing in America: Replicating the Cluster Abroad

Among the four business cases, the Barceló brothers and Gabriel Escarrer (MHI) were the first entrepreneurs to pursue business overseas, despite having followed different paths (San Román, 2017): the Barceló brothers headed for the Dominican Republic while Escarrer went to Bali. It soon became clear that Sebastián and Gabriel Barceló had made the right decision in choosing the American market: cultural affinity and the common language eased the work of the hoteliers. Furthermore, the relative proximity of the Caribbean made it a highly desired sun and beach destination for American and European clients. Wolfgang Beeser, ex-chairman of the German Tour operator Neckermann, properly remarked: 'After Columbus, the Spanish returned to America 500 years later. They were brave enough to do it. The story is identical'.[7]

---

[7]Interview with Wolfgang Beeser (21-11-2013).

3.1. Barceló: The Early Comer

In 1981, Barceló purchased the Spanish tour operator Turavia, which had presence in many countries in Central and South America. With this operation, the Barceló brothers realized the potential of going international, having a strategic knowhow, and a client portfolio. Soon afterwards, Gabriel Barceló travelled to Puerto Rico to explore the possibilities of internationalization.[8] However, Gabriel Barceló did not find Puerto Rico attractive enough to set the first hotel of the company abroad (Barceló Group, 2016). A former employee of Barceló, who lived in Puerto Rico, offered him the opportunity to explore the Dominican Republic (Barceló Group, 2016). This employee introduced Gabriel Barceló to Gabriel Ferrer, a son of Majorcan immigrants who co-owned an important plot of land in association with few partners. Ferrer showed Bávaro Beach to Barceló, who decided to buy a plot of 700 Ha, despite the lack of proper communications and electric power (Pla, 1993). His Majorcan roots were inspirational: 'I was amazed. Bavaro was like Majorca in the 1950s in the Caribbean of the 1980s. I was really amazed'; '[Gabriel Ferrer], being Dominican, spoke Majorcan as if he had been all the life in Majorca. He was my age, 60 years old' (Pla, 1993).

In 1985, the Playa Bávaro, a 400-bed Hotel, opened its doors: it was the first milestone of the Majorcan hotel business in the Caribbean. The Playa Bávaro became the first 'beach resort' built by Spanish companies operating abroad with a new concept of tropical beach hotel. The concept of beach hotel was, subsequently, imitated by other hotel companies.

3.2. Meliá Hotels International (MHI): A Rectified Venture

The internationalization process of MHI started in Bali, Indonesia, in 1985 with the establishment of the Hotel Bali Sol. The company took three years to move to the Caribbean. In the words of the Chairman, Gabriel Escarrer, the main factors that initially prevented the investment in the Caribe were mainly political factors and legal instability, due to governments' volatility and corruption, as well as the lack of infrastructure.[9]

The company soon realized that its choice was not the right one. As the Chairman of MHI stated, cultural links in the Caribbean were stronger than those in Bali, thus offering the opportunity to take advantages of a common language, cultural background and values (Pla, 1993, p. 50). America offered a young market with a great potential for Spanish hotel companies to export their knowhow and expertise. Consequently, in 1988, MHI opened its first hotel in the Dominican Republic, the Meliá Santo Domingo which was soon followed by a second hotel, in Cancun, Mexico. In fact, Gabriel Escarrer was the leader of the Spanish businessman in Mexico together with Pedro Pueyo – owner of Oasis Hotels. They focussed on Los Cabos, Puerto Vallarta and Cancun. Escarrer

---

[8]Interview with Gabriel Barceló (6-9-2013).
[9]"El desembarco en el Caribe, contado por sus protagonistas" en *Preferente* (XXIV, n. 285, February 2015, pp. 50–53).

was also the front-runner in Cuba: in 1987, the Cuban Government established a joint venture with the Spanish group Martinon, a construction company from the Canary Islands owned by Enrique Martinon, that built three hotels in Varadero, and whose management was brought to MHI.[10] The first of these hotels, the Sol Palmeras, was opened in 1990. Of all the Spanish hotel operators, MHI maintains the greatest presence in Cuba.[11]

3.3. Riu: The Strength of an International Partner

The internationalization of Riu started in 1990 with the inauguration of the hotel Riu Taino in Punta Cana, in The Dominican Republic. This meant the first step in RIU Hotels' remarkable growth in America, where they currently own and run over 30 hotels. Along with the Dominican Republic, Mexico has become its main investment destiny (San Román et al., 2020).

Like the other Spanish hotel companies, RIU's early interest on the Caribbean had to do with the similar culture, same language and growth opportunities offered by the American market.[12] Yet, there are some factors that differentiate Riu from the others. The founder had a pioneering vision on the strategic opportunity of having an international partner. That explains the partnership with TUI, which fuelled with key financial and commercial resources the internationalization of the Spanish hotel chain (Fuster, 2010; San Román et al., 2020). Being aware of that asset, the Riu's family took a step forward in strengthening, even further, its alliance with TUI. Both partners founded, in 1993, a hotel management company, RIUSA II S.A, equally owned by TUI and Riu, which assumed the role of co-jointly operating all the Riu hotels (Fuster, 2010).[13]

Riu also pioneered the expansion in Jamaica, where it opened its first hotel in 2001 (San Román et al., 2020). The project embraced some difficulties, as the country lacked basic infrastructure, and the potential of its market was less evident than in the other Caribbean Islands. As explained by Luis Riu, 'it was very difficult for us to get the support of the tour operators'.[14] Now, Jamaica has become a highly appreciated destination by Americans and Europeans. Riu has today a total of three hotels.

3.4. Iberostar: The Last But Not the Least

The accumulated experience and knowledge from the domestic market, its dominant position along with the example of other hoteliers encouraged Miguel Fluxá

---

[10]Interview with Abraham Maciques (10-1-2017). Maciques was the founder of the Joint Venture Cubanacan S.A. and the current President of the Cuban Convention Centre in La Habana.

[11]Today, MHI runs more than 25 hotels in Cuba.

[12]Interview with Carmen Riu (26-2-2016).

[13]'Riu Hotels & Resorts; About Riu'.

[14]Preferente (XXIV, n. 285, February 2015, p. 51).

to internationalize also in America. He followed the advice of the Riu family: 'Luis Riu senior, an extraordinary person, told me that the demand for hotels in Latin America was enormous and the sales there were incredible. With that kind of encouragement, I had no option but to start there'.[15] Luis Riu Güel gave all the information to Fluxá about their business experiences in the Dominican Republic: 'Be quite open. Tell him about the problems and about the advantages too, everything'. Miguel Fluxà spent three nights at the first Dominican hotel of the Riu family and was there given first-hand information about the ups and downs of that process of expansion.[16]

Fluxá proposed the German tour operator to establish a partnership, like they had in Spain, and asked them to fund the building of the first hotel, the Iberostar Bávaro (San Román, 2017; San Román et al., 2021). However, Wolfgang Beeser, Neckerman CEO, turned down the project because of the country risks. Although Neckermann did not finance the internationalization of Iberostar, the German firm contributed to the marketing of the hotels in the Caribbean.[17]

Iberostar opened three hotels in Punta Cana between 1993 and 1997. These hotels were followed by another two in the country, as well as a last one in Punta Cana. The internationalization in the Caribbean was then spread to Mexico, Jamaica and Cuba (San Román, 2017).

3.5. The Main Characteristics of the Cluster Abroad

The last common step observed in the four companies was their internationalization, which occurred in the 1980s and early 1990s. All of them, except Meliá – which quickly revised its strategy – have chosen the Dominican Republic to build their first hotel abroad.

In contrast to other studies, which suggest that competitive hotels tend to isolate themselves in order to internally appropriate their expertise and resources (Henisz & Macher, 2004; Shaver & Flyer, 2000), the four companies opted for regrouping abroad. Specifically, they carried out a replication of the original Majorca's cluster, seeking structures and relationships in the foreign market like those developed at home. In fact, Barceló chose the Dominican Republic because of its similarities to Majorca in the 1950s. The arrival of the three other players allowed them to replicate the dynamics they had at home. Even though their partnerships with the German tour operators were key in developing the domestic cluster, the Spanish hotel companies went abroad alone. The knowledge accumulated in Majorca and their reluctant partners, due to the market risks, explained the sole involvement of the Spaniards in the foreign venture. Yet, their rapid success made the tour operators to reconsider their decision and join their Spanish partners - fully replicating the Majorca's cluster abroad.

---

[15]Interview with Miguel Fluxá (20-3-2013).
[16]Interview with Carmen Riu (26-2-2016).
[17]Interview with Wolfgang Beeser (21-11-2013).

The development of similar structures and relationships in the foreign market seems to be a key element of their successful internationalization. This was, probably, one of the main elements behind Meliá's movement from Bali to the Dominican Republic. The ability of firms to develop international relationships was reinforced by their previous experience in conducting their activities in the original cluster (Kontinen & Ojala, 2011). That is, through their previous experience of specific cluster structures and relationships, firms accumulate knowledge on how to effectively build subsequent similar relationships and how to manage them successfully.

4. Discussion and Conclusions

Tourism destinations are complex units that combine various actors with different individual objectives. However, these actors all share a common goal: to increase the competitiveness of the destination. Thus, tourism destinations can be considered realities where collective entrepreneurship is a central element (Chim-Miki & Batista-Canino, 2017; Timón, 2004). In this chapter, we studied the tourism cluster of Majorca and its connection with collective entrepreneurship, through the cases of the four companies previously analyzed. Specifically, these cases allow us to approach entrepreneurship as a result of a collective action, and context that embeds and shapes entrepreneurship. To do so, we have analyzed the trajectories of the four companies over time and identified common patterns of behaviour amongst them.

The study of the four cases supports Cirer-Costa (2014a, 2014b) in identifying Majorca as a tourism cluster. Specifically, the history of the four companies reflects the reality of an island that meets the characteristics of a Marshallian cluster: the presence of a multitude of companies offering the same service, the availability of a mobile and flexible labour market, the existence of extensive specialized knowledge and the presence of competitive suppliers of complementary products and services (Marshall, 1920). In the case of Majorca, we are dealing with an economy clearly specialized in the tourism sector where the market culture and the flexibility of the production factors made the island a leading destination worldwide, following the boom in mass tourism (Manera et al., 2020). The intensive exploitation of tourism resulted in a network of businesses of all types where the central element was the hotel business, complemented by a multitude of auxiliary businesses – travel agencies, guides, restaurants, shops, leisure services, etc. (Cirer-Costa, 2014a, 2014b).

Once our cases support the idea of Majorca as a tourism cluster, we discuss how these cases contribute to collective entrepreneurship. To do so, it is necessary to identify the characteristics of the Majorca cluster that favoured the flow of information and the continuous interaction between market agents, fostering collective entrepreneurship. In this sense, the two determining characteristics were the proximity between competitors due to the small size of the local market and the specialisation in an activity such as tourism, where it is very difficult to protect innovations with patents. These two characteristics explain the great deal of knowledge and resources shared between companies on an island with a markedly innovative character due to its 'Schumpeterian' business class and its historical commercial tradition (Cirer-Costa, 2009; Manera, 2004; Manera & Valle, 2017). All these characteristics – economic, social, cultural and geographical – reinforced the Majorca cluster and favoured collective entrepreneurship as shown by the common patterns of behaviour of our four cases. This connects with the idea of Cotic-Svetina, Jaklic, and Prodan (2008) on how collective learning flourishes in clusters, due to the geographical, cultural, socio-economic and organisational proximity among their members, which foster mutual understanding and trust.

As Gundolf, Jaouen, and Loup (2006) pointed out, collective strategies in the context of tourism development require the geographical concentration of actors, as well as a common objective and identity. Their insight was illustrated in our study, as the geographical actor deserved special attention. In contrast to the modelling of clusters based on networks (Buchnea, 2016), and on geographies approaches (Porter, 1990), the case of Majorca shows the complementarity between both approaches, by configuring its geography as a central element for the construction of its networks. The concentration of many local companies with a strong sense of belonging, on the island, enabled the cluster to create significant economies of scale. As a result, the cluster was allowed to reduce the costs and to increase their negotiation power with strong foreign companies such as, the European tour operators (Lorgnier & Su, 2014; Van der Zee & Vanneste, 2015). The geographical characteristics of the island have favoured the creation of local networks that, through collective actions, produced dynamics of collaboration, learning and knowledge-sharing (Depret & Hamdouch, 2009; Moulaert, 2013).

We observed how collective entrepreneurship was driven through the continuous interaction between local firms. This interaction between agents in the same market is fundamental to explain the competitiveness that companies have shown when expanding their activity (Cirer-Costa, 2014a, 2014b). Competitiveness was the main characteristic of the Majorcan accommodation market (Cirer-Costa, 2014a, 2014b), forcing companies to be dynamic and innovative, to not be left behind (Hernández-Barahona, San Román, & Gil-López, 2022). However, despite this strong competition, cooperation activities between companies were promoting the joint development of the cluster. As an example, we mentioned the constitution of 'The Confederation of Business Associations of the Balearic Islands', the professional relationship between Escarrer and Fluxá in their origins in the hotel business, or the Riu's support to Fluxá for his internationalization. This simultaneous relationship of competition and cooperation has been defined as coopetition (Brandenburger & Nalebuff, 1996). Firms cooperate to create and to develop a market, competing for market share (Schiavone & Simoni, 2011). This behaviour allows firms to balance the risks of competition with the benefits of cooperation, as well as to develop collective value-creation strategies (Gnyawali & Madhavan, 2001; Lorgnier & Su, 2014). This coopetitive behaviour favours the innovation and the development of the companies (Wilson & Popp, 2003). Thus, the interaction between the agents in the cluster – coopetition – boost the collective entrepreneurship.

Finally, we find that Mallorca's tourism cluster strongly developed, generating a path dependence. When one of the companies takes a decision or carries out an action, this indirectly affects the rest of the companies in the cluster, fostering them to replicate the same behaviour. Tourism destinations are units with a common purpose, co-location, cultural proximity and interconnectedness (Della Corte & Sciarelli, 2012; Kylänen & Mariani, 2012; Taylor, McRae-Williams, & Lowe, 2007). This is the reason why we observe similar trajectories in the case of the four firms studied, reinforcing this chapter's argument that the cluster promoted collective action and entrepreneurship. In this regard, we can note how Barceló's arrival in the Dominican Republic pulled the rest of the companies to expand the Majorca's cluster to the Caribbean.

Building a context of certainty was the main reason behind the replication of the original cluster. This involved choosing conditions such as, a destination with similar cultural and geographical characteristics as Majorca, developing the same original business, sun and sand tourism, and attracting competitors from the local market. Once these conditions were met, the four companies were able to replicate the original Majorca's cluster in the Dominican Republic. The network of relationships, initially developed in the home market, became the driving force behind the companies' successful international expansion (Belso Martínez, 2006; Coviello, 2006; Coviello & Munro, 1995). This replication process highlights, first, how entrepreneurs acting collectively rather than individually are influenced by the environment, but also have the capacity to transform it, driving change, as well as the industrial and economic growth (Lupova-Henry et al., 2021b). Second, this process reflects how the individual actions of the clustered companies influence the performance of the cluster, as a whole, and the rest of its actors. Both points highlight the link between the cluster and the joint action of its members. In the case of the four companies, actors in the Majorca's cluster, their entrepreneurial activity was intertwined with that of the others, resulting in a shared history marked by collective entrepreneurship.

Acknowledgement

Research has benefitted from public research project Spanish Project PGC201S8-093971-B-I00 granted by the Ministry of Science and Innovation Programme for Knowledge Generation, funded by MCIU/AEI/FEDER, UE.

References

Acs, Z. J., & Audretsch, D. B. (Eds.). (2010). *Handbook of entrepreneurship research: An interdisciplinary survey and introduction*. New York, NY: Springer.
Barceló Group. (2016). *Barceló 75 años. Memoria de un viaje compartido*. Madrid: La Fábrica.
Becattini, G. (1990). Alfred Marshall: vida y pensamiento. *Revista de economía, 6*, 11–17.
Belso Martínez, J. A. (2006). Why are some Spanish manufacturing firms internationalizing rapidly? The role of business and institutional international networks. *Entrepreneurship & Regional Development, 18*(3), 207–226.

Brandenburger, A. M., & Nalebuff, B. (1996). *Co-opetition: A revolutionary mindset that combines competition and cooperation in the marketplace*. London: Harper Collins Business, Hammersmith.

Buchnea, E. (2016). Networks and clusters in business history. In J. F. Wilson, S. Toms, A. de Jong, & E. Buchnea (Eds.), *The Routledge companion to business history* (pp. 273–287). London: Routledge.

Casson, M. (2003). Entrepreneurship, business culture and the theory of the firm. In Z. J. Acs & D. B. Audretsch (Eds.), *Handbook of entrepreneurship research* (pp. 223–246). Boston, MA: Springer.

Casson, M. (2010). Entrepreneurship: Theory, institutions and history. Eli F. Heckscher Lecture, 2009. *Scandinavian Economic History Review, 58*(2), 139–170.

Chim-Miki, A. F., & Batista-Canino, R. M. (2017). Tourism coopetition: An introduction to the subject and a research agenda. *International Business Review, 26*(6), 1208–1217.

Cirer-Costa, J. C. (2009). *La invenció del turisme de masses a Mallorca*. Palma: Documenta Balear.

Cirer-Costa, J. C. (2014a). Majorca's tourism cluster: The creation of an industrial district. *Business History, 56*(8), 1243–1261.

Cirer-Costa, J. C. (2014b). The explosive expansion and consolidation of the Balearic hotel sector, 1964-2010. *Revista de Historia Industrial, 56*, 189–216.

Colli, A., Fernández Pérez, P. F., & Rose, M. B. (2003). National determinants of family firm development? Family firms in Britain, Spain, and Italy in the nineteenth and twentieth centuries. *Enterprise & Society, 4*(1), 28–64.

Colli, A., & Rose, M. B. (1999). Families and firms: The culture and evolution of family firms in Britain and Italy in the nineteenth and twentieth centuries. *Scandinavian Economic History Review, 47*(1), 24–47.

Colli, A., & Rose, M. B. (2003). Family firms in comparative perspective. In F. Amatori & G. Jones (Eds.), *Business history around the world* (pp. 339–352). New York, NY: Cambridge University Press.

Cotic-Svetina, A., Jaklic, M., & Prodan, I. (2008). Does collective learning in clusters contribute to innovation? *Science and Public Policy, 35*(5), 335–345.

Coviello, N. E. (2006). The network dynamics of international new ventures. *Journal of International Business Studies, 37*, 713–731.

Coviello, N. E., & Munro, H. J. (1995). Growing the entrepreneurial firm: Networking for international market development. *European Journal of Marketing, 29*(7), 49–61.

Della Corte, V., & Sciarelli, M. (2012). Can coopetition be source of competitive advantage for strategic networks? *Corporate Ownership and Control, 10*, 363–379.

Depret, M. H., & Hamdouch, A. (2009). Clusters, réseaux d'innovation et dynamiques de proximité dans les secteurs high-tech. Une revue critique de la littérature récente. *Revue d'économie industrielle, 128*, 21–52.

Eisenhardt, K. M., & Graebner, M. E. (2007). Theory building from cases: Opportunities and challenges. *The Academy of Management Journal, 50*(1), 25–32.

Fernández Pérez, P., & Colli, A. (2013). *The endurance of family businesses. A global overview*. Cambridge, MA: Cambridge University Press.

Fernández Pérez, P., & Rose, M. B. (Eds.). (2009). *Innovation and entrepreneurial networks in Europe*. Oxford: Routledge.

Ferreira, J. J., Fernandes, C. I., & Kraus, S. (2019). Entrepreneurship research: Mapping intellectual structures and research trends. *Review of Managerial Science, 13*(1), 181–205.

Fuster, B. (2010). Crecimiento internacional de cadenas hoteleras vacacionales españolas desde una perspectiva global: un estudio de casos. *Cuadernos de turismo, 25*, 69–97.

Gadille, M., Tremblay, D. G., & Vion, A. (2013). La méta-organisation territorialisée, moteur d'apprentissages collectifs. *Revue interventions Économiques. Papers in Political Economy, 48*, 2–13.

Gil-López, A., Zozimo, R., San Román, E., & Jack, S.L. (2016). At the crossroads. Management and business history in entrepreneurship research. *Journal of Evolutionary Studies in Business, 2*(1), 156–200.

Gnyawali, D. R., & Madhavan, R. (2001). Cooperative networks and competitive dynamics: A structural embeddedness perspective. *Academy of Management Review, 26,* 431–445.

Gundolf, K., Jaouen, A., & Loup, S. (2006). La place des institutions locales dans les stratégies collectives: le cas du secteur du tourisme. *Revue Française de Gestion, 32*(167), 141–156.

Henisz, W. J., & Macher, J. T. (2004). Firm- and country-level trade-offs and contingencies in the evaluation of foreign investment: The semiconductor industry, 1994-2002. *Organization Science, 15*(5), 537–554.

Hernández-Barahona, J., San Román, E., & Gil-López, Á. (2022). Bricolage and innovation in the emergence and development of the Spanish tourism industry. *Enterprise & Society,* 1–43.

Hollow, M. (2020). Historicizing entrepreneurial networks. *Strategic Entrepreneurship Journal, 14*(1), 66–88.

Jack, S. L., & Anderson, A. R. (2002). The effects of embeddedness on the entrepreneurial process. *Journal of Business Venturing, 17*(5), 467–487.

King, G., Petrenchik, T., Dewit, D., McDougall, J., Hurley, P., & Law, M. (2010). Out-of-school time activity participation profiles of children with physical disabilities: A cluster analysis. *Child: Care, Health and Development, 36*(5), 726–741.

Kipping, M., Wadhwani, R., & Bucheli, M. (2014). Analyzing and interpreting historical sources. In M. Bucheli & R. Wadhwani (Eds.), *Organizations in time: History, theory, methods* (pp. 305–329). Oxford: Oxford University Press.

Kontinen, T., & Ojala, A. (2011). Network ties in the international opportunity recognition of family SMEs. *International Business Review, 20*(4), 440–453.

Kylänen, M., & Mariani, M. M. (2012). Unpacking the temporal dimension of coopetition in tourism destinations: Evidence from Finnish and Italian theme Parks. *Anatolia, 23,* 61–74.

Lehmann, T., & Benner, M. (2015). Cluster policy in the light of institutional context: A comparative study of transition countries. *Administrative Sciences, 5*(4), 188–212.

Lorgnier, N., & Su, C. (2014). Considering coopetition strategies in sport tourism networks: A look at the nonprofit nautical sports clubs on the northern coast of France. *European Sport Management Quarterly, 14*(1), 87–109.

Lupova-Henry, E., Blili, S., & Dal Zotto, C. (2021a). Clusters as institutional entrepreneurs: Lessons from Russia. *Journal of Innovation and Entrepreneurship, 10*(1), 1–27.

Lupova-Henry, E., Blili, S., & Dal Zotto, C. (2021b). Designing organised clusters as social actors: A meta-organisational approach. *Journal of Organization Design, 10*(1), 35–54.

Manera, C. (2004). El model històric de creixement a les Illes Balears: un intent de teorització. *Anuari de la Societat Catalana d'Economia, 18,* 8–18.

Manera, C., Molina, R., Montiel, J. P., & Manera-Salom, M. (2020). El turismo de masas como sistema de producción: la revolución histórica en el Mediterráneo, 1949-2014. *Revista de Historia Industrial, 29*(78), 155–187.

Manera, C., & Valle, E. (2017). Industria y servicios en Baleares, 1950-2015: la desindustrialización regional en una economía terciaria. *Investigaciones de Historia Económica, 14*(3), 210–219.

Marshall, A. (1920). *Principles of economics.* London: Macmillan.

Moulaert, F. (Ed.). (2013). *The international handbook on social innovation: Collective action, social learning and transdisciplinary research.* Cheltenham: Edward Elgar Publishing.

Pla, J. (1993). *Gabriel Barceló: semblanza de un líder.* Palma: Fisa Escudo de Oro.

Popp, A., Toms, S., & Wilson, J. (2006). Industrial districts as organizational environments: Resources, networks and structures. *Management & Organizational History, 1*(4), 349–370.

Porter, M. E. (1990). *Competitive advantage of nations.* New York, NY: Free Press.

San Román, E. (2017). *Building stars. Miguel Fluxá. An Entrepreneurial Story.* Madrid: El Viso.

San Román, E., Gil-López, A., Díez-Vial, I., & Jack, S. L. (2021). Networking from home to abroad: The internationalization of Iberostar group. In T. Leppäaho & S. Jack. (Ed.), *The Palgrave handbook of family firm internationalization* (pp. 327–360). Cham: Palgrave Macmillan.

San Román, E., Puig, N., & Gil-López, A. (2020). German capital and the development of the Spanish hotel industry (1950s-1990s): A tale of two strategic alliances. *Business History*, 1–25. doi:10.1080/00076791.2020.1821658

Schiavone, F., & Simoni, M. (2011). An experience-based view of co-opetition in R&D networks. *European Journal of Innovation Management, 14*(2), 136–154.

Schrammel, T. (2013). Bridging the institutional void: An analytical concept to develop valuable cluster services. *Management Review, 24*, 114–132.

Shane, S. A. (2003). *A general theory of entrepreneurship: The individual-opportunity nexus.* Cheltenham: Edward Elgar Publishing.

Shaver, J. M., & Flyer, F. (2000). Agglomeration economies, firm heterogeneity, and foreign direct investment in the United States. *Strategic Management Journal, 21*(12), 1175–1193.

Taylor, P., McRae-Williams, P., & Lowe, J. (2007). The determinants of cluster activities in the Australian wine and tourism industries. *Tourism Economics, 13*, 639–656.

Timón, D. A. (2004). El concepto de destino turístico. Una aproximación geográfico-territorial. *Estudios turísticos, 160*, 45–68.

Trivellato, F., Halevi, L., & Antunes, C. (Eds.). (2014). *Religion and trade: Cross-cultural exchanges in world history, 1000–1900.* Oxford: Oxford University Press.

Vallejo, R. (2019). Turismo en España durante el primer tercio del siglo XX: la conformación de un sistema turístico. *Ayer: Revista de Historia Contemporánea, 114*(2), 175–211.

Van der Zee, E., & Vanneste, D. (2015). Tourism networks unraveled: A review of the literature on networks in tourism management studies. *Tourism Management Perspectives, 15*, 46–56.

Wilson, J. F., & Popp, A. (2003). Business networking in the industrial revolution: Some comments. *The Economic History Review, 56*(2), 355–361.

Chapter 3

Collective Entrepreneurship and the Development of Private Clinics in Geneva, 1860–2020

Pierre-Yves Donzé

Abstract

The growth of the healthcare industry since the middle of the nineteenth century has offered medical doctors a broad range of opportunities to develop their private practice. However, a major challenge was accessing the new medical technology at the core of this growth, as operation rooms, X-ray machines, laboratories and sterilization equipment were mostly centred in hospitals. Based on the case of Geneva, Switzerland, this chapter discusses the various strategies adopted by medical doctors to benefit from hospital infrastructure for their work. It demonstrates that collective entrepreneurship emerged at the end of the nineteenth century, when groups of doctors started to open collective clinics in response to the impossibility of using the infrastructure of the local public hospital linked to the University of Geneva. This heyday of collective private clinics lasted until the 1990s when listed companies and private investors took over and reorganized these private healthcare organizations.

Keywords: Private clinic; hospital; healthcare; Geneva; collective entrepreneurship; medical technology

1. Introduction

The modern healthcare industry – considered a sector that provides various services to restore or improve the health conditions of individuals and communities – was formed in Western Europe and the United States (US) during the second part of the nineteenth century in a twofold context of social change

Collective Entrepreneurship in the Contemporary European Services Industries:
A Long Term Approach, 29–45
Copyright © 2023 by Emerald Publishing Limited
All rights of reproduction in any form reserved
doi:10.1108/978-1-80117-950-820231003

and technological innovation (Donzé, 2023a). On the one hand, population growth, industrialization and urbanization led to a growing demand for health-care from working classes that needed to cure diseases and recover from injuries to earn a living (Domin, 2008; Labisch & Spree, 2001). On the other hand, technological innovation regarding medical equipment, notably surgery tables, sterilization devices and X-ray machines, changed how medical doctors practised medicine. This new technology, which enabled the treatment of a growing number of patients, involved large financial investments, usually concentrated in hospitals (Howell, 1995; Timmermann & Anderson, 2006).

The consequence of this change was the formation of a growing healthcare market. Previously, hospitalization and healthcare were mostly carried out in a charitable context – that is, in a non-market environment – however, more and more patients were ready to pay to access this new medical technology. Hospital organization and management had to adapt and find ways to ensure the financial basis of their growth (Cherry, 1997; Domin, 2008; Fernandes Péres, 2021; Gorsky & Sheard, 2006).

Another important consequence of this change was related to the daily practice of medicine. The new medical technology was installed in hospitals, but it soon became necessary for medical doctors, who used to work independently and focus on home visits, to use it. They developed various strategies to access this technological infrastructure that had become necessary for their professional practice. Ikai (2010) argued that three major models coexisted in Western countries and Japan: an open hospital model, where independent doctors signed a contract with hospitals to use their equipment for their private needs, as in the United States; a closed model, where hospitals engaged salaried doctors and did not let independent practitioners use their infrastructure, as in the UK and France; and a private model in which doctors create their own individual clinic to access this infrastructure, which is largely dominant in Japan. These three models are basically ideal-types, and a mixture of them can be observed in most European countries (Donzé, 2023b; Faure, 2019; Stevens, 1989). Medical doctors carried out a broad range of collective actions to secure access to the new technological platforms necessary for their professional activities, from lobbying local governments through trade associations to access public hospitals to the foundation of collective private clinics. In this perspective, doctors can be approached as entrepreneurs that take collective actions.

The entrepreneurship of private medical doctors remains an under-studied subject from a historical perspective. Several works in social sciences have addressed this issue, but they assume it is a new phenomenon that emerged world-wide at the end of the twentieth century (e.g. Carlos & Hiatt, 2022; Nagral, 2012; Stone, 1997). However, recent scholarship in the business history of medicine has demonstrated that medical doctors were established as professional entrepreneurs in large hospitals since the late nineteenth century (Donzé, 2023a ; Fernándes Péres, 2021). Similar to the professional managers that transformed American firms into large modern corporations (Chandler, 1977), doctors contributed to making hospital organizations equipped with modern technology and efficiently managed since the 1880s–1900s. However, the collective entrepreneurship of medical doctors was not limited to their actions within hospitals. Private doctors carried out collective actions to create organizations (e.g. trade associations) and enterprises (e.g. private clinics and laboratories) that would strengthen their professional practice. In this sense, they embody the entrepreneurial group, which Rueff (2010) defines teams of entrepreneurs that act collectively against the image of the self-made man to found new ventures.

This chapter explores the collective entrepreneurship of medical doctors through the example of Geneva, Switzerland, during the twentieth century. In 2005, Switzerland was the second country in OECD with the largest density of doctors (3.79 per 1,000 population), behind Austria (4.54) but ahead of the United States (2.43) (OECD, 2022). Moreover, this year, Geneva was the second Swiss canton (among a total of 26) with the highest density of doctors in private practice after Basel (OFS, 2021). Hence, Geneva can be considered as one city with the world's highest density of medical doctors.

Like other countries in Western Europe, Switzerland experienced a fast development of its hospital system during the twentieth century (Donzé, 2023b). The church and philanthropists, local governments and medical doctors engaged in the construction and development of hospitals throughout the country. The modernization of technological equipment (particularly the installation of X-ray devices and new operating rooms) deeply impacted medical doctors' professional practice. Accessing this infrastructure became a key issue during the interwar years and still is today. Moreover, the development of health insurance to cover the costs of hospitalizations ensured a sustainable growth of the hospital system after World War II. Consequently, a growing number of medical doctors, supported by various kinds of investors (real estate owners, private bankers, etc.), organized private clinics in large cities.

The objective of this chapter is to discuss the formation and development of private clinics in Geneva from the early twentieth century until today. Although there is a large state-owned university hospital in this city, it also has several private clinics that developed quickly over time to answer the needs of independent doctors in medtech infrastructure and strong local demand (high-income population and wealthy tourists). The main research questions addressed are: Who were the entrepreneurs who founded private clinics in Geneva? What were their motivations? How did this business change over time? The research is based on primary (hospitals, clinics and local government) and published sources (annual reports and local press).

2. The Heyday of Philanthropy (1860–1890)

In the middle of the nineteenth century, the Geneva medical system showed a strong bipolarization between the healthcare market, which was essentially limited to the outpatient activities of doctors, and the hospital system, which was essentially aimed at the indigent and not part of the market logic. Founded in the sixteenth century, the Geneva General Hospital had been modernized since the end of the eighteenth century, with greater attention given to patients and an increasing number of non-indigents paying to be admitted (Louis-Courvoisier,

2000); however, it was still largely outside the healthcare market. The contributions paid by the patients – which amounted to 12.2% of the hospital's total income in 1850 (Donzé, 2003, p. 47) – were used to cover the costs of board and lodging (food, bedding, hospital staff) and not the actual health care. The doctors of the General Hospital maintained a home practice as a source of income.

In 1856, following a local revolution, the new radical-democratic authorities established the Cantonal Hospital of Geneva, while the General Hospital refocused on public relief. The new hospital was a large organization – 227 beds when it opened – intended to receive all the sick patients of the canton. It also functioned as a university hospital since the 1876 opening of the Faculty of Medicine (Rieder, 2009). The number of inpatients grew rapidly from 1,173 in 1860 to 2,733 in 1890.[1] Yet despite this dynamic, the Cantonal Hospital remained a purely charitable establishment. Most of the patients were indigent people who were offered treatment, and the hospital's doctors, including the professors in charge of clinical chairs, retained private practice as their main source of income (Rieder, 2009, pp. 136–138).

Besides, private philanthropic hospitals were opened by patrician families that lost political power in reaction to the creation of the Cantonal Hospital. The four main establishments were Butini Infirmary (1859), Maison Gourgas for sick children (1869), Rothschild Ophthalmic Hospital (1874) and Priory Infirmary (1876) (Donzé, 2003, pp. 101–107). Their organizational characteristics were similar to those of the Cantonal Hospital: they received indigent patients and had doctors who kept an external professional activity. Their resources were based on charitable donations. This small network of charitable hospitals was very successful, allowing them to compete with the radical state in the field of assistance. Their share of the total number of hospital admissions in the canton rose steadily during 1860–1890, from less than 10% to more than a third (see Table 2).

Although there was strong competition between the Cantonal Hospital and the charitable hospitals, the Geneva medical system was very stable. There was a clear separation between the healthcare market – centred on the private activities of doctors – and the hospital system. The spread of new technologies during 1890–1914 upset this balance, and it made medical doctors' access to hospitals a major issue.

3. The Impact of Modern Technology (1890–1945)

The main results of the transformation of medical technology in Geneva after the 1890s were the fast growth of the Cantonal Hospital, where the most modern technology was concentrated, and the decline of charitable hospitals. Between 1890 and 1945, the market share of the first went from 65.3% of hospitalizations to 88.7% (see Table 2). The healthcare market became highly competitive, and medical doctors had to adapt to this new context to secure their access to modern technology.

---

[1] *Centième anniversaire de l'hôpital cantonal de Genève, 1856–1956*, Genève 1956.

Table 2.   Number of Patients Admitted in Geneva Hospitals, 1860–1945.

	1860	**1875**	**1885**	**1890**	**1914**	**1930**	**1945**
Butini Infirmary	170	200	310	399	300	227	200
Priory Infirmary	–	192	274	279	0	0	0
Maison Gourgas	–	92	156	353	700	788	1,050
Rothschild Hospital	–	286	357	423	476	498	285
Total charitable hospitals	170	770	1,097	1,454	1,476	1,513	1,535
Cantonal Hospital	1,773	2,560	2,638	2,733	7,869	8,019	12,070
Grand total	1,943	3,330	3,735	4,187	9,345	9,532	13,605
Private hospitals as a %	8.7	23.1	29.4	34.7	15.8	15.9	11.3
Cantonal hospital as a %	91.3	76.9	70.6	65.3	84.2	84.1	88.7

Source: Annual reports of the various hospitals.

Note 1: The relative importance of the Cantonal Hospital in 1860 is overestimated because of the existence of a catholic charitable hospital in 1845–1875, which had a capacity of about 300 patients in the mid-1860s. See Droux (2000), pp. 49–61.

Note 2: Author's estimates for the Butini Infirmary and the Maison Gourgas in 1914 and 1945.

3.1. The Dominant Position of the Cantonal Hospital

The Cantonal Hospital underwent a period of reorganization in the years 1890–1914. The number of new departments increased and infrastructure was modernized, with the extension of the buildings (1890), the installation of an X-ray service (1896), the creation of a dermatology department (1898), and then the successive opening of a new maternity ward (1906), a children's clinic (1910), an ophthalmic clinic (1910) and a new surgery clinic (1913). The capacity reached 650 beds in 1910 and allowed 5,267 patients to be treated that year, compared with only 2,733 in 1890. The number of operations increased from 304 in 1889 to 1,350 in 1913.[2]

The professors of medicine who had access to this new infrastructure began to use it for their own purposes. In 1904, newly appointed Professor of Surgery Charles Girard obtained permission to treat his private patients at the Cantonal Hospital (Rieder, 2009, p. 248). The same was true for the professors appointed in the following years. In 1907, the administrative commission issued a regulation on the use of private rooms. As a result, a few professors opened their own private clinic to treat their wealthy patients, the most known being the clinic opened in 1919 by Prof Jacques-Louis Reverdin and his cousin Auguste Reverdin (Rieder, 2009, pp. 136–137). However, it was largely an exception. The integration

[2] *Centieme anniversaire de l'hopital cantonal de Geneve, 1856–1956*, Geneve 1956.

of private practice within the Cantonal Hospital led to strong opposition from self-employed doctors in the city, who did not have access to this infrastructure. Yet, the private clientele of the Cantonal Hospital's doctors still represented only a small proportion of all hospitalizations. In 1910, it accounted for 15% of all days spent in hospital, compared with 82% for state-funded indigent patients and only 3% for people with insurance.[3]

Charitable hospitals tried to integrate new medical technologies but were unable to maintain their competitiveness against the Cantonal Hospital due to their limited financial resources. Priory Infirmary was closed in 1909, while Gourgas and Rothschild hospitals were more fortunate because they specialized in fields for which the Cantonal Hospital had no specific clinics until 1910, namely children's diseases and ophthalmology, respectively. They then enjoyed a quasi-monopoly in treating Geneva's indigents for these specialities (Donzé, 2003). However, they remained essentially charitable institutions that did not provide a professional infrastructure for independent doctors.

3.2. Private Doctors' Access to New Technologies

Access to the new medical infrastructure was a particularly important issue as the number of private doctors increased rapidly in the first part of the twentieth century, making the medical market more and more competitive (see Fig. 1). Between 1890 and 1910, their number increased from 104 to 247. Consequently, in 1892, doctors formed an organised lobby, the *Association des médecins du canton de Genève* (AMG), which worked to defend their professional interests (Ehrenström, 1992). Specifically, it attempted to widen the possibilities of access to the surgical

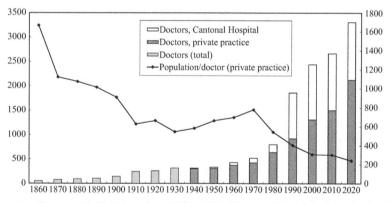

Fig. 1.   Geneva Medical Market, 1860–2020. *Source:* Calculated on the basis of the *Historical Statistics of Switzerland*, Zurich, Chronos, 1996 and FMH statistics (https://www.fmh.ch/fr/themes/statistique-medicale.cfm, accessed 12 July 2022). *Note:* since 1940, doctors of the Cantonal Hospital with a private practice are considered to be private practicians.

---

[3] *Centieme anniversaire de l'hopital cantonal de Geneve, 1856–1956*, Geneve 1956.

clinic of the Cantonal Hospital (Rieder, 2009, pp. 280–282). However, the outcome of lobbying was limited. Consequently, private doctors engaged in another kind of collective action: opening private clinics.

The Clinique Générale SA was founded in 1899 with the aim of providing its members with a hospital infrastructure equipped with the best medical technology. Financially supported by private bankers Pictet, Lombard & Chauvet and philanthropist Agénor de Boissier with capital of 225,000 francs, this company included 22 doctors among its shareholders at the time of its foundation.[4] Several of them had seen their work at the Cantonal Hospital coming to an end in the middle of their careers, which meant they could no longer access its technical infrastructure for their own needs. Examples include Ernest Long, chief physician, 1878–1882; André Jeanneret, assistant physician, 1890–1894; Emile Thomas, unsuccessful candidate for the chair of therapeutics in 1897; and Hector Maillart, assistant physician, 1898–1902. Several of them were also founding members of the AMG.[5] The Clinique Générale was inaugurated in 1901. It was equipped with an operating theatre and included single rooms and four-bed rooms.[6] In 1903, a second establishment, the Clinique La Colline, was also opened. The development of these clinics until the end of the 1910s is unfortunately not documented, but their existence provided private doctors with access to new medical technologies.

3.3. Regulating Competition

The strong competition between healthcare organizations led to financial problems that jeopardized the functioning and development of the medical system. The race for the most profitable patient made it difficult to envisage an increase in pension prices and medical fees that would cover the costs incurred by the constant modernization of technical equipment. Various measures were adopted after 1900 to regulate hospitalization.

First, regarding the indigent, the cantonal government created the Assistance Publique Médicale (APM) in 1900.[7] It provides free healthcare for the indigent, provided they are cared for in the Cantonal Hospital or at home by the University Policlinic. This legislation enabled the Cantonal Hospital to capture the market of needy patients. However, in 1936, the hospital introduced the principle of operating and laboratory fees for indigent patients: the amount varied according to the individual situation.[8]

Second, the hospitalization of the middle classes was encouraged by the development of health insurance. The federal law on health and accident insurance (LAMA) of 1911 provided for the subsidization of state-recognized health

---

[4]Archives of Clinique Générale Beaulieu SA (ACG), Minutes of the meeting of 26 May 1898.

[5]Archives de l'Etat de Genève (AEG), biographical files.

[6]*Journal de Genève*, 8 November 1901.

[7]AEG, Recueil des lois, loi sur l'organisation de l'assistance publique médicale, 21 November 1900.

[8]*Journal de Genève*, 27 May 1939.

insurance funds and the adoption of official tariffs in each canton. In 1916, Geneva's cantonal government drew up a list of medical tariffs after negotiations with the AMG and the Fédération des Sociétés de Secours Mutuels de Genève, an association that gathered healthcare non-profit insurers.[9] This set the rates for medical procedures for patients covered by insurance and thus established equality between the various healthcare institutions in this respect. This list of official medical fees was revised several times (1925, 1939). The number of health insurance organizations in Geneva grew rapidly from 21 in 1914 to 60 in 1928.[10] The proportion of the population covered was certainly on the rise but remained low, increasing from 3% in 1903 to 31% in 1944.[11]

Third, the hospitalization of wealthy patients was a matter of free competition and remained the essential basis of the income for the medical profession (fees) and healthcare institutions (pensions). However, the AMG denounced the unfair competition exercised by the Cantonal Hospital towards independent doctors and private clinics. While first-class patients were subject to the private practice of professors, second-class patients attracted the wrath of the AMG. They were only subject to the operating fees paid to the Cantonal Hospital and were treated without paying doctors' fees. In 1928, the AMG obtained the introduction of fees for doctors, which improved the competitiveness of healthcare institutions.[12]

The evolution of hospitalization conditions in the first third of the twentieth century had two main effects. First, it strengthened the Cantonal Hospital's position in the hospitalization of indigent patients and the consequent decline of philanthropic institutions. The Cantonal Hospital entered a phase of stagnation in terms of hospitalizations after the First World War, with an average of 7,589 patients in the 1920s and 1930s. However, the modernization of its infrastructure and equipment continued with new departments created and a pathological institute opened (1934). The number of doctors increased from 15 in 1922 to 31 in 1935 (Donzé, 2003, p. 181). Moreover, while it attracted more and more private and insured patients after 1910, the Cantonal Hospital retained its status as a care facility for the indigent, who accounted for half of all hospital admissions in 1930 and 1940 (see Table 3).

Under these conditions, philanthropic institutions found it difficult to remain competitive. The administrators of the Butini Infirmary attempted to modernize their equipment, but this did not stop the decline of the establishment, which refocused on elderly people with chronic diseases. Gourgas and Rothschild hospitals remained specialized and shifted from charitable institutions to private clinics, opening their doors to consultations by external doctors (Donzé, 2003).

[9]AEG, Recueil des lois, tarifs médicaux, 25 January 1916.

[10]*Bulletin de la Fédération des Sociétés de secours mutuels de la Suisse romande*, various years.

[11]*Les sociétés de secours mutuels en Suisse en l'année 1903*, Berne 1907 and *Bulletin de la Fédération des Sociétés de secours mutuels de la Suisse romande*, 1944, p. 172.

[12]*Journal de Genève*, 27 May 1939.

Table 3. Coverage of Inpatient Days at the Cantonal Hospital, in %, 1910–1940.

	1910	1920	1930	1940
State (APM)	82	60	50	50
Health insurances	3	8	15	18
Private wards	15	32	35	32

Source: *Centième anniversaire de l'hôpital cantonal de Genève, 1856–1956*, Geneva: Hôpital cantonal, 1956.

However, the business opportunities for private doctors were limited to their specializations.

The second effect of these new conditions of hospitalization was the strengthening of competition between the Cantonal Hospital and private clinics. The development of health insurance companies, whose tariffs are accepted by several private clinics, and the introduction of second-class surgery fees at the Cantonal Hospital, reduced the differences between public and private establishments. This created a more favourable environment for developing private clinics, and several new ones were opened, including the Clinique Beaulieu (1929) and the Clinique des Grangettes (1933). In 1942, the directors of Geneva's clinics joined together to form an Association of Private Clinics to control and unify their fees. Their aim was to strengthen their position in relation to the Cantonal Hospital rather than compete with each other.

The Clinique Générale SA is again a good example of this desire to strengthen competitiveness. It installed a radiology installation (1922), a laboratory (1926), a diathermy machine (1927) and enlarged its main building (1929). In 1935, despite the financial difficulties caused by the economic crisis, the board of directors accepted the project to acquire new surgical devices '*so that our equipment would remain one of the best in Geneva and in order to compensate for the inconvenience of the distance from the clinic by the quality of the work*'.[13] The Clinique Générale also adopted a strategy of diversification into niche activities, opening a nursery (1941) and a dietetics service (1942), which did not exist in Geneva at the time. Moreover, it lowered its boarding prices on several occasions to remain competitive (1924, 1934, 1936) and retain the patients who were '*deserting the clinics and going more and more to the Cantonal Hospital*'.[14]

4. From Stable Growth to Competition (1945–1990)

The regulation introduced during the 1920s and 1930s enabled stable growth of the healthcare industry in Geneva for several decades. However, competitiveness decreased between 1930 and 1970 (see Fig. 1). Despite the slight rise in the number of private doctors, their average number of populations grew over the long term, from 546 persons in 1930 to 778 in 1970. The Cantonal Hospital and

---

[13]AGC, Minutes of meetings of the board of directors, 15 February 1935.
[14]ACG, Minutes of meetings of the board of directors, 29 January 1936.

private clinics experienced a phase of development within a relatively uncompetitive environment, which followed Geneva's demographic growth (from 171,366 inhabitants in 1930 to 331,599 in 1970).[15] The Cantonal Hospital developed quickly to offer healthcare services to this expanding population and answer the needs of the faculty of medicine.[16] It opened new buildings for the new university clinics and medical departments, with the total number of beds growing from 870 in 1940 to 1,960 in 1970. It became a giant organization, employing 3,419 people in 1970, which included an increasing number of academic researchers. As expressed in Fig. 1, the number of hospital doctors without private practice (essentially assistant doctors and university researchers) appeared in the 1940s and became more important during the 1960s. There were 93 in 1970.

Private clinics followed a similar trend until the 1970s, characterized by general growth. The Clinique Générale remained the largest and most important organization open to private doctors. A second major collective clinic was developed after the war, Beaulieu Clinic SA. This hospital was the former clinic of the Reverdin cousins, taken over by a charitable nursing school in 1929. In 1947, a group of investors purchased the clinic to open it more broadly to private doctors. Essentially, the 18-member board of directors appointed that year included doctors.[17] This was the second example of collective entrepreneurship by private doctors in Geneva. In 1956, it opened the first cobalt therapy service in Switzerland.[18] However, other private clinics were mostly small organizations.

The environment of private medicine changed dramatically during the 1970s and 1980s to being more competition-driven by the fast development of Cantonal Hospital. During the 1970s, the management of this organization refocused on high-tech medicine and intensively developed academic research. It adopted a policy of disengagement from chronic and convalescent patients. The cantonal government opened a 320-bed geriatric hospital (1972) and a centre for continuous care (1979). Meanwhile, the Cantonal Hospital developed massively. In 1990, it had nine departments that managed a total of 16 clinics, 21 divisions, 6 policlinics and 6 units. In the same year, it employed 6,030 people, including 937 doctors without private practice (see Fig. 1), which was more than all doctors *with* private practice. Now a giant organization, it adopted new management practices to reduce costs and increase the turnover of healthcare. The total number of beds started to decline after 1970, and the average length of hospitalization dropped from 19.5 days in 1970 to 12.5 days in 1990. At the end of the 1980s, the Cantonal Hospital treated more than 38,000 patients a year and took over 700,000 X-ray images annually.[19]

In these conditions, it became very difficult for private clinics to remain competitive, particularly small-scale clinics that lacked the capital to invest in the modernization of their equipment following the development of CT scanners and MRI devices.

---

[15]Office fédéral de la statistique (OFS), population census.
[16]Hôpital cantonal de Genève, Annual reports, 1945–1990.
[17]*FOSC*, 17 July 1947.
[18]*Journal de Genève*, 23 April 1956.
[19]Hôpital cantonal de Genève, Annual reports, 1945-1990.

To stay competitive against the Cantonal Hospital, private clinics had to expand the scale of their business. This led to two major developments: the merger of Clinique Générale and Beaulieu Clinic, and the foundation of a new private hospital.

First, in 1981, Clinique Générale and Beaulieu Clinic, the two largest private hospitals in Geneva, decided to merge into a new joint stock company, Clinique Générale Beaulieu SA (CGB) and open new modern medical facilities. The following year, the board of directors had 11 members, including 7 doctors, which suggests that private doctors continued to invest in their clinic. In 1983, the capital increased from 290,000 CHF to 2.5 million CHF, but private doctors kept the majority on the board.[20] This investment enabled CGB to remain a major private hospital in Geneva and continue developing its technological equipment.

Second, in 1976, a new 250-bed private clinic, La Tour Hospital, opened in Geneva. It was founded by private investors, charitable gifts, and the participation of Gourgas Hospital, which was merged with this project. When it started its operations, it employed only six salaried doctors but was open to private doctors established in Geneva.[21] However, this ambitious project was unprofitable, and the clinic was sold in 1980 to the US for-profit healthcare company Humana Inc.[22] During the 1980s, this firm invested millions of CHF in Switzerland and developed La Tour, despite various scandals related to over-priced services.[23]

These two largest private hospitals embody well the turning point of the 1980s for private hospital business: while the first one can still be considered as the outcome of collective entrepreneurship by private doctors, the second resulted from the foreign investment of a US corporation looking for short-term financial profit. Moreover, most of the smaller private clinics disappeared during this period. In 1952, Geneva had at least 13 private clinics, mostly very small organizations[24]; by 1990, half had vanished (see Table 4). However, some doctors identified specialized activities as an opportunity to open new ventures during this period; for example, the Champel-Elysée Clinic, a private hospital that specialized in outpatient surgery.[25] Nevertheless, this was an exception, as it was taken over in 1998 by CGB.

5. Neo-Liberalism and the Growing Big Business of Private Clinics (1990–2020)

The 1990s were a turning point in the organization of the Swiss healthcare system, characterized by the adoption of a new federal law on health insurance that introduced the principle of hospital planning in each canton to reduce over-equipment and try to control the increase of healthcare costs (Donzé, 2017). This led to

---

[20]*FOSC*, 27 July 1983.
[21]*Journal de Genève*, 19 March 1976.
[22]*FOSC*, 12 March 1980.
[23]*Journal de Genève*, 17 December 1982, 14 November 1986 and 25 March 1988.
[24]*Journal de Genève*, 4 February 1952.
[25]*FOSC*, 3 March 1983.

Table 4.   Private Clinics in Geneva, 1990.

	Number of Beds	
L'Arve	21	Merged by La Tour (1998)
Grangettes	84	Taken over by Hirslanden (2018)
Vert-Pré	23	Independent
Générale-Beaulieu	104	Taken over by Swiss Medical Network (2016)
La Colline	62	Taken over by Hirslanden (2014)
Belmont	21	Independent
Champel-Elysée	15	Merged by Générale-Beaulieu (1998)
La Tour	132	Taken over by Colony Capital (2007) and private investors (2013)

Source: *La santé en chiffres: Recueil de statistiques socio-sanitaires sur le canton de* Genève, Genève: Office cantonal de la statistique, 1995, p. 143; *Le Temps*, 12 November 1998, *Bilan*, 11 February 2013.

the creation of healthcare networks through the merger of several organizations at the regional level and a stronger concentration of public investment in a few major university cantonal hospitals.

In Geneva, this policy gave birth in 1995 to a new giant public organization, Hôpitaux Universitaires de Genève (HUG, *Geneva University Hospitals*), through the merger of all public healthcare organizations, from general hospital to psychiatry and geriatrics (Donzé, 2003). It employed 7,623 people for a budget of about 1 billion CHF in 1995.[26] In 2020, the number of employees had increased to 12,838 with a 2.1 billion CHF budget.[27] The workforce included a slightly increasing number of doctors without private practice: 937 in 1990 and 1,181 in 2020 (see Fig. 1). However, although HUG was established as one of the most important healthcare centres in Geneva and Switzerland, access to its infrastructure by independent medical doctors was still impossible.

Yet, at the same time, the number of private doctors entered a period of fast growth, increasing from 923 in 1990 to 2,125 in 2020. The market's competitiveness, which had developed dramatically in the 1970s and 1980s, continued to expand. In 2020, there was an average of 239 inhabitants per private doctor in Geneva, compared to 404 in 1990 (see Fig. 1). The issue of access to medtech infrastructure led to new business opportunities. However, unlike in the pre-1980s era, it became more and more difficult for a group of doctors to establish their own collective private clinic. The construction and daily management of a clinic with high-tech equipment that could compete with HUG required massive investments that went

---

[26] *Le Nouveau Quotidien*, 7 May 1996.
[27] HUG, Rapport d'activité 2020, https://panorama.hug.ch/html/2020/rapport-dactivite-2020/ (accessed 20 July 2022).

beyond the means of independent doctors. Table 4 reflects the consolidation process that occurred in the private clinic business in Geneva after 1990. Except for two small clinics that remained independent – one refocusing on the treatment of dependencies, a specialty that does not require massive technological investment – all other clinics were either merged (by CGB or La Tour) or taken over by listed companies.

Clinique Générale-Beaulieu SA (CGB) was reorganized in 1994. The following year, its new official objective was stated as '*the exploitation in Geneva of clinic managed according to the principles of liberal private medicine […]. This clinic is open to doctors and surgeons practicing regularly in Canton Geneva and expressly authorised by the board of directors*'.[28] There were a total of 478 doctors under contract with CGB in 2000.[29] Renamed Clinique Générale Beaulieu Holding in 1998, its capital was raised to 7 million CHF, and it took over another private clinic, Clinique de Champel-Elysée, founded in 1984 and specialized in ambulatory medicine and in-vitro fertilization (IVF) (Donzé, 2003).[30] At the same time, a real estate company with a capital of 29 million CHF was founded to take over and modernize the property of the CGB (Donzé, 2003). Besides CGB, other clinics in Geneva experienced a slight development, although none could achieve a similar development. They remained small organizations accessible to a smaller number of patients.

The case of CGB showed the necessity to move towards a new type of organization to offer private doctors access to hospital infrastructure. Investors from finance took advantage of the growing market of private medicine in Switzerland. Their objective was not to have the infrastructure necessary for their professional practice but to look for financial profit. Moreover, the scope of their action was no longer local but national, even sometimes international. After 2000, two major private companies entered the market of private clinics in Geneva.

The first is Swiss Medical Network SA (SMN), a wholly owned subsidiary of Aevis Victoria SA, a company listed on the Zurich stock exchange, active mainly in the healthcare, luxury hotel and media industries (Agefi).[31] SMN is better known by its former name, Genolier Group. It was founded in 2004 by Geneva-based investors who had acquired a stake in the Genolier Clinic two years earlier, a hospital founded in 1972 in the neighbourhood of Geneva. Since 2007, it has been headed by the former ambassador and conservative politician Raymond Loretan. Since then, the group has invested heavily. It acquired CBG in 2016, and owned a total of 22 private hospitals in Switzerland by 2020. In addition, Aevis founded a real estate division (Swiss Healthcare Properties AG) in 1997, which owns, among other things, the hospital buildings it rents to its own clinics. It also controls an ambulance company in the canton of Geneva (Ambulances Services SA). The development of turnover illustrates this strong development: for the health

---

[28]*FOSC*, 4 September 1995.
[29]ACG, undated documents.
[30]*FOSC*, 16 June 1999.
[31]Aevis SA, annual reports, 2001–2021, https://www.aevis.com/en/news-reports/financial-reports/ (accessed 20 July 2022).

sector (clinics), it rose from 117 million francs in 2007 to 547 million francs in 2020. Aevis is also extremely profitable: the hospital division had a gross profit rate (ebitdar) of 18% in 2020.

The second is Hirslanden, Switzerland's largest private hospital group, headquartered in Zurich. Founded in 1990 with the merger of four hospitals, it has grown continuously since then. Specifically, it has acquired two hospitals in Geneva, Clinic La Colline (2014) and Clinic Les Grangettes (2018).[32] In 2020, Hirslanden owned a total of 17 clinics, representing more than 1,850 hospital beds, almost twice the capacity of its competitor SMN. The formation and development of this group of private clinics was made possible by capital from the Union Bank of Switzerland (UBS) and later from British investors. Then, in 2007, Hirslanden was taken over by Mediclinic International, a South African company listed on the London Stock Exchange, which also owns private hospital networks in South Africa and the Middle East. The Hirslanden subsidiary is a very large business, generating a turnover of over £1.4 billion in the 2020 fiscal year.[33]

The growth of listed companies as major actors in the healthcare market in Geneva and Switzerland results from two major factors (Donzé, 2017). First, there have been changes in the regulation of the healthcare system and hospital financing due to the federal healthcare insurance law, which has led to private clinics receiving some public funding. In some cantons, private clinics are recognized as being of public interest by the cantonal authorities and receive funding to fulfil a public policy; that is, to treat patients without private insurance to relieve public hospitals. This type of measure became widespread in 2012, since the federal law allows access to private clinics for patients with only basic insurance in certain cases, according to the principle of free choice of hospital. However, the accounts published by SMN and Hirlsanden do not allow for an assessment of the financial importance of these hospitalizations.

Second, it should be remembered that the high average income of the Swiss is a factor that favours the development of private clinics. Despite the continuous increase in basic insurance premiums, there is also an increase in expenditure on supplementary insurance. According to the Swiss Insurance Association (Association Suisse d'Assurances, ASA), total premiums for private health insurance rose from CHF 6.6 billion in 1997 to CHF 11.2 billion in 2020, an increase of more than 50%.[34] The evolution of the number of people benefiting from this coverage is not known, and it is likely an ever smaller proportion of the population has access to private care. However, these general figures show that the private medical market is not in crisis.

---

[32] *Tribune de Genève*, 4 September 2018.
[33] Mediclinic International, Annual report, 2020, https://investor.mediclinic.com/static-files/af844f8e-575b-4339-b82e-c2282b1db9fc (accessed 20 July 2022).
[34] ASA, Statistics, https://www.svv.ch/fr/lasa/publications/chiffres-et-faits/chiffres-et-faits/affaires-dassurance-directe (accessed 20 July 2022).

6. Conclusions

The long-term development of private clinics in Geneva analyzed in this chapter enabled emphasis on the nature of collective entrepreneurship carried out by medical doctors. As a liberal profession, doctors were strongly attached to individual practice but engaged in collective actions when it became necessary to defend or promote their business. However, this does not mean all these activities can be consider 'entrepreneurship'. For example, when private doctors gathered in a professional association in 1892, they did not aim to start a business. They intended to simply lobby the cantonal authorities, for example, to open the surgical clinic of the Cantonal Hospital (failed) or regulate hospital fees to stop unfair competition by professors of medicine (succeeded). Their objective was to ensure good conditions for their individual professional practices.

However, at the turn of the twentieth century, private doctors engaged in a new kind of collective action: the funding of Clinique Générale SA, a private hospital that would offer them the high-tech medical environment – including X-ray equipment, a laboratory and a surgical room – necessary for their work. They invested capital in this project, which can hence be considered the result of collective entrepreneurship by individual doctors. In the following years, other private clinics were founded based on similar models, although on a smaller scale. They developed steadily over several decades until they started to reach the limit of their business model in the 1970s and 1980s. New medical technology, notably CT scanners and MRI equipment, was necessary to stay competitive in the healthcare market but it was too costly for small-scale organizations. The crisis of private clinics then became an opportunity for new actors with large financial means to enter the business of private hospitals and reorganize it. However, they were no

Table 5.   The Development of Private Clinics in Geneva, 1860–2020.

	1860–1890	1890–1945	1945–1990	1990–2020
Structure of the healthcare market	Home visits-based	Hospital-based	Hospital-based	Hospital and private practice-based
Level of competition	Low	Very high	High	Very high
Institutional environment	Free competition	Regulation of fees	Regulation of fees	Regulation of fees; private clinics accessible by all population
Dominant type of private hospitals	Charitable; individual clinics	Charitable; collective clinics	Collective clinics	Collective clinics
Entrepreneurship	Individual doctors	Groups of doctors	Groups of doctors	Listed companies; private investors

longer private doctors but listed companies and investors outside healthcare who took the opportunity to invest in a fast-growing business. The collective entrepreneurship of medical doctors in Geneva was hence a phenomenon timely limited, which answered specific needs in a specific environment, as expressed in Table 5.

Hence, medical doctors acted as an entrepreneurial group (Rueff, 2010) to build collective private clinics between the 1890s and the 1990s. However, other forms of entrepreneurship also impacted the development of the modern healthcare industry. In the case of private medicine, individual entrepreneurs, although in a limited number, represented the dominant type during the period 1860–1890, when the technological infrastructure necessary to carry out modern medicine was still basically limited to a simple operating room. Moreover, after the 1990s, teams of doctors gave way to new kinds of entrepreneurs in the healthcare industry: investors looking for a high financial return on their investment, unlike doctors who were expecting infrastructure for their own professional practice.

References

Carlos, W. C., & Hiatt, S. R. (2022). From surgeries to startups: The impact of cultural holes on entrepreneurship in the medical profession. In C. Lockwood & J. F. Soublière (Eds.), *Advances in cultural entrepreneurship* (pp. 137–156). Bingley: Emerald Publishing Limited.

Chandler, A. D. (1977). *The visible hand: The managerial revolution in American business.* Cambridge, MA: Harvard University Press.

Cherry, S. (1997). Before the national health service: Financing the voluntary hospitals, 1900–1939. *The Economic History Review, 50*(2), 305–326.

Domin, J. P. (2008). *Une histoire économique de l'hôpital (XIXe-XXe siècles): Une analyse rétrospective du développement hospitalier.* Paris: Comité d'histoire de la sécurité sociale.

Donzé, P. Y. (2003). *Bâtir, gérer, soigner: histoire des établissements hospitaliers de Suisse romande.* Geneva: Georg Editeur.

Donzé, P.-Y. (2017). *Histoire des politiques hospitalières en Suisse romande.* Neuchâtel: Ed. Alphil-Presses univ. suisse.

Donzé, P.-Y. (2023a). The healthcare industry. In M. Kipping, T. Kurosawa, & E. Westley (Eds.), *Oxford handbook of industry dynamics,* forthcoming.

Donzé, P.-Y. (2023b). *The formation of the Swiss hospital system (1840-1960): An analysis of surgeon modernisers in the canton of Vaud.* Singapore: Palgrave Macmillan.

Droux, J. (2000). *L'attraction céleste: la construction de la profession d'infirmière en Suisse romande: XIXe-XXe siècles.* Unpublished PhD dissertation, University of Geneva, Department of General History.

Ehrenström, P. (1992). Affirmation et structuration de la profession médicale, Genève, 1880-1914. *Revue suisse d'histoire, 15*(2), 220–226.

Faure, O. (2019). *Les cliniques privées: deux siècles de succès.* Rennes: Presses universitaires de Rennes.

Fernández Pérez, P. (2021). *The emergence of modern hospital management and organisation in the world 1880s-1930s.* Bingley: Emerald Group Publishing.

Gorsky, M., & Sheard, S. (Eds.). (2006). *Financing medicine: The British experience since 1750.* London: Routledge.

Howell, J. (1995). *Technology in the hospital: Transforming patient care in the early twentieth century*. Baltimore/Londres: Johns Hopkins University Press.

Ikai, S. (2010). *Byoin no seiki no riron [The theory of the hospital century]*. Tokyo: Yuhikaku.

Labisch, A., & Spree, R. (Eds.). (2001). *Krankenhaus-Report 19. Jahrhundert: Krankenhausträger, Krankenhausfinanzierung, Krankenhauspatienten*. Frankfort: Campus Verlag.

Louis-Courvoisier, M. (2000). *Soigner et consoler: la vie quotidienne dans un hôpital à la fin de l'ancien régime, Genève 1750-1820*. Geneva: Georg Editeur.

Nagral, S. (2012). Doctors in entrepreneurial gowns. *Economic and Political Weekly, 10–12*.

OECD. (2022). *Health care resources: Physicians*. Retrieved from https://stats.oecd.org/#. Accessed on July 11, 2022.

OFS. (2021). *Effectif et densité des médecins, des cabinets dentaires et des pharmacies, par canton, table je-f-14.04.05.02*. Retrieved from https://www.bfs.admin.ch/bfs/fr/home/ statistiques/sante/systeme-sante/emplois-professions-sante.assetdetail.20044855. html. Accessed on July 11, 2022.

Rieder, P. (2009). *Anatomie d'une institution médicale. La Faculté de médecine de Genève (1876–1920)*. Geneva: Georg Editeur.

Rueff, M. (2010). *The entrepreneurial group: Social identities, relations, and collective actions*. Princeton: Princeton University Press.

Stevens, R. (1989). *In sickness and in wealth: American hospitals in the twentieth century*. Baltimore: Johns Hopkins University Press.

Stone, D. A. (1997). The doctor as businessman: The changing politics of a cultural icon. *Journal of Health Politics, Policy and Law, 22*(2), 533–556.

Timmermann, C., & Anderson, J. (Eds.). (2006). *Devices and designs: Medical technologies in historical perspective*. Gordonsville: Springer.

Chapter 4

The Transfer of the North American Ideas of Hospital Management to Europe in the 20th Century: The Case of Spain

Paloma Fernández Pérez[1]

Abstract

This chapter contributes to a better knowledge of the role played by the collective entrepreneurship of networks of scientists and doctors in the transfer and adaptation of ideas on hospital organization and management for modern hospitals with new technology, from Western Europe and above all the United States. Literature about new medical technology has demonstrated how medical innovations required changes in human capital and organization in hospitals, to benefit patients in the private and the public hospitals after World War II. The chapter provides an analysis about the origins of the modern North American ideas about professionalization and hospital accreditation, in the consolidation of a modern hospital management and organization. In particular, the focus is in demonstrating how networks of scientists' entrepreneurs were fundamental drivers in the process of knowledge transfer and the dissemination of these ideas to the large Western European hospitals. More specifically, the chapter studies the diffusion of the new ideas about the large hospital organization and management from the United States to the Western Europe, applied to the Spanish context. Informal networks of doctors applied new ideas developed in the United States to new clinics and hospitals in Spain. Some of them occupied official positions in the key public health administrations and were crucial to introducing the hospital accreditation systems and the US ideas in Spain.

[1]Research has benefitted from public research project Spanish Project PGC201S8-093971-B-I00 granted by the Ministry of Science and Innovation Programme for Knowledge Generation, funded by MCIU/AEI/FEDER, UE.

Collective Entrepreneurship in the Contemporary European Services Industries:
A Long Term Approach, 47–59
doi:10.1108/978-1-80117-950-820231004

Keywords: Collective entrepreneurship; hospital management; networks; North America; Spain; medical innovations

1. Introduction

Americanization has been analyzed in close relationship with industry, finances and in business history (Kipping & Bajnar 1998; Kipping & Engwall 2002; Kudo, Kipping & Schoter 2003; Tiratsoo & Tomlinson 1997, 1998). Previous scholars have paid particular attention to the complex transfer of a diversity of management models from the United States (Carew, 1987; Engwall & Zamagni, 1998; Fridenson & Yui, 2002; Gemelli, 1998; Gourvish & Tiratsoo, 1998; Killick, 1997; Kipping, 1999; Kipping & Bjarnar, 1998; Kipping & Engwall, 2002; Kudo, Kipping, & Schröter, 2003; Sahunn Anderson & Engwall, 2002; Tiratsoo, 2000; Tiratsoo & Tomlison, 1997, 1998; Tiratsoo & Kipping, 2018; Zeitlin & Herrigel, 2000).

However, there is little research devoted to the influence of the Americanization in the health sector from a historical perspective, before the 1960s (Schleiermacher, 2019). Yet, the management consultants close to the well-known theories of Frederick Winslow Taylor, and the hospital managers of the large hospitals, were very soon aware of the new ways of organization and management in the factories, in the United States since the decade of 1910, and how they could be used in other sectors, like the health sector (MacEachern, 1935; Martin & Mayo, 1922). Hence, a process has started, before World War II, with the new large hospitals accepting with optimism the ideas of standardization, measurement, and control (Kauffmann, 1990, Donzé & Fernández, 2019). This acceptance brought forward a belief that a strict and professional standardized organization and managerial control were crucial factors required to reach efficiency and to reduce financial costs in the health centres (Fernández Pérez, 2021a, b).

The early pioneers in this new belief, now in debate and under serious criticism since the late 1980s, understood that, regardless of the city or country, standard models of efficiency in hospital organization could be easily transferred across borders. Moreover, for these pioneers to adopt, this belief in the new hospitals institutional isomorphism was the clue (Kipping, 1997).

These ideas were elaborated in scientific and professional seminars, congresses, organizations and associations, in the Americas and in Europe, as well as in Japan or Australia, between the 1910s and the 1990s, and their transference and dissemination started to be studied from a business perspective. More specifically, business historians have started to study the hospitals, as the central hubs of health care products and services, in the twentieth century until now (Donzé & Fernández, 2019; Pérez Castroviejo, 2002; Pons-Pons & Vilar-Rodríguez, 2021; Fernández, 2021a, b; Zarzoso, 2021; Sabaté, 2017; Risse, 1999).

This chapter contributes to a better knowledge of the process of transference and dissemination of the ideas about hospital efficiency and management. To do so, it provides an analysis about the origins of the modern North American ideas about professionalization and hospital accreditation, in the consolidation of a modern hospital management and organization. In particular, the focus is in demonstrating how networks of scientists' entrepreneurs were fundamental drivers in the process of knowledge transfer and the dissemination of these ideas to the large Western European hospitals. From a business history perspective, this study demonstrates how collective entrepreneurship contributes to shape the modern hospital managerial ideas and centres.

This chapter studies the diffusion of the new ideas about the large hospital organization and management from the United States to the Western Europe, applied to the Spanish context. Spain has one of the longest life expectancies of the world, despite the relatively reduced investment on the health expenditure over GDP (Fernández Pérez, 2021).

The study starts with the implementation of the new ideas about modern hospital organization, across some European countries, before World War II, for which the chapter uses secondary sources of outstanding impact worldwide, like the 1910 and 1912 Flexner reports on the medical education in North America and in Europe, and the 1932 Newsholme book about the state of the medical practice in Europe (Flexner, 1910, 1912; Newsholme, 1931).

Further on, the chapter shows an example of the direct acceptance and application of the American ideas about modern hospital organization, in the Western Europe after the World War II, with sources stemming from journals of medicine, associations of surgeons and physicians, and publications from within the network of physicians and hospital managers who fully adopted the North American ideas in the accreditation and management of the large hospitals in Spain.

2. Modern Ideas on Hospital Management, Organization and Accreditation: The US Before the 1930s and Dissemination in Western Europe Before World War II

The construction of the United States as a new nation took place during the nineteenth century in the context of a mass migratory movement that moved millions of people between continents. Similarly, a fast industrialization process scaled to face the challenge of necessary mass distribution, mass production, and mass organization and management. The US civil war, the war between the United States and Spain in Cuba at the end of the nineteenth century, and the expansion to the South in Mexican territory, all increased the wounded, infected and deadly tool of soldiers. Many immigrants and soldiers, who returned with health problems, were arriving to the large cities, like San Francisco and New York. In these cities, the management of the injured and sick masses of people became a political priority due to the social (and racial) conflicts that the lack of effective help to the affected people was creating (Fernández Pérez, 2021). New technologies requiring new organizational routines also pressed in that direction (Howell, 1995). The US Army Medical Department often declared in official documents that the public health sector would have to coordinate with the national private actors so that the new drugs, technologies, and the graduates in Medicine could be coordinated to solve the many health problems of the new nation.[2]

Very early in the twentieth century, W. Taylor's disciples, Frank and Lillian Gilbreth (1911–1914), applied the ideas about measurement, control, and standardization from the industrial and commercial sectors to the health sector, aiming to reduce time losses and inefficient allocation of the specialized human workforce to the surgical room of hospitals. Gilbreth's articles on motion studies of nurses and doctors in the surgical room have started in 1912 the theory about the scientific management in the hospital.[3]

In parallel to this stream of research, experts in education, sponsored by philanthropic foundations like the Carnegie or the Rockefeller Foundation, and many of immigrant origins with personal networks with educational institutions in Germany, France, the United Kingdom, Switzerland, or Italy became aware of the many routines in place in Western Europe that could be adapted to the North American reality, but only if the educational system of the country could help disseminate standard ways and routines that could be later applied in the professional life.

It was exactly in this context that the new Johns Hopkins Medical School opened its doors in 1898, under the influence of the German models of long-term, specialized, and scientific-based medical education. With the donation of 7 million dollars from the businessman Johns Hopkins and William Osler's medical leadership, the new school set a model for the world that would be enduring until now. Osler, a Canadian son of immigrants from Wales, studied Medicine in Toronto and at the MacGill University of Montreal, then expanded his postgraduate studies in London and Berlin, where he met the famous professor of the German's Charité Hospital, Rudolf Virchow, one of the founding fathers of the modern pathology and cells (Robert Koch studied his Ph.D. with Virchow). In the 1870s, William Osler learned from direct eyesight how the clinical analysis was organized in the hospitals, in Berlin and Vienna, and in the General Hospital of London. Back in Canada, he actively supported the modernization of the National Library of Medicine in Bethesda, and became Professor of Medicine at Johns Hopkins in 1889. He was one of the first professors of the new Johns Hopkins School of Medicine in 1893, being recognized crucial to transfer German and British traditions of performing autopsies in the hospital to verify accurate diagnosis and effects of medical treatments, and hospital routines of clinical analysis (Fernández Pérez, 2021, p. 43).

It was in this context, that Simon Flexner's brother (a highly regarded bacteriologist and virologist working for the Rockefeller Institute for Medical Research),

---

[2]Fernández Pérez 2021, 38-39; US Army Medical Department/Office of Medical History website.

[3]Archives and Special Collections, The Frank and Lilliam Gilbreth Library of Management Research and Professional Papers. https://archives.lib.purdue.edu/repositories/2/archival_objects/9120 (accessed December 16th 2019). Fernández Pérez 2021, 35–36.

Abraham, a graduate in classic studies of Johns Hopkins University, in 1886, with postgraduate studies in Germany, was commissioned to write two books about the state of the medical education in the United States and Canada and in Western and Eastern Europe in 1910 and 1912, respectively (Flexner, 1910, 1912).[4] In these books, Abraham Flexner advocated for extending the model of medical education inspired by the scientific and practical clinical expertise of Germany, France and the United Kingdom in the United States, in Canada, and in the Northern hemisphere. He believed that this model of medical education increased the time and improved modern scientific foundations of the medical students who practiced medicine in clinics and hospitals in North America, before World War I. Flexner, who travelled to Europe extensively and knew firsthand the practices of modern European medicine and the hospitals, had the support of private and public institutions in the United States. The aim of the President of the United States was to increase the coordination and cooperation of the thousands of actors involved in the practice of medicine in the army, and in the civil society. Thus, in line with Flexner, the Johns Hopkins Medical School, the Carnegie Foundation, the Rockefeller Foundation, and the US President, many other young doctors believed in the necessary professionalization of the medical profession. For instance, Ernest A. Codman defended that the professional hospital staff had to closely take care of every patient, and to learn how to avoid medical failures from the direct observation of the patients, not just from the theory. Codman had learnt this lesson during his visits to the medical centres in Europe, after graduation in the Harvard Medical School in 1895, and after he returned to the United States, he worked in the Massachusetts General Hospital in 1899 (and from 1902 to 1914), lecturing at the Harvard Medical School (1913–1915). Edward Martin, President of the Clinical Congress of North America, encouraged Codman to integrate the new Committee on Hospital Standardization, whose work was behind the new American College of Surgeons in 1913. This College was one of the top leading professional medical associations in the United States, that resiliently worked towards spreading the standardization wave in the hospital organization and management under the general direction of Franklin Martin, from 1913 to 1935. As a graduate from the Chicago Medical College (which became Northwestern University Medical School later), Martin served in the Mercy Hospital in Chicago, and was appointed by President Woodrow Wilson to serve in the National Advisory Commission of civilian leaders, becoming the medical representative to improve the standardization of

---

[4]Carnegie Foundation. Archive. Abraham Flexner 1910, *Medical Education in the United States and Canada. A report to the Carnegie Foundation for the Advancement of Teaching. With an introduction by Henry S Pritchett, President of the Foundation.* Bulletin number four (1910). New York City, The Carnegie Foundation for the Advancement of Teaching. And from same author, *Medical Education in Europe. A report to the Carnegie Foundation for the Advancement of Teaching,* 1912. Retrieved from http://archive.carnegiefoundation.org/pdfs/elibrary/Carnegie_Flexner_Report. pdf. Accessed on June 18th 1919.

the hospitals.[5] During Martin's directorship, the American College of Surgeons published in 1919 the seminal document 'Minimum Standard', still cited in the medical literature. Five key points were mentioned as basic cornerstones of the modern hospital organization: (1) the organization of medical staff in the hospitals; (2) the requirement to have graduates in medicine in the medical staff of a hospital; (3) the need to have a shared set of rules as a standard practice; (4) and that each hospital had to have, as in modern Western European hospitals, an X-Ray Department; and (5) a clinical laboratory.[6]

A good friend and colleague of Franklin Martin was doctor William James Mayo, born and raised in a family of medical doctors. He has graduated in medicine, in 1883 from the University of Michigan Ann Arbor, and has worked with his brother, Charles Horace Mayo, at St. Mary's Hospital in Rochester until 1905, and later in the clinic that would become the famous Mayo Clinic (Fernández Pérez, 2021). Martin and Mayo were commissioned by the American College of Surgeons to travel to South America on behalf of the association in 1921 and, again, in 1922 with letters of presentation from the highest North American medical and the political authorities, to be introduced and meet the South American Presidents, the South American associations of doctors, and their health centres. The goal of these meetings was to increase the membership of the US American College of Surgeons. Also, to observe the diversity of hospital practices and traditions of medical education and training, learning what was in their eyes better practice than the one they knew in the United States, and transfer rather humbly their own ideas about how the United States was experimenting the modernization of their hospital organization and management.

The American College of Surgeons believed that the standardization of the high-quality medical education and the professional hospital organization had to expand beyond the US borders to reach the North, Central and South America. During times of fast expansion of the North American foreign direct investment in the continent, and the rapid and massive migratory waves reaching the shores of the United States, medical doctors became convinced that exchanging and sharing new knowledge about standardization and modern hospital organization would benefit, not only the North American health systems and citizens, but also the health system of their neighbors.

Martin and Mayo have travelled twice, as said above, in 1921 and 1922, on behalf of the American College of Surgeons, from Panama in the North to Chile in the South, and from the Andean republics in the West to Brazil in the East. The data collected from the observed reality has been described in a book about the concentration of the inequality in the distribution of the modern medicine and the hospital routines in South America in the 1920s. They described, on the one hand, the excellent endowment of the great surgeons and the hospitals in

---

[5]American College of Surgeons Digital Archives. Https://wwwfacs.org/about-acs/archives/pasthighlights/martinhighlight (accessed December 16th 2019).
[6]American College of Surgeons Digital Archives, Https://www.facs.org/about-acs/archives/pasthighlights/codmanhighlight; https://www.facs.org/about-acs/archives/pasthighlights/minimumhighlight (accessed December 16th 2019).

some cities, like Buenos Aires or Lima, and the US military centres in Panama, or in the big mining sites of Chile, owned by the US multinationals. On the other hand, they portrayed the poor medical assistance that was offered in most of the dominant rural areas of the continent.[7]

The League of Nations' archive contains abundant digitized documents that confirm the impressions of Martin and Mayo in the 1920s. Also, the documents reveal how the South American doctors and surgeons not only travelled regularly to Europe but also steadily established permanent contacts with the international associations to which they asked about alternative models of construction and organization of hospitals[8].

Western and Eastern Europe had a diversity of new clinics and hospitals that had been introducing modern scientific medicine, and professionalization, since the last four decades of the nineteenth century (Fernández Pérez, 2021). But ideas do not travel alone, nor easily replace tradition in Medicine, as in so many sciences. New ideas need human vectors to enact them and evidence to support them. To develop new ideas towards the establishment of new routines and beliefs, struggle and resistance have to be minimized. These are culturally and educationally manageable within a cross-cultural way, and can adapt to the different realities. In this context, '*Hybrid scientific entrepreneurs*', were the most successful human vectors in the first third of the twentieth century, convincing medical practitioners of the efficiency of the innovative outcomes in in the Medicine and the Hospital organization of that time. These innovations were applied, across various departments, in many hospitals and faculties of Medicine in Europe, North and South America, Asia, and in the Middle East.[9] Open minded doctors and surgeons travelled between these hospitals and faculties were anonymous human vectors who made the hybridization of new ideas possible. One of these doctors that contributed to such movement of relevant ideas, and to their hybridization, between the United States, Canada, and Europe, was Sir Arthur Newsholme (1857–1943). He was born

---

[7]*South America from a Surgeon's Point of View*, New York and Chicago, Fleming H. Revell Company 1922 (downloadable in https://babel.hathitrust.org/cgi/pt?id=hvd.32 044080373640&view=1up&seq=7, accessed January 2020).

[8]United Nations Archive in Geneva. League of Nations. Digital documents 1921-1934. Temporary access online granted, due to the covid 19 pandemic, is greatly acknowledged.

[9]Hybrid entrepreneurship, a concept introduced by this author in other publications (Fernández Pérez 2019), will be here defined as 'the cultural and educational capacity to translate new practices and ideas from science, business, or other sciences, in a way that people from different educational and cultural backgrounds can absorb and efficiently introduce and adapt in different institutional contexts with reduced rigidities. Hybrid entrepreneurship reduces the time in the dissemination of innovations across borders. Also, hybrid entrepreneurship reduces the frequent struggle and resistance that takes place in processes of dissemination of innovation across territories, institutions, companies, entrepreneurs, and social communities. Hybrid entrepreneurship increases the efficient adaptation of innovations in institutions or territories considered to be backward in the adoption of innovations in a given field of science or economic application of ideas'.

at Haworth in England, as an orphan. He had scholarships before becoming an apprentice for a Bradford practitioner and entering at St. Thomas's Hospital, while the modern surgery was developing (American Journal of Public Health Editorial, 1943). As a house-surgeon at that hospital, he was appointed as a part-time MOH for Clapman in 1883, and as a full-time MOH for Brighton. He has worked in Brighton for twenty years. He then retired from Whitehall in 1919, when he was invited by the W. H. Welch to go to the United States. Welch had been the first director of the School of Hygiene, the Public Health and the Institute of the History of Medicine in the United States, President of the Congress of American Physicians and Surgeons in 1897 and of the American Medical Association in 1910.

As one of the big four 'founding fathers' of the pioneering Johns Hopkins Hospital, Welch had travelled and studied at German Universities in the late 1870s. He became one of the chief advisors to the US Army's medical department, and served as a president of the board of directors of the Rockefeller Institute for Medical Research, from 1901 to 1932, where he advised John D. Rockefeller in the establishment of the Peking Union Medical College (https://publichealth.jhu. edu/about/history/heroes-of-public-health/william-henry-welch).

Welch invited the English Newsholme to lead the new school of hygiene at Johns Hopkins and in this position had a significant influence on the US new models of the public health. It was in this position that the Milbank Fund sponsored his visits to Europe and that led him to analyze and gather quantitative and qualitative precious evidence about the changes in the hospitals and in the health system of Europe.

He has published *Red Medicine*, with J. A. Kingsbury, in 1933, a vital book with data not found anywhere else about the innovations in the preventive medicine in the Communist Russia during the Russian revolution, (1) the presence of women directors of large hospitals, (2) the regular use of X-Ray technology, pediatric incubators, and coordination of local and regional health officers, and (3) the introduction of preventive measures of health at all levels, with public system of payment of health assistance for workers (Fernández Pérez, 2021). Newsholme also wrote three volumes of books on *International Studies on the Relation between the Private and Official Practice of Medicine with special reference to Public Health*, covering with rich empirical evidences the changes in health insurance, public health, programs and practices of Medical students, and the organization with strengths and weaknesses of the hospitals and the clinics (general and specialized ones) in more than a dozen Western and Eastern European countries. Volume 1 contained his observations about the Netherlands, Norway, Germany, Denmark, Sweden, Austria and Switzerland. Volume 2 refers to Belgium, France, Italy, Jugoslavia, Hungary, Poland and Czechoslovakia, and Volume 3 includes England, Scotland, Wales and Ireland. The books had a foreword by William H. Welch, and were published in London and in Baltimore (Newsholme, 1932). Only a few years after the works of Flexner in the early 1910s, and the activity and travels of Franklin Martin with William Mayo in the 1920s, coinciding with the maturity of the United States and European associations of the hospital superintendents, surgeons, obstetricians, nurses, a close colleague, Malcolm MacEachern, published what would become the 'bible' of the modern hospital organization and management in the world, for the rest of the twentieth century (Fernández Pérez, 2021).

The ideas that crossed the borders between Europe, America, and Asia, between an elite of expert doctors and specialized associations and publications, started to filter down, and were considered a model to be achieved: excellence in the modern medical clinical education, connection between hospitals and faculties of medicine, professionalization, hierarchy, hospital centralization, coordination, standardized routines, measurement, controls, cost efficiency rules. What so many believed was the key to progress, whose strength was not questioned by the elite hospitals, and whose weaknesses were criticized and slowly abandoned in many health systems after the late 1990s.

3. The Diffusion of the US Modern Ideas of the Hospital Organization and Management: The Case of Spain

American ideas of productivity and efficiency in business arrived very soon to Spain through large public business groups and firms, as well as to small family firms (Puig, 2018). Spanish physicians used to travel to learn new techniques of diagnosis and therapy of a diversity of illnesses, something very common in the field of Medicine since the early modern times.

During the seventeenth and eighteenth centuries, doctors from the Catholic countries had travelled to the Protestant countries where autopsies or anatomic studies were allowed and where Inquisition did not kill heretic professionals, who dared to challenge the authority of the Church. The knowledge from the traditional Asian medicine, or the advanced medical practice from the Islamic countries, and the traditional use of plants and animals to heal from the Americas and Australia travelled to Europe, between the seventeenth and nineteenth centuries, and was shared, though not always taught in the official academic world. The true dissemination of modern science in the field of biology, pharmacy, and medicine, only came when a true reform of the University education took place in Europe, since the last third of the nineteenth century. The revolution in medical education paved the way for the revolution in medical practice.

A new generation of doctors, trained in the new programmes of medicine in the reformed schools in Spain, with exchange periods in Germany, France, the United Kingdom, some in the United States, started to see new ways of hospital design, organization, and management abroad. Valentí Carulla was a central hub of change in the management of the new Hospital Clínic of Barcelona created in 1906; Wenceslao López Albó did a similar role in Santander in the new Marqués de Valdecilla Hospital in 1929, as did Carlos Jiménez Díaz in the Instituto Médico of Madrid, in the 1930s (Fernández Pérez, 2021, p. 108).

Carles Soler Durall, a key pioneer in the dissemination of the North American ideas about hospital accreditation, medical education and training, and hospital management, acknowledged in many of his articles and conferences his debt to Franklin Martin, to Abraham Flexner, and to Malcolm MacEachern (Barceló-Prats, 2021; Bohigas, 1996, 2021; Soler-Durall, 2010). Soler Durall combined all the ideas he learned from his readings, and travels to the United States, to the organization of the Hospital General de Asturias in 1961 where, since then, the modern system of education of Medicine in Spain was formally established. This model was based on the specialization in education and training in a hospital, under the strict evaluation and control criteria to guarantee excellence and quality as well as the efficiency of the allocated resources in a hospital. The sanitary assistance was a high-quality service to be supplied as a citizens' right, not as a charity, with a transparent acknowledgement of the rights and duties of the doctors, the nurses and the patients, with salaries ranking according to needs and expertise, a council board, and a general manager (García González, 2011).

As Barceló's work has consistently demonstrated, in Spain until the early twentieth century, the public hospital and the health system was organized at the provincial level, with a relative concentration of resources in the large provincial capital, and a relative lack of staff and centres in the countryside. Between 1917 and 1938, the industrial regions were the ones with more openness to the international trade and business and also to travels through which scientists, created informal and invisible networks of cooperation and knowledge transfer.

This chapter proposes that the Industrial districts of the nineteenth century in Europe were the key factor that favoured the early creation of modern health districts in the nineteenth century. This is a hypothesis that will be checked with international comparisons in future works. In Catalonia, this is particularly well known in the vast literature from the History of Medicine in the region, with open-minded physicians, individuals who were passionately eager to modernize their region's economy, society, policy, and their health system.

Since the early twentieth century, many physicians were among the top officers in the regional or local government, in the chancellorship of the Universities (e.g. University of Barcelona), as presidents of civil associations, and directors of new journals and magazines. In Catalonia, doctors were at the cutting-edge with ideas from abroad, and these were being exchanged their institutions, associations, and centres. As a result, in the 1920s and 1930s, the first efforts to organize a modern health system with new models of organization and management took place in the Basque country, more precisely in Santander and Catalonia (Sabaté 2017; Barceló-Prats, 2021). Following on the associations of physicians in Germany and in France, the Sindicat de Metges de Catalunya was founded in 1920, becoming a powerful union of physicians with a bulletin, as well as their insurance firm to protect their families from poverty (in case of incapacity, retirement, and death). The union's members represented almost all the graduated physicians of the region, since the fragmentation of Franco's regime. Their bulletin, 'Butlletí del Sindicat de Metges de Catalunya', was monthly published with the new ideas about education, specialization, science, and hospital organization. It was a powerful tool that helped spreading innovations that arrived from the Faculty of Medicine and from the leading countries' journals of Medicine to the local libraries.

4. Conclusions

From the 1920s and 1930s until the 1960s, depending on the region, and the country, new ways of defining excellence in a doctor's education and in the design, organization, and management of a hospital took place across the world. In a relatively not well-known effort of collective entrepreneurship led by the medical profession and the hospital staff, innovations spread that contributed to increase the well-being of the population.

Pioneers, like Florence Nightingale in Crimea, used rationale planning in contexts of scarcity to organize resources more efficiently than in the past, to maximize space, and to reduce the time of moving bodies. Florence started modern education for nurses, the most direct resource patients need in times of unprecedented needs like wars, or pandemics. Her example is still followed in the clinics and hospitals.

In a similar way, the past wars in the Empires' age of the nineteenth century have pressured the handling of millions of wounded and infected people, the supply chain of medicines, and the accountability standards. Doctors in the army had the opportunity to experiment with new products and processes to accelerate or to prevent thousands of deaths from infectious diseases. The Medical Unit of the US Army sent since the late nineteenth century top officers to Europe to learn medical innovations, in order to adapt them to the emerging and urgent needs of a bruised country that had lost hundreds of thousands of lives in its recent Civil War and then in the War against Spain in Cuba. Modern hospitals were built and others reformed, in the East and the West coast, and in the Central America, supported by the US Army. Doctors Franklin and Mayo described the army's hospital in Panama as one of the largest and most modern in the world when they attended the US soldiers in the early 1920s. They also described to have seen in some Chilean mines, owned by US multinationals, nurses and technology, rarely seen in many US hospitals.

Newspapers, and specialized journals and magazines, were describing to the European readers how the United States was reaching great achievements in all the fields. In the 1920s, and after the 1930s, some young doctors had travelled to observe the magnificent new hospitals of New York and San Francisco, the specialized clinics of the Mayo brothers, the organization, equipment, staff behaviour, and the performance of the surgeries. Some young doctors, like Carulla, López Albó, Jiménez Díaz, Soler Durall, Plana, among many others, returned to Spain and applied the new knowledge to new clinics and hospitals. Most of the pioneers, in Barcelona, brought back books, articles, and the imprinting of the new ideas they had captured on site. They adapted the new ideas to the old continent, with many local resistances to abandon the old practices as in Germany (Schleiermarcher, 2010), scarce money, and a few convinced followers at the beginning (Barceló-Prats, 2021). It was, indeed, a powerful wave, and some of the key actors who occupied official positions in the key public health administrations, as Soler Durall in Asturias, or Bohigas in Catalonia, were crucial to introducing the hospital accreditation systems and the US ideas in the hospitals in Spain (Bohigas, 1996, 2021).

References

American Journal of Public Health Editorial. (1943). Obituary of Sir Arthur Newsholme. *33*(8), 992–993.

Barceló-Prats, J. (2021). Genealogía de la reforma hospitalaria en España: la gestación de una nueva cultura hospitalocéntrica de la sanidad. *Dynamis, 41*(1), 27–51.

Bohigas, L. (1996). *L'acreditació dels hospitals catalans*. Barcelona: University of Barcelona.

Bohigas, L. (2021). How self-government in Catalonia has integrated private not for profit care in the public healthcare service. *Journal of Evolutionary Studies in Business, 1,* 263–280.

Carew, A. B. (1987). *Labour under the Marshall plan: The politics of productivity and the marketing of management science.* Manchester: Manchester University Press.

Donzé, P.-Y., & Fernández, P. (Eds.). (2019). *Health industries in the twentieth century.* Special Issue in *Journal Business History.* London: Routledge.

Engwall, L., & Zamagni, V. (Eds.). (1998). *Management education in historical perspective.* Manchester: Manchester University Press.

Fernández, P., & Zarzoso, A. (2021). A mixed model of hospital services: Catalonia, 1870s-2010s. *Journal of Evolutionary Studies in Business, 6*(1), 1–19.

Fernández Pérez, P. (2021a). *The emergence of modern hospital management and organization in the world 1880s-1930s.* Bingley: Emerald Publishing.

Fernández Pérez, P. (2021b). How to evaluate the capacity of hospital systems in a very long term international comparative perspective? Hospital beds per inhabitant in Catalonia 1900s-2010s. *Journal of Evolutionary Studies in Business, 6*(1), 182–226.

Flexner, A. (1910). *Medical education in the United States. A report to the carnegie foundation for the advancement of teaching.* New York, NY: The Carnegie Foundation.

Flexner, A. (1912). *Medical education in Europe. A report to the Carnegie Foundation for the Advancement of Teaching.* New York, NY: The Carnegie Foundation.

Fridenson, P., & Yui, T. (Eds.) (2002). *Managerial enterprise and organisational adaptability in France and Japan.* London: Routledge.

García-González, J. (2011). *La implantación del hospital moderno en España. El Hospital General de Asturias, una referencia imprescindible.* Oviedo: Nobel.

Gemelli, G. (Eds.). (1998). *The Ford Foundation and Europe (1950's-1970's): Cross-fertilization of learning in social science and management.* Brussels: European Interuniversity Press.

Gourvish, T., & Tiratsoo, N. (Eds.). (1998). *Missionaries and managers: American influences on European management education, 1945-60.* Manchester: Manchester University Press.

Kauffmann, C. J. (1990). The push for standardization: The origins of the Catholic Hospital Association, 1914–1920. *Health Progress, 71*(1), 57–65.

Killick, J. (1997). *The United States and European reconstruction, 1945–1960.* Edinburgh: Keele University Press.

Kipping, M. (1997). Consultancies. Institutions and the diffusion of taylorism in Britain, Germany and France, 1920s to 1950s. *Business History, 39*(4), 67–83.

Kipping, M. (1999). American management consulting companies in Western Europe, 1920 to 1990: Products, reputation and relationships. *Business History Review, 73*(2), 190–220.

Kipping, M., & Bjarnar, O. (Eds.). (1998). *The Americanisation of European business.* London: Routledge.

Kipping, M., & Engwall, L. (Eds.). (2002). *Management consulting: Emergence and dynamics of a knowledge industry.* Oxford: Oxford University Press.

Kudo, A., Kipping, M., & Schröter, H. (Eds.). (2003). *Transforming the American model: German and Japanese industry during the boom years.* London: Routledge.

MacEachern, M. (1935). *Hospital organization and management.* Chicago, IL: Physicians Record Company.

Martin, F., & Mayo, W. (1922). *South America from a surgeon's point of view.* Chicago, IL: Fleming H. Revell Company. Retrieved from https://babel.hathitrust.org/cgi/pt?id=hvd.32044080373640&view=1up&seq=7. Accessed on January 2020.

Newsholme, A. (1932). *Medicine and the State. The relation between the private and official practice of medicine, with special reference to public health*. London: Unwin Brothers Ltd.

Pérez Castroviejo, P. (2002). La formación del Sistema hospitalario vasco, administración y gestión económica 1800–1936. *Transportes, Servicios y Telecomunicaciones, 3–4*, 73–97.

Pons-Pons, J., & Vilar-Rodríguez, M. (2021). The historical roots of the creation of the Catalan private-public hospital model: c.1870–1935. *Journal of Evolutionary Studies in Business, 6*(1), 30–66.

Puig, N. (2018). The Americanisation of a European latecomer: Transferring US management models to Spain, 1950s–1970s. In N. Tiratsoo & M. Kipping (Eds.), *Americanisation in Europe in the 20th century. Business, culture and politics* (pp. 259–275). Lille: Open Editions Book.

Risse, G. B. (1999). *Mending bodies, saving souls: A history of hospitals*. New York, NY: Oxford University Press.

Sabaté, F. (2017). Public health in Catalonia between 1885 and 1939. *Catalan Historical Review, 10*, 43–57.

Sahun-Andersson, K., & Engwall, L. (Eds.) (2002). *The expansion of management knowledge: Carriers, flows and sources*. Stanford, CA: Stanford University Press.

Schleiermacher, S. (2019). 'Importance of Germany to countries around and to World Economy makes it impossible to ignore' – The Rockefeller Foundation and Public Health in Germany after WWII. *Business History, 61*(3), 481–497.

Soler-Durall, C. (2010). Reflexiones sobre el hospital: su función en la formación de los médicos. *Educación Médica, 13*(2), 71–75.

Tiratsoo, N. (2000). The United States technical assistance programme in Japan. *Business History, 42*(4), 117–136.

Tiratsoo, N., & Kipping, M. (Eds.). (2018). *Americanisation in Europe in the 20th century. Business, culture and politics*. Lille: Open Editions Book.

Tiratsoo, N., & Tomlinson, J. (1997). Exporting the 'Gospel of Productivity': United States technical assistance and British industry 1945–1960. *Business History Review, 71*, 41–81.

Tiratsoo, N., & Tomlinson, J. (1998). *The conservatives and industrial efficiency, 1951-64. Thirteen wasted years?* London: Routledge/LSE.

Zarzoso, A. (2021). Private surgery clinics in an open medical market: Barcelona 1880s–1936. *Journal of Evolutionary Studies in Business, 6*(1), 67–113.

Zeitlin, J., & Herrigel, G. (Eds.). (2000). *Americanization and its limits*. Oxford: Oxford University Press.

Chapter 5

Evolution of Public Services: The Case of UK Leisure Centres in the Late 20th Century

Alex G. Gillett and Kevin D. Tennent

Abstract

This chapter focusses on entrepreneurship and policies of public services in England, specifically leisure centre provision in the UK during the late twentieth century. The central role played by local authorities in sport provision was complimented by an increasing cadre of leisure sector professionals and with increasing architectural interest in the provision of leisure. The institutional context was framed by the Sports Development Council (SDC) after 1965 together with the broader action of local authorities who aimed to provide their ratepayers with access to improved sport and leisure services. The resulting leisure centres were perhaps a way to signal the prestige of local authorities but were expensive investments. The capability of local authorities was boosted by the local government reforms of the 1970s, which merged districts, pooling their resources. The possibility of support from private capital and after 1973 from the European Economic Community (EEC) also provided new opportunities for the organizational form. Eventually, there was a shift in emphasis from the provision of organized sport to that of more individualized and commercialized "leisure" as a product. Whether or not this achieved the long-term aims of central government, to improve access to sport and to tackle urban challenges, remains questionable. However, the story of leisure provision in the UK remains one of remarkable public sector entrepreneurship within an institutional context.

Keywords: Leisure management; leisure centres; public services; sport; policy; United Kingdom

Collective Entrepreneurship in the Contemporary European Services Industries:
A Long Term Approach, 61–76
doi:10.1108/978-1-80117-950-820231005

1. Introduction

Following Gillett and Tennent (2020) who outline sport as a lens through which to view management history, this chapter focusses on entrepreneurship and evolving policies of public services in England, specifically leisure centre provision in the late twentieth century. Overall, we chart the development of the UK's sport and leisure provision in the second half of the twentieth century, expanding on the work of Houlihan (1991) who identified the central role played by local authorities in sport provision. This was complimented and reinforced by an increasing cadre of leisure sector professionals (Torkildsen, 2005, pp. 562–569) together with increasing architectural interest in the provision of leisure, which fit the broader post-war reconstruction movement (Saumarez Smith, 2019). We also explore the role of football clubs (FCs) as representative bodies for local government to outsource some of its leisure centre provision, to highlight how the public sector engaged with elite sport organizations, which have a quasi-public character. Gillett and Tennent (2018) demonstrate that such collaborations led to local government efforts to protect these FCs because of their community value. We draw upon archival sources from FCs and sports halls dating from the 1980s, as well as internet resources, market/industry reports, and secondary literature on sport politics and policy, leisure and tourism, and business/management history.

We undertook exploratory and inductive research, consistent with the work of Wond and Macaulay (2011) who champion longitudinal research in the public management field. This draws on the work of Rose (1993) who identified the importance of temporality and geography in lesson-drawing for public policy.

2. Creating the Leisure Centre – Establishing the Institutional Context

The post-1945 period in the UK was associated with rapidly rising prosperity for working people despite the prevailing austerity in the immediate post war years. However, the introduction of universalized secondary education in the 1944 Education Act together with an increasingly assertive 'youth culture' saw the creation of the *teenager* and the rise of an associated moral panic that youth were dropping out of physical activity after leaving school (TSSLP, n.d.). The 1944 Act also indirectly contributed to British sport by placing statutory responsibility on local education authorities to provide the facilities for games and physical education, which led to setting standards of provision for gymnasia and playing fields, and from now on young people were guaranteed a grounding in sport. Some areas of sport had historically been considered amateur, gentlemanly pursuits with ties to the education system. While a few elite sports, most notably association football and rugby league, had professionalized or reluctantly accepted some professionalism, as with cricket (Stone, 2022). Although some athletes competed for financial prizes or otherwise found ways to make money from their abilities, some sports more closely affiliated to the Olympics such as athletics, swimming and gymnastics also retained an amateur image, effectively barring participation at elite events such as the Olympic Games to a large part of the population.

Government involvement in sport and recreation was new but became more common in the post-war era as sport was considered a way to enhance British 'soft power', as well as to solve domestic social problems. In 1947, the Ministry of Education agreed to help finance the salaries of some national coaches affiliated to the Amateur Athletic Association, the forerunner for the government funding available to coaches that expanded in later years (Coghlan & Webb, 1990).

The establishment of dedicated sporting facilities in structured institutions separate from schools or from existing sporting clubs, whether professional, semi-professional or amateur, and largely (though not exclusively) aimed at young and mature adults was in many parts of the UK a new departure. From the mid-1950s, experts in the Physical Education field started to encourage the establishment of multi-sport facilities, including sports halls which could host multiple indoor activities such as volleyball, basketball, badminton, indoor tennis, table tennis, handball and five-a-side football. These could be combined with more traditional outdoor playing fields and sometimes a swimming pool or other water-based facilities or even an ice rink (TSLLP, n.d.; Saumarez Smith, 2019). Professional instructors provided training for the public and organized competitions, while often the presence of a café or licensed bar provided a small revenue stream. Such centres became an important part of the post war British landscape, often serving as one of the focal points of a community, but converting advocacy into action was not always a straightforward process. This was partly because of the lack of a national funding structure for sport and recreation activity, but also to some extent because local authorities did not have a statutory duty to provide such facilities.

The Central Council of Physical Recreation (CCPR) was a non-governmental body founded in 1935, with the social objective to encourage as many men and women as possible to participate in sport and physical recreation, and the administrative objective to provide the separate governing bodies of sports with a central organization to represent and promote their individual and collective interests. It was further grant aided by the Ministry of Education to foster physical recreation activities among those who had left school, which it did by providing training for coaches and school-leavers, as well as opportunities for adults to take up new sports, and running three 'National Recreation Centres' which provided a resource for the governing bodies of sport (Wolfenden Committee on Sport, 1960, pp. 16–17). Following the progress of sport and leisure coverage and availability and advances in provision, the CCPR considered it important to assess what existed and what more should be done. Thus, in October 1957, it appointed an independent Committee to examine the general position of sport in the UK and to recommend the steps that should be taken by statutory and voluntary bodies. Sir John Wolfenden, a British educationist, and Vice Chancellor of Reading University, agreed to Chair the Committee, which comprised scholars and representatives of different English countries, but no sportsmen or sportswomen. The Wolfenden Committee on Sport and Community reported in 1960 and was debated in Parliament in 1961. While the CCPR itself provided physical training courses for nearly 50,000 leaders or coaches a year, there was little structure for national dissemination. It made many recommendations, including the establishment by Government of a national strategy and governing body and the provision of more indoor and outdoor facilities (playing fields, sports arenas, swimming pools, and so on), and that these should be undertaken by local authorities and voluntary organizations working in partnership, together with central Government (Coghlan & Webb, 1990; Hansard, 1961).

Wolfenden Committee on Sport (1960, pp. 25–29) diagnosed a clear educational need, that a 'gap' existed between young people leaving school and establishing themselves in adult recreational activities, and that the availability of facilities, often provided by private or industrial sports clubs, and instruction for this was often lacking. Wolfenden also cited and agreed with the Albemarle Report of 1960, which established the field of youth work, but also pointed to the potentially positive role of physical recreation. As a response, sport (which in the second half of the twentieth century became a social service) was increasingly used as a tool to tackle societal problems associated with deprivation in urban or inner-city areas (Coghlan & Webb, 1990; Gillett & Tennent, 2018), although the Conservative government of Harold Macmillan did not prioritize recreation in the structured way their successors would. Wolfenden did not propose a centralized approach to sport but rather recommended the strengthening of the CCPR together with more cooperation between local authorities and sporting bodies. Facilities in general needed to be strengthened. More floodlit pitches for playing games in all weathers were required as well as more swimming baths, but most urgent of all was the provision of 'barns' for indoor games, which could be supported by 'the establishment of experimental multi-sports centres (Wolfenden Committee on Sport, 1960, p. 108). It was thought that multi-sports centres could offer economies of scale and scope because indoor facilities could be used for many different activities, including for instance dance, competitive sport, and coaching, allowing individuals to try different pursuits and also attracting family membership. Multi-sports centres therefore had a potential community role, and the example of a 4,000 member sports club in Copenhagen was used as an example of international best practice (Wolfenden Committee on Sport, 1960, pp. 38–39).

3. 1960s–1970s – Early Steps

Wolfenden recommended that the building of multi-sports centres would partly be supported by a new 'SDC' which would receive up to £5 million of government funding a year, with powers to disperse grants to the various bodies involved (Wolfenden Committee on Sport, 1960, p. 112). This was not implemented immediately but was introduced in an advisory only form by Denis Howell in 1965 with executive powers to encourage the knowledge and practice of sport being granted to the body through a Royal Charter in 1972. This move, which originally proposed that the Sports Council would absorb the CCPR, which was an independent charity although in receipt of government funding, was not without controversy (Department for the Environment, 1971). The CCPR had endorsed the Wolfenden Report, but its own committee, including its patron the Duke of Edinburgh, its General Secretary, Phyllis Colson, and its Chair (and FIFA President),

Sir Stanley Rous remained sceptical of the implementation of a government led strategy for sports and recreation (TSLLP, n.d.), perhaps fearing public sector over-reach or unnecessary intervention or duplication of the existing structure of voluntary and professional bodies (Coghlan & Webb, 1990). The CCPR operated its own multi-sport centre at Crystal Palace, in London, jointly with the Greater London Council, together with several sites for training instructors and outdoor pursuits across the country. The government proposed that these sites and their staff, which were funded by central government, be absorbed by the Sports Council, and their instructors transferred to the civil service pay scale from the further education pay scale. Ultimately, though, after intervention from the Duke of Edinburgh and others, the CCPR was allowed to continue as a charity providing an umbrella body for the governing bodies of sport (Department for the Environment, 1971). However, this move signalled the maturing of a hybrid model of state funding and local provision which had evolved since the early 1960s.

Wolfenden's emphasis on multi-activity provision encouraged the building of local authority leisure centres even before the establishment of the Sports Council. The first, which had been in development since the mid-1960s, was the Harlow Sportcentre, developed around an indoor sports hall opened in the new town of Harlow in Essex in 1964 on local authority and development corporation rather than national initiative. The Harlow project, which included provision for football, athletics, cricket and hockey, as well as an all-weather training pitch and even a dry ski slope, was taken as the model for the development of multi-sport provision after the introduction of the Sports Council. Governance of the centre was placed in the hands of a charitable organization, the Harlow and District Sports Trust while the first manager, George Torkildsen, was an influential thinker in sports and leisure who worked with the sports clubs using the facilities as well as organizing coaching and centre programmed activities. As it grew, the Harlow centre was credited with producing instructors and managers who would go on to manage other centres around the UK (TSLLP, n.d.). By doing so, Torkildsen and his colleagues helped to build a distinct profession of leisure centre management which grew out of the academic discipline of Physical Education, first established in the UK at the University of Birmingham in 1946 and further encouraged by the expansion of higher education in the 1960s. Instruction and then leisure centre management would provide employment opportunities for the graduates of these programmes. The managers and their assistants had varied roles – they hired instructors, worked out schemes of charges, ran the buildings, encouraged clubs, organized activities and did much 'soft work' with communities to encourage them to use the leisure centres (SLLP, n.d). Instructors were salaried under the existing Further Education grading structure already used by local authorities in technical colleges and were expected to work flexible hours in evenings and weekends, aligning with the leisure hours of the public (The Guardian, 1966). Indeed, one of the controversial aspects of the Sports Council taking over the CCPR's centres, including the National Sports Centre at Crystal Palace (which was managed jointly with the Greater London Council) in south London, was that instructors would be moved to the Civil Service paygrades from the Further Education structures (Department for the Environment, 1971).

Early centres tended to be built in towns dominated by (and often specifically developed for) the steel or chemical industries, where the local authorities, although smaller than today, had considerable disposable rateable income. These included the Teesside towns of Billingham, Stockton, Thornaby and Eston, as well as Port Talbot in Wales, all of which had benefited from the increasing concentration of industry as industrial policy encouraged corporate mergers and green-field facilities to maintain competitiveness against overseas firms (Owen, 1999). The formula, which usually consisted of the provision of a multi-use sports hall together with all-weather and grass pitches, proved successful with users and was soon imitated across the UK. These early centres were very impactful – the Afan Lido centre in Port Talbot spun out a professional FC who later played in the League of Wales, while the Teesside cluster fostered a new local interest in table tennis, hosting international matches in the sport. Afan Lido also innovated by broadening the emphasis from participation in competitive sport to leisure generally, including a spa, a gym and the large central area was fitted with a rising stage and moveable seats for large concerts, and in the 1984–1985 miners' strike, the site was used for union rallies. On Teesside, Billingham Forum went further and provided an ice rink with seating for 1,000 spectators as well as a 650-seat theatre separate from the sports hall, and a restaurant, snack bar and licensed bar run by Scottish & Newcastle Breweries (SLLP, n.d.). Leisure centres were taking on a more communal role in providing public space. The new towns created for urban overspill would also pioneer provision so as to attract new residents from the large cities and other parts of the UK; in 1973, the Economist noted that of the five Scottish new towns, East Kilbride, Irvine and Glenrothes had already built or were in the course of building sports centres. One of the two centres in East Kilbride even featured an Olympic size swimming pool (Economist 1973a), while Irvine touted its new leisure centre scheme to attract inward investment (Economist, 1973b).

Soon after, the creation of the SDC as an advisory body finally happened in 1965, following an election manifesto pledge to do so by the incoming Labour government. The SDC, with parallel Scottish and Welsh equivalents, and regional councils beneath it (Coghlan & Webb, 1990), controlled the allocation of £5m worth of government funding for sports facilities per year through a process of competitive grants (SLLP, n.d.). This competition was open to local authorities, charitable bodies, or sports clubs to establish facilities for the public good.

Following the change of government in 1964, the establishment of the SDC had finally fulfilled the Wolfenden proposals, although the ideas for direction of travel and initial progress had occurred under the previous Conservative government, and it would be inaccurate to credit it all to the political shift. Nevertheless, the extent and rapidity of progress appear to have increased thereafter, perhaps due to Labour's plans but also due to progress in Continental Europe. Since 1959, West Germany's Olympic Society had presented a 'Golden Plan for Health, Play and Recreation'. This stemmed from the founding of the Institute for Sports Facility Construction in the mid-1950s, which bought together local authorities, sports associations, and town planners. A Federal Statistical Office study revealed a significant shortfall in the provision of recreational, games and sports facilities per capita, resulting in the 'Golden Plan...', which aimed to overcome the shortfall over a 15-year period, with a multi-billion Deutschemark investment. Although this went far beyond the British approach, it appears to have set a tone amongst other developed European nations (Sport Structures Limited, 2011).

It should also be mentioned that similarly to Germany, much autonomy about how to meet provision was left to the local authorities, with the SDC fulfilling the role of coordinating and providing some grant funding. Most of the commissioning and financing of facilities was left to the initiative of local government, the SDC merely offering a fraction of funding to catalyze developments or to help them reach the specifications of the sports' governing bodies, or to add extra facilities. Arguably, this was the most democratic way to 'do' sports and leisure strategy as social service, with the ability for flexibility and adjusting to local needs that local authorities knew best. However, without the same investment as occurred in West Germany, it also created a 'postcode lottery': the most deprived areas, whose residents had the most to gain from such facilities (if viewed through the social service lens), had the most demands on finances and proportionally least to spend on sport and leisure (Coghlan & Webb, 1990). Although sports and leisure facilities could attract a lot of users (for instance, the Billingham Forum received 10 million visits in its first six and a half years), sometimes travelling in from other boroughs, public subsidy remained necessary to maintain usage fees at a level to maintain accessibility to the public, meaning that the centres maintained a utility maximizing ethos. For instance, in the 1970–1971 financial year, Teesside County Borough provided continued grant funding of £99,500 to Billingham Forum, even though the centre attracted a total income of £273,676 (SLLP, n.d.).

It is inaccurate though to think that the central government's approach to sport and leisure is by now only concerned with tackling inner-city problems or education. After World War II, there was also renewed focus on the treatment and rehabilitation of paraplegics. This was particularly stimulated by responsibility to those returning from war, but with benefits for the broader community of spinal injury and disabled people. As well as advances in medical treatment and equipment, the national centre for spinal injuries at Stoke Mandeville in Buckinghamshire emphasized sport for rehabilitation. This involved looking internationally to draw upon ideas and 'best practices' from other countries, notably America. Patients were encouraged to participate in sports that could be adapted to wheelchair mobility such as basketball, fencing, and archery. Competitions were held between patients and then with other UK institutions, with leagues and sports days organized. Overall, standards and specifications were shared for accessibility to buildings, to sport, and to the workplace. Public sector organizations were encouraged to accommodate these standards in workplaces and leisure facilities to optimize opportunities for disabled communities. The profile of disabled sport and leisure was boosted as ambitions of Stoke Mandeville became reality, and their sports day spawned regular international paraplegic 'Olympics' from 1960, the inaugural event held in Rome, Italy (these games were eventually co-opted by the International Olympic Committee as the Paralympics and held quadrennially in tandem with the Olympic Games) and Paraplegic Commonwealth Games starting in Perth, Australia, in 1962 although the only disability allowed at this time was spinal injury (The Cord, 1947–1982).

It is important to realize that infrastructure development was happening at a time when the UK, and other nations around the world, were implementing national plans and new deals to modernize urban areas and stimulate their economies. The election of Harold Wilson's Labour government in the Autumn of 1964 meant a change of ethos towards centralized planning which was fundamental to the Wilson view of the economy. In the British context, Wilson's National Plan of 1965 meant stimulus and corrective intervention in the economy through control of public investment, nationalized industries and encouragement of technological change (Tomlinson, 2004), rather than the outright command and control approach favoured by the Communist nations (Gillett & Tennent, 2017). An important element of government policy was to invest heavily in Science and Education. Unlike today, where responsibility for sport and leisure exists within distinct government department (Digital, Culture, Media and Sport – or DCMS) sport was under the purview of the Department of Education and Science (DES) and after 1970 was moved to the Department for the Environment. As Tennent and Gillett (2016) explain, the government's role in funding the FIFA (soccer) World Cup in 1966 was part of this expansion of Education and Science funding, and sport formed only part of a broader portfolio in which education and science were the main responsibilities (Howell, 1990). The World Cup is relevant when considering the tensions between the provision of facilities for professional sport and for recreation facilities: in Newcastle-Upon-Tyne, which had opened its own distinctive sports hall, the Lightfoot Centre in the inner-city district of Walker in 1965, the ambitious council leader T. Dan Smith came into conflict with the local soccer team Newcastle United FC, who leased the St. James' Park stadium from the council. Smith wanted to upgrade the stadium to a municipal multi-sport arena which could be used seven days a week, rather than the sole domain of the club (Foote Wood, 2010; Joannu, 2000, p. 270). This appears to have been an attempt to replace an athletics stadium that would have been demolished by a motorway project (Newcastle Corporation, 1964). The club resisted, and the stadium lost the right to host World Cup games.

The full benefits of the 'white heat of technology', based on the application and development of science and technology in education and work (Wilson, 1963), never quite came to fruition as the British economy developed more slowly than those of continental Europe and Asia, and entire industries and regions faced relative decline. Visionary architects' schemes for modern living were often either practically problematic or otherwise compromised by the budgets available, and the resulting concrete jungles created by ring roads, underpasses, flyovers, and blocks of flats and offices compounded existing problems of urban regeneration, meaning even greater need for community cohesion initiatives and the supposed benefits from sport and leisure and other social services (Coghlan & Webb, 1990).

Sport and leisure was the zeitgeist, or at least one of them! In 1968, The Council of Europe adopted the idea of the right to sport for all, an inclusive and democratic approach to sport and leisure whereby all citizens, regardless of age, colour or capability, would have the opportunity to participate (Coghlan & Webb, 1990). This was adopted across the continent including in the United Kingdom, where the national policy of 'sport for all' promoted inclusion and aimed to use sport and recreation for improving public health. Compared to other European nations, in the UK its application did not receive the same amount of public funding, with organization delegated to quasi-autonomous public bodies, voluntary organizations, and local authorities, rather than central planning or funding through national lotteries (Coghlan & Webb, 1990).

The growth of the sector was further boosted by the Royal Charter awarded to the Sports Council in 1972 together with the transfer of the sport portfolio to the Department for the Environment (Civil Service, 1997) and the local government re-organization in 1974, which was intended to tidy up urban sprawl. This reform consolidated the many small Rural and Urban District councils as well as County Boroughs into larger Metropolitan Borough and District Council units, deepening the resources of some while spreading others more thinly. Some policy confusion did arise from the reforms, however. New Metropolitan County Councils were created in the larger conurbations with strategic powers over land use planning. These councils also took an interest in recreation with a view to standardizing provision between constituent Boroughs/Districts, though attempts to do so directly (for instance where Greater Manchester County attempted to influence the recreation policies of Manchester City Council) were often resented as 'interference' by the districts (Flynn, Leach, & Vielba, 1985). Scotland saw a similar re-organization into a two-tier system of regions and districts in 1975 and saw a considerable expansion on its five existing centres. In Northern Ireland, an existing two-tier system was re-organized into 26 single-tier districts and a statutory duty to provide facilities for recreation was introduced. In 1974, Northern Ireland had just two sports centres, in Antrim and Craigavon (SLLP, n.d.), but this would soon grow as a strategy to distract from the Troubles, which were at their most violent in the early 1970s. This was partly due to availability of central government funding but also because leisure remained a local government power, whereas responsibilities for more 'strategic' services such as housing were removed to deter their political misuse (Saumarez Smith, 2019, p. 187; Sugden & Barnier, 1986).

In 1969, there had been 27 centres across England and Wales; by 1973, there were 170; and by 1979, there were around 600 public leisure centres (SLLP, n.d.). The years 1967 and 1975 had seen an especial surge in schemes opening as some local authorities that were being abolished built centres to provide legacies to their existence, while new authorities sought to mark their formation. Centres combined municipal trading with the provision of services, charging the public for their use as well as receiving financial subsidies, remaining subject to the frameworks of local authority organization, many remaining directly operated by local authorities until the 1990s. Local Councils acted, sometimes forming partnerships with sporting organizations such as FCs, because of the previous failure of government to develop a coherent national policy (Cobham Report, 1973).

The linkage to professional sport was at times pivotal in encouraging the growth of the movement. From mid-1970s, central government wanted the Sports Council to target its resources at specific groups in society. Then, an investigation in 1978 showed a need for 2,900 local indoor sports halls in England (Gillett & Tennent, 2018). That year, Denis Howell met with representatives of the

Football League, League Clubs Secretaries Association and Sports Council, to discuss plans for public financing of development schemes at clubs, in response to another moral panic, that of spectator violence at football games, which some linked to bigger societal problems especially in the inner-cities. Money would be provided to the Football League to assist with the development of facilities at clubs' grounds that would benefit the community, such as sports halls and similar facilities that the public and community groups could access. Funding of £1.6million was made available for the Football and Community Development Programme (Gillett & Tennent, 2018) paid via the Sports Council, which had full support from English Football's main governing institutions. Fifty-seven of the 92 professional league clubs expressed interest before 29 (and 8 rugby league) clubs were selected to receive funding in the scheme's first year. Schemes included providing synthetic-surfaced pitches, floodlighting, and converting existing facilities for community use, such as those at Sheffield United and West Ham United. Later in 1978, The Football Grounds Improvement Trust matched this funding with a further £250,000 to enable more clubs to participate (Coghlan & Webb, 1990). The most successful schemes relied on the development of close links with local authorities, and some also received money from the Training Agency, such as between Calderdale Council and Halifax FC (Gillett & Tennent, 2018).

More significantly, the clubs Manchester City and Aston Villa built and operated indoor training and leisure centres for club use, but those could also be opened to the public and community user groups, such as teams and clubs for children and the disabled (Gillett & Tennent, 2018). They were seen as key to reaching communities, making use of their tangible (land and built facilities) and intangible (skills and knowledge of sport and managing sport facilities) to help meet commitments for leisure provision per geographic area and head of population).

4. National Diffusion – 1980s and 1990s

After 1979, this move towards outsourcing public leisure provision was re-emphasized by the incoming Conservative government, headed by Margaret Thatcher. Indeed, the broad move towards managerialism in the public sector has been observed internationally and described as the new public management (NPM) (Hood, 1991). Thatcher's government applied ideas such as compulsory competitive tendering (CCT), which introduced market forces to the procurement of public goods and services (Gillett, 2016, p. 16). Although the provision of leisure facilities had become normative, central government support was cut during the recession of the early 1980s. One of the first actions of the new UK government was to reduce Sports Council funding – this reduced the potential grants available to FCs for sports hall/leisure centre projects and left some club's schemes in a precarious position.

However, sport and leisure continued to be a field for government intervention. New initiatives such as 'Action Sport', piloted in 1982, were introduced to encourage communities to participate in sports, including football. Finance was made available to assist local authorities in metropolitan areas to provide new or improved facilities (Houlihan, 1991). The Sports Council continued to target the growth of sports centres, especially in smaller communities and adjusted its grant aid appropriately, with the target that one sports centre might serve 20,000 people, whereas the 1972 target had been one for 40–50,000 people (Coghlan & Webb, 1990, p. 201). Through Action Sport, there were attempts to boost participation through group work, emphasis on drawing non-participants into activity using Sports Leaders, and the development of activities in non-purpose-built sports spaces. However, in the hands of local authorities that did not want sole control, the schemes failed to thrive, funding was ultimately withdrawn, and partnerships were dissolved (Watson, 2000).

Although Walters and Hamil (2013) assert that the political economy of the 1980s was typified by these increasingly free-market rather than interventionist principles, in reality it was not uncommon for *local* authorities, rather than central funding, to assist their local professional sports teams. In fact, a memo distributed by the Association of District Councils (ADCs) evidence that they were encouraged to do so (Association of District Councils, 1984). One club that suffered from the cut in Sports Council grant funding was Middlesbrough, the club then carried the burden of constructing a multi-use sports hall scheme with a reduced grant, a situation that arguably contributed to the club's insolvency a few years later and left the area without the facility needed for several years (Gillett & Tennent, 2018). A 1974 survey of the Cleveland County funded by the Sports and Arts councils showed that the four other sports centres in the county, perhaps most notably the multi-activity facilities at Billingham and at Eston (Gillett & Tennent, 2018), all drew a considerable number of members from the Middlesbrough district, which lacked an indoor sports centre of its own (SLLP, n.d.).

Partnerships with professional sports clubs were though just one strand of sport and leisure provision. Indeed, usage surveys such as the Cleveland survey and a more comprehensive survey undertaken in Atherton, Lancashire, in 1981 demonstrated that formal clubs which fed into the bigger professional sports such as football, rugby and cricket often carried on as before (SLLP, n.d.). The demand for public sector leisure provision had started to shift from the focal point of club activity envisaged at pioneering centres such as Harlow and Afan Lido to more casual, smaller scale participation in more individualized activities such as swimming or keeping fit. Indoor provision of this sort was a major participation success, with up to 1 million more adult women and 600,000 more men participating in indoor physical exercise between 1983 and 1988, indicating that between a quarter and a third of the adult population were now participating. An example of demand-based provision was the interest in playing squash in the early 1980s – local authorities found that squash users were willing to pay higher fees for a half hour rental than players of other sports, making it easier to repay the capital costs of courts (Coghlan & Webb, 1990, pp. 199–200). A further trend, encouraged by the videos of the American actress Jane Fonda as well as exercise segments on breakfast television was the renewed popularity of keeping fit for its own sake (Mansfield, 2011; TV-am, 1984), providing the opportunity for classes and the provision of equipment.

Reflecting this the emphasis of many schemes had started to move away from sport towards an integrated model of leisure time provision from the mid-1970s onwards, and overall, expansion continued apace, and by the mid-late 1980s, there were around 1,200 leisure sites, expanding to an estimated 1,600 by 1994 and 1,800 by 1999 (SLLP, n.d). By this point, many towns had built flagship centres which had tourism value and were expected to draw people from outside of the commissioning borough. The first to move in this direction is considered to have been the 'new city' of Milton Keynes, whose Bletchley Leisure Centre complex, opened in 1984, was centred on a glass pyramid containing a 'free-form' swimming pool not designed for sporting use, but rather to replicate the conditions indoors of a sub-tropical beach environment with palm trees and a waterside (Saumarez Smith, 2019, pp. 188–191). This form of design, usually including a wave machine to simulate being at the seaside, proved popular with local authorities and architects, and through the 1980s and 1990s, more leisure pools were opened on this model around the UK. Sunderland's Crowtree leisure centre had a wave machine so powerful that in early testing it flooded the street outside, while the Coral Reef in Bracknell, opened in 1989 went so far as to include a pirate ship for children to play on (SLLP, n.d.). These projects usually continued to cater for other sports too, with the Crowtree's sports hall being used to host a professional basketball team (Daily Mirror, 1979) though away from the pool there was an increasing interest also in fitness and wellbeing for its own sake – weight training rooms and running machines were provided to allow users to build muscle mass, while saunas and solariums boosted relaxation.

The turn towards an explicitly leisure-oriented approach, which aimed to attract non-ratepaying tourists gave the opportunity for new funding models including private capital and EEC funding which did not involve central government. These new complexes could also be used to promote the local economy to prospective inward investors. Scunthorpe Leisure Centre promised to create a 'tropical paradise' – it opened in 1984 at a cost of £3.5 million, and was opened by the England footballer Kevin Keegan, who had played for the local FC. The local authority co-funded the centre with a merchant bank, but the long lead time for the centre, first planned in the mid-1970s, meant that by the time, it opened the local steel industry was facing a downturn, with local unemployment reaching 25%. The borough council used the facility to promote the town to American and Japanese visitors, including representatives of Nissan who were interested in building a car factory in the UK; unfortunately for Scunthorpe, they chose to invest in Washington near Sunderland instead (The Guardian, 1984a). The same year in Yorkshire, Doncaster council was funded by the European Commission for a feasibility study into an ambitious plan for a centre costing £22 million, which would include some elements of sports provision but also an emphasis on 'fun rather than hearty sporting activity' (The Guardian, 1984b). The council was funding the project by selling land but also aimed to attract further EEC funding together with investment from the Regional Tourist Board and the Sports Council. The EEC also provided £673,000 towards an attraction which aimed to appeal to a UK wide audience (The Guardian, 1982), the Rhyl Sun Centre in North Wales, which overall cost £4.25 million to build. This centre, located on the beach, opened in 1980 and included three pools including an indoor surfing pool and attractions including a remote-control car circuit, a nightclub and even a 200-metre suspended monorail (SLLP, n.d.). This was an attempt to revive a declining seaside town where male unemployment had reached 26.5%, though the centre proved expensive to maintain in the long run as local holiday camps started to build their own swimming pools, and it eventually closed in 2014 after the local authority withdrew its subsidy (BBC, 2016). Many of the leisure pool focussed centres eventually suffered a similar fate as the novelty subsided.

The establishment of a national system of centres, whether leisure or sport focussed, was essentially completed by the year 2000. This encouraged the formalization of the profession which had grown out of university PE departments with the formation of professional organizations, including the Association of Recreation Managers, which after a series of mergers with other bodies in the field, was eventually chartered in 2013 as the Chartered Institute of Sport and Physical Activity (CIMSPA, 2021). By the 1990s, the sports centre context and the profession that supported it was considered so well established that it were reflected by the BBC in television comedy. The series 'The Brittas Empire', set in a fictional new town leisure centre, ran for 52 episodes between 1991 and 1997. The central character, Gordon Brittas, was an idealistic PE graduate who believed that by organizing leisure activities he could lead society to a higher purpose, but of course this rarely went according to plan – the programme perhaps also lampooned late twentieth century managerialism (Lewis & Stempel, 1998).

The turn of the millennium coincided with an apparent growth of private sector sports centres and gyms as disposable income grew; as provision became more abundant, there was less of a need for subsidised centres. Private sector gyms brought a sense of exclusivity and additional segmentation to the marketplace. There was also increasing hybridity as local authorities hived off direct operation of their provision to charitable bodies or non-profit making company structures, allowing publicly financed facilities more commercial freedom outside of public sector procurement and accounting rules. For instance, in 2011, Doncaster Metropolitan Borough Council moved all its leisure provision into a new body, the Doncaster Culture and Leisure Trust. The trust has subsequently expanded its fitness and cultural business to compete with the private sector, providing among other facilities gyms, a bowling alley, and even buying a local public house and music venue (DCLT, 2022). Other institutions such as universities moved towards hybrid forms of provision too, such as the University of York, which opened its two sports centres to the public, branded as 'York Sport' in partnership with the City of York Council in 2012 (York Sport, 2022). These trends reflected the eventual movement away of the government from the direct funding of sport and leisure, despite the formation of a designated Department for National Heritage with specific responsibility for sport in 1992.

5. Conclusion: The Building of a Profession

By the year 2000, access to dedicated, multi-sport and leisure facilities was expected by British citizens across the four nations. We have focussed here on examples and vignettes from around the country as well as summarizing the national story, which is in total one of institutional entrepreneurship within a public sector framework. The institutional context was framed by the provision of grants by the SDC after 1965 together with the broader action of local authorities who aimed to provide their ratepayers with access to improved sport and leisure services. The tethering of this system to the framework of instruction through further education Pay-scale provided opportunities for promotion and created a form of exchangeable labour market, encouraging PE graduates to commit themselves to a long-term career in the profession. Furthermore, although centres proved over time to become more expensive investments for local authorities (and often, perhaps a way to signal the prestige of that local authority), the capability of local authorities was boosted by the local government reforms of the 1970s which merged districts, pooling their resources. The form also proved durable enough to shift its emphasis from the provision of organized sport to the provision of more individualized and commercialized 'leisure' as a product, although the extent to which this ultimate outcome achieved the aims of central government, following Wolfson, to improve access to indoor sporting facilities and to tackle 'the youth problem', remains questionable. The possibility of support from private capital and, after 1973, from the EEC, also provided new opportunities for the organizational form. However, the story of leisure provision in the UK remains one of remarkable public sector entrepreneurship within an institutional context.

References

Association of District Councils. (1984). Circular no: 1984/39 dated 29 February 1984.

BBC. (2016, August 27). *Rhyl Sun Centre: No more waves in the lagoon pool*. Retrieved from https://www.bbc.co.uk/news/uk-wales-north-east-wales-36833354. Accessed on August 16, 2022.

CIMSPA. (2021). *A history of CIMSPA – at the heart of the sport and physical activity sector*. Chartered Institute of Sport and Physical Activity. Retrieved from https://www.cimspa.co.uk/about/a-history-of-cimspa. Accessed on June 26, 2021.

Civil Service. (1997). *The civil service yearbook*. London: Dandy Booksellers.

Cobham Report. (1973). *Second report of the select committee of the house of lords on sport and leisure*. London: HMSO.

Coghlan, J. F., & Webb, I. (1990). *Sport and British politics since 1960*. Abingdon: Routledge.

Daily Mirror. (1979, 30 January). 'Halt the Hulk' is a tall order, p. 27.

DCLT. (2022). *About the trust*. Retrieved from https://www.dclt.co.uk/about-dclt/about-the-trust/. Accessed on August 16, 2022.

Department for the Environment. (1971). Steering Group on the Future of the Central Council for Physical Recreation (CCPR) and the Sports Council: National sports centres. The National Archives, reference HLG 120/2553.

Economist. (1973a, 29 September). Ring in the new: A survey of Scotland, pp. 40–43.

Economist. (1973b, 10 March). Nerve-centre of what will be one of Europe's most advanced New Towns, p. 39.

Flynn, N., Leach, S., & Vielba, C. (1985). *Abolition or reform? The GLC and the metropolitan county councils*. London: George Allen & Unwin.

Foote Wood, C. (2010). *T. Dan Smith 'voice of the north': Downfall of a visionary*. Bishop Auckland: Northern Writers.

Gillett, A. G. (2016). Multiple relationships with multiple stakeholders: The scope of relationship marketing for public services. *Journal of Services Research, 16*(2), 1–28.

Gillett, A. G., & Tennent, K. D. (2017). Dynamic sublimes, changing plans, and the legacy of a megaproject: The case of the 1966 Soccer World Cup. *Project Management Journal, 48*(6), 93–116.

Gillett, A. G., & Tennent, K. D. (2018). Shadow hybridity and the institutional logic of professional sport. *Journal of Management History, 24*(2), 228–259.

Gillett, A. G., & Tennent, K. D. (2020). Sport and project management: A window into the development of temporary organizations. In K. Bruce (Eds.), *Handbook of research on management and organizational history* (pp. 169–191). Cheltenham: Edward Elgar Publishing.

Hansard. (1961). Volume 369, debated 28th April 1961. Retrieved from https://hansard.parliament.uk/commons/1961-04-28/debates/fb1305b5-ac14-44a4-809c-15e611868bc5/Sport(WolfendenCommitteeSReport)]

Hood, C. (1991). A public management for all seasons? *Public Administration, 69*(1), 3–19.

Houlihan, B. (1991). *The government and politics of sport/Barrie Houlihan*. London: Routledge.

Howell, D. (1990). *Made in Birmingham: The memoirs of Denis Howell*. London: Queen Anne.

Joannu, P. (2000). *Newcastle United, the first 100 years & more*. Leicester: Polar Print Group.

Lewis, J. E., & Stempel, P. (1998). *Cult TV: The comedies: The ultimate critical guide*. San Francisco, CA: Pavilion.

Mansfield, L. (2011). 'Sexercise': Working out heterosexuality in Jane Fonda's fitness books. *Leisure Studies, 30*(2), 237–255.

Newcastle Corporation. (1964). Minute Book. *Plan Proposed New Bridge Street Motorway*, undated insert. Tyne & Wear Archives, City of Newcastle-upon-Tyne Corporation Minute Books.

Owen, G. (1999). *From empire to Europe: The decline and revival of British industry since the Second World War*. London: Harper Collins.

Rose, R. (1993). *Lesson-drawing in public policy: A guide to learning across time and space*. Chatham: Chatham House Publishers.

Saumarez Smith, O. (2019). The lost world of the British leisure centre. *History Workshop Journal, 88*, 180–203.

Sport Structures Limited. (2011). *Benchmarking – German report*. Retrieved from https://www.sportstructures.com/media/1332/sport_structures_german_benchmarking_report_-_germany_09092011.pdf>

Stone, D. (2022). *Different class: The untold story of English cricket*. London: Repeater.

Sugden, J., & Barnier, A. (1986). Northern Ireland: The politics of leisure in a divided society. *Leisure Studies, 5*(3), 3419–3452.

Tennent, K. D., & Gillett, A. G. (2016). *Foundations of managing sporting events: Organising the 1966 FIFA world cup*. London: Routledge.

The Cord. (1947–1982). Examples and articles can be throughout the entire run of volumes archived by Buckinghamshire Council Archive, holding: D-IWAS/11/1/1-5, 80-81

The Guardian. (1966, January 7). Classified Ad 17: Essex: Harlow and District Sportcentre, p. 6.

The Guardian. (1982, May 22). Seaside resort's tide of unemployment, p. 5.

The Guardian. (1984a, March 31). A tropical heat wave over Scunthorpe...but it's cold cold cold in the market place, p. 7.

The Guardian. (1984b, December 17). Councils plan rival leisure centres, p. 4.

The Sports Leisure Legacy Project. (TSLLP). (n.d.). The Sports Leisure Legacy Project: Harlow to K2 and Beyond. *The story of the UK Sports & Leisure Centre Past, Present and Future*. Retrieved from https://sportsleisurelegacy.co.uk/. Accessed on August 16, 2022.

Tomlinson, J. (2004). *Economic policy*. Manchester: Manchester University Press.

Torkildsen, G. (2005). *Leisure and recreation management*. London: Routledge.

TV-am. (1984). Lizzie Webb with TV-am technicians. Retrieved from https://www. youtube.com/watch?v=BeAv-1tnePQ&list=PLDQnWpHQh7h9cnxmp6p34O-sJrPPOq6nv&index=3. Accessed on August 16, 2022.

Walters, G., & Hamil, S. (2013). The contests for power and influence over the regulatory space within the English professional football industry, 1980–2012. *Business History*, *55*(5), 740–767.

Watson, N. (2000). Football in the community: 'What's the score. *Soccer and Society*, *1*(1), 114–125.

Wilson, H. (1963). Labour's plan for science. Reprint of speech by the Rt. Hon Harold Wilson, MP, Leader of the Labour Party, at the Annual Conference, Scarborough, Tuesday, October 3rd, 1963. Retrieved from http://nottspolitics.org/wp-content/uploads/2013/06/Labours-Plan-for-science.pdf

Wolfenden Committee on Sport. (1960). *Sport & the Community: The Report of the Wolfenden Committee on Sport*. London: Central Council of Physical Recreation.

Wond, T., & Macaulay, M. (2011). Extending time–Extended benefits: Using longitudinal research in public management evaluation. *Public Management Review*, *13*(2), 309–320.

York Sport. (2022). York sport 10 year anniversary. Retrieved from https://www.york-sport.com/york-sport-and-you/ys10/. Accessed on August 16, 2022.

Chapter 6

Alliances as a Coopetitive Strategy of the Airlines: The Case of Iberia (1980–2020)

Javier Vidal Olivares

Abstract

Alliances between companies are an example of a collaborative strategy adopted in anticipation of highly uncertain markets. Since 1980, the commercial airline industry has been affected by a progressive liberalization worldwide. In this historical context, most airlines reacted with defensive movements in the face of high competition. In the case of airlines in the Spanish market, one of the largest in the world due to the weight of the tourism sector in its economy, airlines responded in various ways to the intensification of competition. Iberia, the main Spanish airline, established different defensive alliance policies. In the 1980s, alliances were mainly collaborative. Since 1998, airline alliances have become coopetitive in nature, as was the case with the creation of One World group (American Airlines, British Airways, Cathay Pacific, Qantas and Iberia). The partners began to interact in a more horizontal way, maintaining various agreements (code-sharing, handling, schedule coordination, shared sales, fleet maintenance) without renouncing their independence in the face of global competition. Iberia has subsequently modified the composition of its portfolio to move towards a more vertical collaboration with the integration into the *IAG Group* (Iberia, British Airways, Air Lingus and Vueling). This second phase is a quest to increase market power with deep changes in the nature of its alliances while maintaining coopetitive alliances.

Keywords: Airlines; coopetitive alliances; collective entrepreneurship; Iberia; flag carriers; Spanish airlines

Collective Entrepreneurship in the Contemporary European Services Industries:
A Long Term Approach, 77–93
Copyright © 2023 by Emerald Publishing Limited
All rights of reproduction in any form reserved
doi:10.1108/978-1-80117-950-820231006

1. Introduction

The liberalization of the commercial aviation markets, after 1978, led to a period of transition in airline competition. The airlines, still largely publicly owned on an international scale, embarked on a path of privatization and organizational change. These internal changes were accompanied and driven by the new regulations that were developed from the institutional framework. First the United States, and then the European Union, implemented the modifications that marked the new rules of airline organization in different chronological phases (Dobson, 2017, p. 1; Doganis, 2001; Hanlon, 2007).

The phases were characterized by an initial transition between 1980 and 2000, when the foundations for the regulatory transformation were established, followed by a subsequent one, from 2000, characterized by a remarkable growth of competition in the aviation markets, culminating in the USA-EU *Open Skies Treaty* in 2008. This agreement marked the culmination of the objectives set out by the European authorities, which envisaged the overcoming of the national barriers to commercial air navigation, giving way to a single, fully competitive market for all the EU airlines, in which all domestic flights would be considered cabotage (Dobson, 2007; Staniland, 2008).

Each of the phases until the final progressive liberalization of the airline markets was dominated by a policy of deploying strategies developed by the airlines. From the late 1980s onwards, the most common practice – in the meantime, the airlines were being privatized, as were large parts of the world market (except for the US airlines) – was the implementation of code-sharing agreements.

Codes and other commercial mechanisms can be seen as a practice fully integrated within the theory of *collective entrepreneurship* (Ribeiro-Soriano & Urbano, 2009) although the different approaches applied to airline behaviour integrate it into more classical theories (defensive movements) or into new approaches such as those based on the theory of dependency resources that use the concept of *coopetition* strategy (Mehmet, Yildiz, Okumus & Barca, 2019; Walley, 2007).

The aim of this chapter is to apply new approaches based on the development of alliances in the airline industry, from an evolutionary perspective, combining modifications of the institutional environment and adaptations of the airlines. The use of strategies based simultaneously on cooperation and competition was the response of airlines such as Air France or Qatar Airways to the uncertainty existing in the air market (Chiambaretto & Fernández, 2016; Chiambaretto & Wassmer, 2019). The case study of Iberia, the Spanish flag carrier until the end of the twentieth century, which is addressed here, shows this transition from the alliance models applied by companies from commercial ones to those of a strategic nature. The merger of Iberia into the IAG conglomerate (British Airways and Iberia) with other airlines shows the success of the use of collaborative and coopetitive strategies. These combinations have continued to be present in the portfolios of the integrated airlines, increasing the equity capital, and appropriating resources in their relationship with the alliance network. It is the positive management of the alliance network that brings more resources to the social capital of the airlines that form it (Casanueva, Gallego, Castro, & Sancho, 2013).

2. Theoretical Visions of Alliances in the Airline Sector

There is a changing nature to the evolution of alliances in the commercial aviation sector that is correlated with the different periods of the market regulation. Until the 1980s, when the strict control of the air navigation system prevailed, competition between airlines was not relevant. In a context of reduced competition, airlines, most of them under state control and ownership, were only able to increase their traffic through bilateral agreements with other airlines. The agreements only provided for frequency increases, usage of larger aircraft or technical and financial cooperation. Fares were generally not affected and remained at high levels. These agreements developed under the control of the cartel represented by IATA were the best guarantee that the regulatory environment meant commercial profitability for all the airlines (Doganis, 1991).

The alliances between airlines only began to vary when competition from charter airlines appeared from the 1960s. The tourism market, which had taken off rapidly and intensely, since the mid-1950s, brought a series of airlines that operated irregularly, with seasonal flights and in perfect symbiosis with the Tour Operators/Inclusive Tours that were created in the main tourists' countries of origin. In the receiving countries, the flag carriers tried to compete with these airlines with transport agreements and with hotels and Tour Operators/Inclusive Tours to win passengers in this growing market, but without much success.

Theoretical views on the reasons for and contents of alliances in the airline industry can be divided between those that emerged during, and after, the 1980s and 1990s (Burton & Hanlon, 1994). The former was dominated by an approach more focussed on the commercial aspects, through which airlines entered into their agreements. The scholars advocating this approach were those who focussed on the analysis of the various contents of the most common practices in the airline operations (Doganis, 1991, 2001; Hannegan & Mulvey, 1995; Morrish & Hamilton, 2002; Oum & Park, 1997; Park, 1997) with clearly two sub-periods: 1978 to 1992 and 1992 to 2001. The first period comprised the early stages of the development of liberalization, with the widespread commercial practices such as the use of code-sharing (Zou & Chen, 2017). The second period corresponded to the deepening of these practices, moving to the full strategic agreements where the most important aim was to share the increasing revenue (Evans, 2001) (Table 6).

Doganis (1991, 2001) argued that, in essence, alliances took on a defensive character in the face of the progressive liberalization of the international system from 1980. The key commercial practices were aimed at consolidating deals that would prepare airlines for increased competition. The predominant agreements focussed on code share, interline/prorate, mutual ground handling, frequent flyers programmes, block space, common sales, ticketing outlets, schedule capacity coordination and joint engineering and joint flights. The application of these practices, within an alliance configuration, has been seen as a positive phase for the airlines, increasing load factors and overall productivity levels (Brueckner, 2001). At the same time, there was a relative decrease in fares, generating profits for the airlines (Morrish & Hamilton, 2002). For their part, studies on the code-sharing practices

Table 6.   Common Practices in Airline Operations.

1978–1992	1992–2001	2001–2020
Commercial Alliance	Transition to Strategic Alliances	*Strategic* Alliances
Interline/Pro-rate	Common Sales/ Ticketing Oulets	Common Branding
Mutual-Ground handling	Schedule/Capacity co-ordination	Joint Cargo and passengers services ventures
Frequent-flyer programmes	Joint Engineering	Full Mergers
Code share	Joint Flights	Global
Block Space	Franchising	Collaborative and coopetitive alliances

Source: Own elaboration based on R. Doganis (2001, p. 74).

showed significant success, alongside the integration of agreed operations between the airlines and common marketing actions implied a success of the alliance policy. Other gains also came from new traffic stimulated by the increased competition amongst alliances and between alliances and other airlines operating, without being integrated into any (Hannegan & Mulvey, 1995).

The alliances implemented in the early stages of the liberalization were the natural outcome of the model built by the flag carriers, based on the issuance of flights through a *hub spoke* framework (Adler & Smilowitz, 2007; Brueckner, 2001). The alliances increase competition with this system, narrowing the cost/ price margins on the long-haul flights to compensate for the decrease in competition on the short-haul flights (Bicen, Hunt, & Madhavaram, 2021; Burton & Hanlon, 1994). During the 1990s, it was this distribution system that subsequently concentrated and consolidated the airlines and was the main impetus for the formation of the alliances. Alliances have been encouraged by the persistence of regulation in some markets and at the same time by the speed of deregulation in others (Pels, 2001).

During the last 20 years of the twentieth century, Oum and Park (1997) carried out the systematic study of the alliances, showing that airline agreements have become a permanent practice. They created value for the passengers and opportunities for the airlines. Hence, these alliances would not only continue but also become much stronger in the future. However, there was consensus at the beginning of the twenty-first century that alliances in the airline industry were beginning to undergo changes. The rapid pace of the liberalization and the strong development of the international commercial aviation have increased the degree of the uncertainty and risk in the airline business. In parallel, pressures to enforce anti-trust regulations have grown. The result was a decline in the number of the strategic alliances that led to the emergence of global alliances, in which the major airlines have joined in (Fan, Vigeant-Langlois, Geissler, Bosler, & Wilmking, 2001; Gaggero & Bartolini, 2012). This has been the result of the changes of the early twenty-first century, in which the implementation of a rapid pace of deregulation has given way to an uncertain and complex alliance climate. A progressive shift was taken place, from commercial to strategic agreements, leading to high competition (Agusdinata & De Klein, 2002). The instability of the alliances and, at the same time, the configuration of the global agreements, including a large number of airlines, have finally led to the emergence of mergers.

Since the beginning of the twenty-first century, competition has grown substantially in the air transport market, with advances in the deregulation processes and increasing pressure to apply antitrust legislation following the emergence and consolidation of the global alliances in the air transport. In this new context, characterized by an acceleration of competition in the sector, theoretical explanations were based on the analysis of the alliances as coopetitive practices, i.e. where there was both collaboration and competition with the partners in the agreement, and with other airlines with which independent agreements were reached. In the first decades of the twenty-first century, airlines have maintained and developed bilateral relationships with other airlines that are not in their own alliances but with others with which they compete.

This new scenario has been explained by applying the resource dependence theory, according to which, when resources are scarce to be shared, firms look for mergers or alliances. It is the high uncertainty in markets that triggers these responses. Alliances can involve either pure partners or competing partners; and the interactions between them can be either horizontal – between equals – or vertical – larger and smaller partners – or a mixture of both. It was under this approach that the theory of coopetitive alliances has been increasingly important since the late 1990s (Dahl, 2014; Devece, Ribeiro-Soriano, & Palacios-Marqués, 2019; Ghobadi & Ambra, 2011; Mehmet et al., 2009; Walley, 2007; Wassmer, 2010). Coopetitive approach and its application to airline's case studies showed how the combination of collaboration and competition in companies strategic portfolios yields better results for the airlines. Airlines used coopetitive strategies more than exclusively collaborative ones. This explanation is that high levels of uncertainty due to increased competition in airline markets have led to a greater focus on the combination of collaboration and competition, rather than increased reliance on collaborative alliances alone. The key to explaining the increased profitability of coopetitive alliances is the increasing competition in the airline market and the scarcity of resources to be shared.

Case studies in the airline industry have showed that coopetitive alliances have generated positive results for the airlines that have combined them with the collaborative alliances. In the case of Air France, Chiambaretto and Fernandez (2016) have explained how this airline, in the period 2000–2011, resorted to changes in its alliance portfolio with coopetitive alliances predominating over collaborative ones. The reasons for this change were based on the fact that the airline faced the prevalence of periods of high uncertainty in the airline market during the early twenty-first century. This could be seen from the extensive use of the horizontal agreements with the other airlines; agreements that sought to overcome problems of overcapacity on many of the routes offered. The agreements' approach was abolished when Air France succeeded in increasing its load factors, thereby increasing competition. This made it possible to practise a policy of alliances, both as a partner with other airlines and as a competitor, when they were organized on one aspect only (code share) but not on the others (network extension agreements). The French airline used horizontal agreements for the most part – but also vertical and mixed[1] – throughout the period under consideration, which supports the above assertion that increased risk and uncertainty led to greater use of the coopetitive alliances as part of the agreement options used by the company to achieve its strategic objectives.

The trajectory presented by Qatar Airways, from an analysis based on the internal resource management factors, validates the explanations based on coopetitive alliances (Chiambaretto & Wassmer, 2019). Qatar's trajectory showed a combination of the horizontal and vertical alliances that were managed to generate their own resources. Managers combined both strategies to improve their efficiency and the competitive quality of their product, even if at the final stage, they resorted more to vertical agreements that led precisely to improvements in their own resources. The case of Qatar can illustrate how the alliance strategies in the airline industry are not only defined by the impact of external factors on the airlines but also by the way alliances are defined internally by the airline managers.

Alliances in the airline industry thus show their changing nature, where scarce resources force collaboration and competition at the same time. Changes in the competitive environments are managed by the governance of the airlines that are able to improve their resources and restructure them continuously to adapt to the change in the market conditions. The most recent empirical applications of the dynamics of coopetitive alliances showed positive results. For instance, using the *hub-and-spoke* system shows how these agreements imply beneficial and stable outcomes for the companies involved, reduce infrastructure duplication and generate positive revenues in most of the scenarios considered (Ankit, Kohar, & Jakhar, 2021)). Other work, in Europe, shows how cooperation and coopetition involve complex interaction depending on whether the alliances involve sharing access to many markets in competition or in cooperation (Klein, Semrau, Albers, & Zajac, 2020).

3. From the Flag Carriers Era to an Open Market, 1944–1978

The different approaches to the airline alliances and to their diverse nature are directly related to the conditions under which they operated throughout the industry's

---

[1]The most common horizontal agreements between airlines are code-sharing agreements in which the airlines involved seek to reduce the excess capacity offered on different routes in order to increase passenger loads. Verticals are alliances between airlines that seek to expand the network of flights by taking advantage of those of the partner. Mixed alliances are a mixture of both, seeking greater efficiency on the part of the partners involved.

historical phases. In addition, there were other conditioning factors of political nature, international expansion strategies or cultural relations. This is explained by the nature of the airlines that emerged after World War II, which for the most part were organized independently of those of the United States as public companies directed and managed with criteria that were not directly linked to the market. Strict regulations, based on the bilateralism between airlines, diplomatic agreements on granting rights to flights, schedules, capacity, fares and aircraft models restricted competition, and in many cases, prevented it. The Chicago agreements of 1944, and the creation of IATA, were the central elements around this system of regulations,which remained in force until 1978, when the United States abolished some of the restrictions. The subsequent liberalization process was also applied to the European markets and progressively to the rest of the world (Dobson, 2017; Doganis, 1991).

During this long period, the airline alliances were mostly bilateral and, to a lesser extent, involved several airlines. The nature of the pacts was aimed at increasing the traffic of the passengers and generating higher revenues for the airlines, as well as the use of loan fleet, granting of credits for the acquisition of new aircraft, aircraft maintenance, and wet and dry leasing of fleet. Given the characteristics of the bilateral deals' system, international relations played a central role. The countries involved in the agreements often used their flag carriers as instruments of policy and international relations interest. The alliances sought to promote areas of influence, gain political support or boost the airline industry, especially during the reconstruction process, after World War II, or from the beginning of bloc politics with the onset of the *Cold War* (Svik, 2020).

These alliances were commercial and horizontal in nature, seeking to complement airlines in technical or in logistical support, including commercial advice, development assistance and information platform sharing to boost sales networks. In many cases, airlines also adopted horizontal alliances to defend markets threatened by the introduction of more technologically advanced aircraft. The use of the jet-engine aircraft in the early 1960s and the new wide-body aircraft, in the early 1970s, provoked reactions among lagging airlines that took protective measures in their markets. Bilateral agreements with the larger airlines were changed, and new conditions for the acquisition of the new fleets were negotiated.

The technological renewal of the civil aeronautics and the emergence and consolidation of the non-scheduled flights due to the boom in tourism, in the 1960s, eroded the mechanism for regulating air markets that had been in place since 1944 (Dobson, 2017; Lyth & Dierikx, 1994). The alliances remained, despite some commercial and political limitations (Vidal, 2008a; Morales, 2021). These limitations prevented the uncertainty of resource scarcity by resorting to more vertical alliances or directly favouring mergers or acquisitions. The public nature of many of the airlines was an insurmountable obstacle since buying a foreign airline's shareholdings involved political negotiations to exchange the shareholdings or required privatizations of the companies' capital. Alliances remained essentially collaborative, and commercially oriented, but without recourse to strategic pacts, given the impossibility of resorting to other types of alliances. Competition remained limited, and only a change of the system, as a whole, or progressive reforms could change the way airline alliances were organized.

The high protectionism of the bilateral agreements and the existing regulation of the market were threatened from two angles. First, from the strong role of the charter sector and, especially, also from the European efforts to create its own aviation industry. The first threat could hardly be contained in Europe where the seasonal but growing flow of tourists made it difficult for the scheduled airlines to capture this traffic. Second, the successful creation of the pan-European Airbus project company (in which Germany, France and Spain collaborated) deepened the collaboration between the flag carriers to acquire larger aircraft. In the 1970s, this made it possible to absorb the growing demand of passengers in Europe. The beginning of the end of regulation in the global commercial airline industry began with the passage, in October 1978, of the *Airline Deregulation Act* in the United States by President J. Carter. In any case, as Dierikx argues (Dierikx, 2008), in addition to these two aspects, liberalization was the solution requested by internal US organizations and was the result of a series of factors: the industrial crisis of 1973; the increase in the competition in the market with the introduction of a larger aircraft (Boeing 747 and Douglass DC 10); the monetary instability associated with the collapse of the dollar in 1971; the crisis associated with the exorbitant increase in the oil prices, which had a significant impact on fare increases, especially on long-haul flights. The latter led to the renegotiation of the bilateral agreements of most airlines, particularly those of the United States, aiming to absorb more traffic and mitigate the increase in costs. In this context, new prospects for the international aviation opened up completely.

4. Global Alliances as a Coopetitive Driver After 1978

The process of implementation of the free competition in the airline industry, after the beginning of the passage of legislation in the US domestic market, was not as rapid as expected. Throughout the 1980s, there was a gradual process of relaxation of the rules governing civil aviation in the international markets. Deregulation meant that Europe, the United States and the rest of the world gradually dismantled the system that had prevailed since 1944, relaxing flight conditions and replacing bilaterals with broader agreements involving different countries. The United States began to apply it with some bilaterals, such as those with the Netherlands and Belgium.

In 1979, Europe began to consider the possibility of opening its own markets to the airlines from the different European member countries of the Common Market, initiating a process that was definitively consolidated in 1987 with a first phase in which European airlines could fly in the continental market, as an extension of the national cabotage under the control and supervision of the European Commission. From 1993, a new phase was opened in which European airlines could fly without restrictions as long as they were majority-owned by European capital. Differences between European countries remained due to differing national interests regarding the existence of *flag carriers,* which defended the need for a period of protection from the external competition. In 1997, the European Community introduced the abolition of restrictions. This period brought along a double process of privatizations of the European flag carriers and the bankruptcy of several of them. Privatization was opened by British Airways in 1979, and closed by the Spanish airline Iberia, in 1996, although many others opened their capital to the markets, such as Lufthansa, Air France or KLM. Sabena and Swissair disappeared because they could not cope with the fierce competition that opened up in Europe with the implementation of the different phases of the liberalization process (Dobson, 2007).

In parallel, charter airlines became scheduled airlines with European deregulation. Of the large number of non-scheduled airlines, many of them were linked to Tour Operator groups, which proliferated from the 1960s through the 1980s in the UK, Germany, Spain and in the Scandinavian countries, some became scheduled airlines (Lyth, 2009; Vidal, 2008b). As a result, in the 1990s, there was a strong growth of new airlines that were born with a different organizational set-up, aiming for direct flights, without hubs, and with a structure based on cost reduction. This is how the no-frill and the low-cost airlines, such as Ryanair and Easy Jet, were born. Their business model differed from the traditional airlines. To some extent, these airlines were responsible for the intensification of the competition in the European market since the 1990s. Their formula replicated some of the airlines' that had started to apply this model in the United States, with Southwest, as a role model to imitate in the European market, which was already beginning to function as a single market (Doganis, 2001, pp. 147–195).

At the end of 1990s, uncertainty was the common denominator in the airline markets. The crisis in the Asian countries, economic downturns in some European markets, and the rise in the oil prices generated significant losses for the airlines, especially due to the decline in traffic due to the higher fares. The attacks on the twin towers in New York, in 2001, introduced a very high risk environment for the airline businesses. In this context, airlines responded by having increased commercial alliances due to the uncertainty. From 2001, there were more agreements between airlines to form more stable alliances, which also included coopetitive pacts. This was a move in a direction that had begun with the deregulation of the airline industry in 1978; this process 'marked the beginning of the most uncertain period in their existence' as Dierickx has underlined (Dierikx, 2008, p. 111).

The airlines deepened their moves to generate the interline agreements and pacts, culminating in the formation of global alliances. The latter emerged from 1997 to 1998, with the creation of three major airline clusters: *Star Alliance* (1997), *Oneworld* (1999) and *Skyteam* (2000). All three global alliances have gradually incorporated more partners, with the pioneers' of airlines as the initial drivers. All of them emerged with the same characteristics: one partner from the United States and one from Europe, and each had their its allies on the other continents. Many airlines acted before the formation of the global alliances as regional operators, feeding from Latin America, Asia or Africa the basic hubs of the air traffic: the United States and Europe. Originally, these global alliances maintained the individual agreements of each airline, combining in their portfolio those of a collaborative nature with a coopetitive nature; their intention was to strengthen the aspects that benefited the network structure of most of the pioneering and central companies (Iatrou & Alamdari, 2005). However, the persistence of the risks and uncertainties in the commercial aviation landscape was visible, alongside the permanent institutional change that justified the recourse to competition through agreements with other competing airlines, either without being part of any of the global alliances or with airlines included in the opposing alliances. The latter continued to occur in those markets that were complementary but essential to maintain competition from the larger airlines.

The process leading to the creation of the global alliances had different alternatives, with continuous changes and subject to the strategies of each airline. Until their consolidation, in the first decade of the 2000s, there were exits and entries of different airlines in each of them, break-ups of commercial relations after many years and permanent exchanges of ownership stakes between the airlines. There were also merger processes leading to the creation of large airlines. As Doganis explained, 'the beginning of the 21st century witnessed permanent changes in the airline alliances, the aim of which was to try to develop survival strategies' (Doganis, 2001, pp. 84–86).

5. Iberia's Alliances, Integration into the Oneworld Alliance and the Merger with British Airways

Since 1940, Iberia has maintained a policy of bilateral agreements with three preferential geographical areas: Europe, the United States and Latin America. Under the rules of the Chicago's Convention of 1944, the agreement strategies were guided by commercial objectives and political orientations, given Iberia's character as a flag carrier (Vidal, 2008a). Until the 1970s, these agreements included some European airlines that fed the expanding tourism flows. From the 1970s, Iberia became linked to the European *flag carriers* with the most traffic and political influence, especially Air France and Lufthansa. These agreements were linked to the aeronautical industrial policy of the French and German governments, which were launching the Airbus project. The Spanish government supported Spain's entry into the Airbus project, committing to the financial support, industrial participation and orders for its first aircraft for Iberia. In addition, Spain's support was confirmed for the Atlas Group, created in 1969 by Air France, Alitalia, Lufthansa and Sabena, for the technical coordination of the long-haul aircraft maintenance. During the 1970s, Iberia and progressively included the eastern area, with agreements developed with the national airlines of Poland, Hungary, Czechoslovakia and Bulgaria. Iberia also deployed agreements with African airlines (Royal Air Maroc, Air Afrique and Nigeria Airways) and Middle Eastern airlines (Jordan Air) in an attempt to capture transit traffic to Latin America and the North Atlantic.

The liberalization of the international air market and the development of the first packages of legal changes in the European Economic Community set in motion a first phase of changes in the Iberia's commercial and organizational structure. In addition, Spanish's political transition process forced the configuration of a different policy for the public companies. With this new scenario, a period of permanent uncertainty opened up in which the main concern of Iberia's management was to try to increase its size to prepare for a possible scenario of takeovers between the European airlines. This scenario followed the implementation, in the medium term of the privatization, advocated by the European

Commission and the initial step of liberalizing the fares and capacity within the European market.

Given the open change process in Europe, Iberia established a plan to acquire the airlines in Latin America, taking advantage of the privatization's process in most of the countries in the region; in the second half of the 1980s, Iberia acquired equity stakes in the airlines of Argentina, Chile and Venezuela with the explicit support of the Spanish government (Vidal, 2008a). Moreover, Iberia held 20% of the air traffic between Europe and Latin America, and was commited to consolidate these markets and grow in size and traffic as a decisive bet to strengthen its position. It was also a way to face a possible merger with one of the larger European airlines. The process of converting Iberia into a multinational company (with the acquisition of Aerolíneas Argentinas, Ladeco in Chile and Viasa in Venezuela) was not as successful as expected. Initiated in 1988, Iberia's conversion generated financial problems for the company, and forced the Spanish state-owned airline to request authorization from the European Commission to increase its capital and offset the losses caused by the Latin American operation. Iberia tried to reduce the market uncertainty with an acquisition strategy that proved unsuccessful, however, it did manage to increase its position in the South Atlantic market and defend its market share with the bilateral agreements with the other Latin American airlines.

The failure of the Latin American's operation and the losses incurred by Iberia, opened the way to accelerate the privatization of the airline's capital. The Spanish government initiated the process with a twofold objective: first, to bring private capital into the ownership structure, without losing control to foreign investors; and second, to seek partners among the airlines that would fit in the scenario that was opening up in the world's commercial aviation that of strong competition and the configuration of the global alliances. In parallel, Iberia continued to develop alliance proposals and,simultaneously, to explore agreements with the other European airlines to strengthen its position. Iberia was used by the state to cement the intra-European relations, deepening the Airbus industrial project in the 1990s. In 1987, Iberia participated in the creation of a booking software called *Amadeus*, in which the European airlines created their alternative to the US airlines' reservation system. Iberia, Air France and Lufthansa moved forward in this dual industrial and logistical arrangement for the distribution of travel and hotel services.

Iberia bilateral agreements with Air France, for the long-haul traffic in Asia and southern Europe, were collaborative, but at the same time, the two airlines competed for passengers' traffic between Europe and Latin America. These coopetition arrangements continued throughout the 1990s and extended into the early twenty-first century. At the same time, as airlines' movements within Europe began to point towards the creation of large alliance groups in combination with US airlines,[2] Iberia was looking for a stable

---

[2]The aim was to put pressure on the European Commission to open up European skies more quickly to the alliances that were being launched. Association of European Airlines. *Airline alliances and competition in transatlantic airline markets*, August 21, 1998.

core of shareholders through the split sale of its assets. In the context of 'absolute frenzy in alliance formation' during the second half of the 1990s (Hanlon, 2007, p. 302), the Spanish company initiated talks with American Airlines (AA) and British Airways (BA), and formalized an exchange of 10% of Iberia's capital (1% AA and 9% BA), as part of the airline's privatization process in September 1999. Shortly before that, in 1996, the American and British airlines initiated the *Memorandum of Understanding* to implement their agreements, which led to the creation of the global alliance: *Oneworld* (OW), Iberia's entry into OW did not mean the end of Air France attempts to merge with trying to form, together with Alitalia, a large southern European carrier. This initiative preceded the merger of Air France with the Dutch airline KLM, which was formalized in 2004. Iberia continued its strategy of inserting itself into OW through more developed agreements with the other alliance partners, in particular BA. In 2002, Iberia launched an agreement with BA for the joint development of the route Madrid-London and Barcelona-London. The agreement meant agreeing fares and schedules and was a step towards further collaboration, in a context of similar agreements between European airlines, such as Lufthansa, SAS and Austrian Airlines. Iberia bilateral agreements with US airlines further complicated Iberia's bilateral relationship landscape, especially when the Spanish airline was looking to deepen its alliance with Swiss.

The final 'open skies' agreement between the United States and the European Union, in 2007, meant that Iberia was able to implement the pact it had been trying to develop with American Airlines, but which had been delayed by European and US disagreements over the antitrust immunity. In this context, both the Global One World alliance and the Iberia, American Airlines and British Airways were able to launch a general pact operation, signed in 2008, to develop exclusive relations on the North Atlantic routes (Ustaömer, Durmaz, & Lei, 2015). This operation involving commercial, operational and marketing activities, was formally investigated by the European Commission in 2009, and was the prelude to merger moves between Iberia and British Airways. The merger of these two airlines was proposed at the end of 2009, and after a two-year process, the IAG Group (which holds the ownership rights over the two airlines) was formally created and approved by the European Commission and the US authorities. In 2010, it was also approved the joint route operating agreement with the merged airlines in the North Atlantic (Canada, USA, Mexico and Puerto Rico; including the European Union, Norway and Switzerland). The merger of these two major airlines preceded the integration of the other airlines into IAG group, such as Vueling and Air Lingus. In the early 2020s, the merger process left Europe with three major airlines: Lufthansa; British-Iberia and Air France-KLM with their different hubs.

Since the beginning of the international airline market liberalization, Iberia had undergone very rapid changes – both endogenous and especially exogenous – ranging from privatization to joining the One World global alliance and the merger with British Airways, although its alliance portfolio has not changed significantly since 1996. Most relevant is how it maintained a clear focus on linking to European airline movements, while maintaining its core interests in the Atlantic markets, including the Latin America. The changes that can be seen of lesser significance are those related to limited codeshare agreements with European, Asian and African airlines. This can be seen from a comparison of Iberia's alliances between 1996 and 2022 (Table 7).

Table 7 highlights how collaboration agreements were maintained within the alliances with partners belonging to the other global groups. This collaboration agreements underline the coopetitive character that was included in Iberia's commercial portfolio strategies. Iberia sought to diversify its portfolio of alliances, seeking complementarity of resources and learning between organizations (Cobeña, Gallego, & Casanueva, 2019). Here again, the preferential nature of Latin America, as a market, is of particular importance. The cases of AVIANCA and Transportes Aéreos de Centro America TACA, (Star Alliance) or Latam (Delta Airlines and Sky Team) show this dual collaborative and competitive character of Iberia agreements. AVIANCA and LATAM have become the largest airlines in Latin America and the Caribbean. The former has built an extensive network in the last decade, with several hubs, that covers Colombia and Central America, having absorbed several airlines in the region, including Brazil's GOL. LATAM is an airline resulting from the merger of Chile's LAN and Brazil's TAM (2012) and was partially acquired by Delta in 2019, triggering LATAM's exit from Oneworld. Iberia has maintained collaborative alliances with these two major airlines in the region for flights to Spain and Europe, while competing with them in the same markets and within the broader competition of the major global carriers.

Table 7. Iberia Alliances (1997–2022).

1990		2011		2020	
American Airlines	C	Avianca	C	One World	C
British Airways	C	Gol	C	Latam	L
Japan Airlines	L	Lan	C	Avianca	L
Royal Air Maroc	C	Malev	C	TACA	L
El Al (Israel)	L	TACA	C	Boliviana	L
		One World	C	Copa	L

Note: C = Complete; L = Limited.

Source: Own elaboration based on S. Mills, 'Airline Alliance survey', Airline Business, Sept (2011).

6. Conclusions

Alliances between companies constitute one of the central points of the analyses carried out by the theorists of collective entrepreneurship. Most approaches focus on the collaborative character that inter-firm pacts have historically acquired, especially those developed between the airlines. The persistence of an airline market regulation, between 1944 and 1980, limited competition a great deal with a majority set of state-owned airlines restricted airline alliances to market sharing. The abolition of market regulations initiated in 1978 by the United States gradually put an end to the system of bilateral agreements between airlines. It paved the way for a wave of institutional changes at the international level.

Changes in the rules of the international airline market regulation produced important change in competition. One of the most important was the implementation of a new system of alliances, with characteristics that progressively changed as market liberalization progressed. Initially, alliances were collaborative in nature, with code-sharing and other commercial arrangements between the companies. Increasing uncertainty and the risks of a changing and uncertain market gave way to strategic alliances that, eventually, led to the creation of global agreements with several airlines involved. In their latest development, these alliances led to mergers with creation of the large airlines from originally state-owned airlines to, eventually, being privatized.

The historical analysis of the evolution of alliances has received significant attention, especially in the field of airlines. The predominant focus was on cooperation and the external factors that determined its implementation. In contrast, some endogenous elements regarding to how airlines have historically used their alliance strategies to manage their own resources, have been neglected. In this sense, the coopetitive approach, embedded in the resource dependence theory, explains more rigorously the behaviour of airlines throughout the period of start-up and during the consolidation of the commercial aviation market, since the end of the twentieth century. Coopetitive alliances have been the dominant resource when the periods of uncertainty faced by airlines were greatest. In this regard, the case studies showed that airlines have resorted to using network resources to remain profitable and have combined alliances with the other companies to improve their efficiency, expanding their product to wider markets. At other times, the airlines have maintained mixed alliances, combining partial collaboration agreements in certain aspects, but with competition in markets for the other products.

The case of Iberia shows how the liberalization of the air market, from 1978, impacted the airline's history evolution from two perspectives. First, the company had to adapt to a new competitive environment, in which most airlines were still publicly owned and their objectives were subject to the State criteria, not necessarily those of profitability. Second, to design a survival strategy that involved changes in the organization and structure of the airline. The adaptation of the organization made it necessary to develop a strategy based on increasing its size to be able to compete in the market. To this end, an internationalization process was launched based on the acquisition of airlines in Latin America, the company's main market. Between 1985 and 1992, this strategy proved unsuccessful, forcing the company to increase its capital and to accelerate the privatization process committed to with the European Commission.

During the transition period (1996–2002), Iberia's collaborative alliances focussed on Europe, especially, on cementing a closer partnership with British Airways and American Airlines, for the North Atlantic. The general target was to maintain its market leadership between Europe and Latin America, apply a strategy of a coopetitive nature, especially with Latin American airlines. Depending on demand, Iberia combined the different alliances, collaborating when uncertainty, risk and low occupancy threatened its profitability. The change in economic conditions generated a return to coopetitive agreements. The Iberia case shows that the airline strategies in changing contexts were not only those associated with collaborative commercial arrangements such as code-sharing and other forms. The intensification of competition allowed for strategic agreements with intermediate steps and permanent changes.

Collaboration between airlines was compatible with competition, even with the same airline in different global alliances, as was the case for Iberia with AVIANCA and LATAM. The intensification of risks and the persistence of uncertainty allowed for merger processes such as the one between Iberia and British Airways at the end of 2009, along the same lines as that between KLM and Air France in 2004. The maintenance of post-merger agreements within the IAG Group of Iberia and British Airways allowed for increased resourcing by improving the quality of their networks, structures and positions. Indeed, it allowed for a positive influence on the airlines' social capital, which is part of the holding company.

Acknowledgement

Research has benefitted from public research project Spanish Project PGC201S8-093971-B-I00 granted by the Ministry of Science and Innovation Programme for Knowledge Generation, funded by MCIU/AEI/FEDER, UE

References

Adler, N., & Smilowitz, K. (2007). Hub-and-spoke network alliances and mergers: Price-location competition in the airline industry. *Transportation Research Part B: Methodological, 41*(4), 394–409. doi: 10.1016/j.trb.2006.06.005

Agusdinata, B., & De Klein, W. (2002). The dynamics of airline alliances. *Journal of Air Transport Management, 8*(4), 201–211. doi: 10.1016/S0969-6997(01)00052-7

Ankit, S., Kohar, A., & Jakhar, S. K. (2021). Profit maximizing hub location problem in the airline industry under coopetition. *Computers & Industrial Engineering, 160*, 107563. doi: 10.1016/j.cie.2021.107563

Bicen, P., Hunt, S. D., & Madhavaram, S. (2021). Coopetitive innovation alliance performance: Alliance competence, alliance's market orientation, and relational governance. *Journal of Business Research, 123*, 23–31. doi: 10.1016/j.jbusres.2020.09.040

Brueckner, J. K. (2001). The economics of international codesharing: An analysis of airline alliances. *International Journal of Industrial Organization, 19*(10), 1475–1498. doi: 10.1016/S0167-7187(00)00068-0

Burton, J., & Hanlon, P. (1994). Airline alliances: Cooperating to compete? *Journal of Air Transport Management, 1*(4), 209–227. doi: 10.1016/0969-6997(94)90013-2

Casanueva, C., Gallego, Á., Castro, I., & Sancho, M. (2013). Airline alliances: Mobilizing network resources. *Tourism Management, 44*, 88–98. doi: 10.1016/j.tourman.2014.02.011

Chiambaretto, P., & Fernandez, A. S. (2016). The evolution of coopetitive and collaborative alliances in an alliance portfolio: The Air France case. *Industrial Marketing Management, 57*, 75–85. doi: 10.1016/j.indmarman.2016.05.005

Chiambaretto, P., & Wassmer, U. (2019). Resource utilization as an internal driver of alliance portfolio evolution: The Qatar Airways case (1993–2010). *Long Range Planning, 52*(1), 51–71. doi: 10.1016/j.lrp.2018.02.004

Cobeña, M., Gallego, Á., & Casanueva, C. (2019). Diversity in airline alliance portfolio configuration. *Journal of Air Transport Management, 75*, 16–26. doi: 10.1016/j.jairtraman.2018.11.004

Dahl, J. (2014). Conceptualizing coopetition as a process: An outline of change in cooperative and competitive interactions. *Industrial Marketing Management, 43*(2), 272–279. doi: 10.1016/j.indmarman.2013.12.002

Devece, C., Ribeiro-Soriano, D. E., & Palacios-Marqués, D. (2019). Coopetition as the new trend in inter-firm alliances: Literature review and research patterns. *Review of Managerial Science, 13*, 207–226. doi: 10.1007/s11846-017-0245-0

Dierikx, M. L. J. (2008). *Clipping the clouds. How air travel changed the world.* Westport: Praeger.

Dobson, A. (2007). *Globalization and regional integration. The origins, development and impact of the single European aviation market.* London: Routledge.

Dobson, A. (2017). *A history of international civil aviation: From its origins through transformative evolution.* London: Routledge.

Doganis, R. (1991). *Flying off course. The economics of international airlins.* London: Routledge.

Doganis, R. (2001). *The airline business in the twenty first century.* London: Routledge.

Evans, N. (2001). Collaborative strategy: An analysis of the changing world of international airline alliances. *Tourism Management, 22*(3), 229–243.

Fan, T., Vigeant-Langlois, L., Geissler, C., Bosler, B., & Wilmking, J. (2001). Evolution of global airline strategic alliance and consolidation in the twenty-first century. *Journal of Air Transport Management, 7*(6), 349–360. doi: 10.1016/S0969-6997(01)00027-8

Gaggero, A. A., & Bartolini, D. (2012). The determinants of airline alliances. *Journal of Transport Economics and Policy, 46*(3), 399–414. doi: 10.1287/mnsc.1120.1591

Ghobadi, S., & Ambra, J. D. (2011). Coopetitive knowledge sharing: An analytical review of literature. *Electronic Journal of Knowledge Management, 9*(4), 307–317.

Hanlon, P. (2007). *Global airlines. Competition in a transnational industry.* Oxford, UK: Routledge.

Hannegan, T. F., & Mulvey, F. P. (1995). International airline alliances: An analysis of codesharing's impact on airlines and consumers. *Journal of Air Transport Management, 2*(2), 131–137. doi: 10.1016/0969-6997(95)00029-1

Iatrou, K., & Alamdari, F. (2005). The empirical analysis of the impact of alliances on airline operations. *Journal of Air Transport Management, 11*(3), 127–134. doi: 10.1016/j.jairtraman.2004.07.005

Klein, K., Semrau, T., Albers, S., & Zajac, E. J. (2020). Multimarket coopetition: How the interplay of competition and cooperation affects entry into shared markets. *Long Range Planning, 53*(1), 101868. doi: 10.1016/j.lrp.2019.02.001

Lyth, P. J. (2009). Flying visits: The growth of british air package tours, 1945-1975. In L. Segreto, C. Manera, & M. Pohl (Eds.), *Europe at the seaside. The economic history of mass tourism in the mediterranean* (pp. 11–30). New York, NY: Berghahn.

Lyth, P. J., & Dierikx, M. L. J. (1994). From privilege to popularity the growth of leisure air travel since 1945. *The Journal of Transport History, 15*(2), 97–116. doi: 10.1177/002252669401500202

Mehmet, A. K., Yildiz, M., Okumus, F., & Barca, M. (2019). The intellectual structure of coopetition: Past, present and future. *Journal of Strategy and Management, 12*(1), 2–29. doi: 10.1108/JSMA-07-2018-0073

Morales, E. (2021). *Cuba et le monde: une histoire aérienne (1945-1979)*. Thèse de doctorat. Université Sorbonne Nouvelle.

Morrish, S. C., & Hamilton, R. T. (2002). Airline alliances-who benefits? *Journal of Air Transport Management, 8*(6), 401–407. doi: 10.1016/S0969-6997(02)00041-8

Oum, T. H., & Park, J. H. (1997). Airline alliances: Current status, policy issues, and future directions. *Journal of Air Transport Management, 3*(3), 133–144. doi: 10.1016/S0969-6997(97)00021-5

Park, J. H. (1997). The effects of airline alliances on markets and economic welfare. *Transportation Research Part E: Logistics and Transportation Review, 33*(3), 181–195. doi: 10.1016/S1366-5545(97)00013-6

Pels, E. (2001). A note on airline alliances. *Journal of Air Transport Management, 7*(1), 3–7. doi: 10.1016/S0969-6997(00)00027-2

Ribeiro-Soriano, D., & Urbano, D. (2009). Overview of collaborative entrepreneurship: An integrated approach between business decisions and negotiations. *Group Decision and Negotiation, 18*(5), 419–430. doi: 10.1007/s10726-008-9134-x

Staniland, M. (2008). *A Europe of the air? The airline industry and European integration*. Lanhman, USA: Rowman & Littlefield Publishers.

Svik, P. (2020). *Civil aviation and the globalization of the cold war*. Torino: Palgrave Macmillan.

Ustaömer, T., Durmaz, V., & Lei, Z. (2015). The effect of joint ventures on Airline competition: The Case of American Airlines, British Airways and Iberia Joint. *Procedia - Social and Behavioral Sciences, 210*, 430–439.

Vidal, J. (2008a). *Las Alas de España. Iberia, líneas aéreas (1940-2005)*. Valencia: Publicaciones de la Universidad de Valencia.

Vidal, J. (2008b). Cielos abiertos. Las aerolíneas charter españolas en el mercado europeo, 1959-1994. *Revista de Historia de la Economía y de la Empresa, 2*, 237–252.

Wassmer, U. (2010). Alliance portfolios: A review and research agenda. *Journal of Management, 36*(1), 141–171. doi: 10.1177/0149206308328484

Walley, K. (2007). Coopetition: An introduction to the subject and an agenda for research. *International Studies of Management & Organization, 37*(2), 11–31. doi: 10.2753/imo0020-8825370201

Zou, L., & Chen, X. (2017). The effect of code-sharing alliances on airline profitability. *Journal of Air Transport Management, 58*, 50–57. doi: 10.1016/j.jairtraman.2016.09.006

Chapter 7

Building an Enterprise for the Future Through Network Bricolage and Memories of the Past

Águeda Gil-López, Elena San Román, Sarah L. Jack and Ricardo Zózimo

Abstract

This chapter explores how network bricolage, as a form of collective entre-preneurship, develops over time and influences the shape and form of an organization. Using a historical organization study of SEUR, a Spanish courier company founded in 1942, the authors show how network brico-lage is implemented as a dynamic process of collaborative efforts between bricoleurs who draw on their historical experience to build and develop an organization. Our study offers two main contributions. In combining net-work bricolage with ideas of collective entrepreneurship, the authors first extend knowledge about the practice of bricolage and the role of the bri-coleur in the entrepreneurial context beyond start-up. Second, the authors show that, while entrepreneurs' decisions are historically contingent, it is how entrepreneurs wed past experience with current context which informs their actions in the present, shaping the enterprise for the future.

Keywords: Network bricolage; social embeddedness; collective entrepreneurship; historical organization study; courier company; Spain

1. Introduction

The lens of bricolage has been applied in entrepreneurship work to enhance under-standing about how individuals – bricoleurs – combine and recombine resources

Collective Entrepreneurship in the Contemporary European Services Industries:
A Long Term Approach, 95–116
Copyright © 2023 by Emerald Publishing Limited
All rights of reproduction in any form reserved
doi:10.1108/978-1-80117-950-820231007

for entrepreneurial activities, especially when facing challenges (Baker & Nelson, 2005; Janssen, Fayolle, & Wuilaume, 2018; Stinchfield, Nelson, & Wood, 2013). Zooming in on network bricolage (McKague & Oliver, 2016), we see a growing view that entrepreneurs, as bricoleurs, activate socially embedded ties to solve their early-stage resource problems (Baker & Nelson, 2005; Desa & Basu, 2013; Kwong, Cheung, Mauzoor, & Rashid, 2019). Nevertheless, we still know little about how network bricolage, as a form of collective entrepreneurship, plays out over time and across different historical contexts (Duymedjian & Ruling, 2010; Garud & Karnøe, 2003; Hernández-Barahona, San Román, & Gil-López, 2022).

Combining network bricolage (Baker & Nelson, 2005; Fisher, 2012) with ideas of socially embedded ties (Jack & Anderson, 2002), we step back from current perspectives and, taking an historical view, we consider *how entrepreneurs draw on their past, on their experience of network bricolage, to build an organization for the future?*

Through an historical organization approach (Maclean, Harvey, & Clegg, 2016; Wadhwani & Bucheli, 2014, p. 4), we consider the Spanish courier company SEUR and show how an entrepreneurs' past experience of using bricolage shapes their present decisions and the organization's future. SEUR is the oldest courier company in Spain. It was founded in 1942, at the beginning of Franco's dictatorship, by two entrepreneurs who, through economic constraints, enacted socially embedded ties to pioneer the provision of express delivery services (Gil-López, 2015; Tàpies, San Román, & Gil-López, 2012). From the late 1960s, ambitions for growth saw these entrepreneurs being joined by others who co-operated informally so that by the mid-1980s, SEUR constituted over 50 independent businesses. The entrepreneurs of SEUR saw their position wane when in 2004, GeoPost, a subsidiary of the French postal operator, bought a number of these independent businesses, weakening the social underpinnings characterizing SEUR's growth while simultaneously internationalising and professionalizing its organization. By 2020, Geopost owned over 70% of SEUR, employing 8,100 employees, operating more than 1,000 stores with a fleet of 4,600 vehicles covering more than 230 countries worldwide while remaining a well-known brand in Spain.

We review the history of SEUR between 1970 and 2000. This period comprises an initial context of resource constraints in Spain (up to 1985), mainly caused by the oil shocks and the Spanish transition to democracy, then economic expansion and resource abundance, driven by the Spanish incorporation into the European Union. This changing context helps us consider how the entrepreneurs' past experience of using network bricolage in times of constraints shaped their decisions and actions in more prosperous times.

This study offers two main contributions. We first extend knowledge about how network bricolage, as a form of collective entrepreneurship, unfolds over time and beyond start-up (Garud & Karnøe, 2003; Kwong et al., 2019; Tasavori, Kwong, & Pruthi, 2018). We show bricolage as a practice that involves the 'putting together', i.e. the forming and reforming of socially embedded ties for a new purpose. Unlike earlier work, we show that as an experienced practice, bricolage can endure through time. Second, we show that while entrepreneurial decision-making is historically contingent (Baker & Nelson, 2005; Wadhwani & Jones, 2014), it is through balancing past experience and future aspirations that entrepreneurs find ways to practice in the present and thus shape their organization's future (Garud, Kumaraswamy, & Karnøe, 2010).

2. Theoretical Framework

2.1. Bricolage and the Entrepreneurial Context

Levi-Strauss (1966) idea of bricolage has come to be associated with creating something from nothing by making do with the resources at hand to grasp opportunities and solve problems (Baker & Nelson, 2005; Desa & Basu, 2013; Kwong et al., 2019). Within the context of entrepreneurship, Baker and Nelson (2005) argue that three things are necessary for the practice of bricolage. First, an understanding that the environment does not create the future but instead needs to be actively engaged to create opportunities. Second, entrepreneurs do not start from scratch but instead apply the resources they already have in new ways. Third, in being bricoleurs, entrepreneurs seek out resources which can be acquired freely or cheaply for future use. What this emphasizes is the relevance of the stock of resources at hand, gathered with no clear purpose or intended use over time and the recombination of resources for new purposes when the entrepreneur is faced with constraints (Baker & Nelson, 2005; Duymedjian & Ruling, 2010; Kwong et al., 2019).

Bricolage, therefore, seems to describe what entrepreneurs do in creating entrepreneurial organizations seemingly out of nothing (Stinchfield et al., 2013). However, it seems to be a practice which occurs out of necessity and is invoked when no other alternative for resource acquisition is available (Desa & Basu, 2013). This highlights an important dimension of entrepreneurship in relation to resource acquisition, where the bricoleur becomes embedded in his/her community and closely aligns with others who have undergone similar kinds of socialization and lived experiences (Duymedjian & Ruling, 2010). Hence, what bricolage does is to build on ideas of social exchange, reciprocity, the conditions under which relationships exist and emerge and the strength of social bonds (Levi-Strauss, 1966).

There is a growing interest about the social dimensions of a bricolage approach to entrepreneurship. However, there is limited work drawing on this concept, which explains why and how some entrepreneurs manage to create something from nothing and/or prosper in times, situations and circumstances, perceived as constraining (Kwong et al., 2019). Hence, in spite of its popularity, it has been said that the idea of bricolage and the network dimension of bricolage lack systematic exploration and development (Duymedjian & Ruling, 2010; Senyard, Baker, Steffens, & Davidsson, 2014; Stinchfield et al., 2013). This is especially the case when it comes to understanding how it might link to the development of entrepreneurial organizations.

2.2. Network Bricolage as a Form of Collective Entrepreneurship

Entrepreneurship is relational and transformative by nature (McKeever, Anderson, & Jack, 2014). It offers a socially situated process which influences how entrepreneurs perceive and exploit opportunities (Jack & Anderson, 2002; Kim & Aldrich, 2005), as well as how organizations emerge and develop over time (Dodd, Anderson, & Jack, 2013; McMullen & Dimov, 2013). Network bricolage is part of this process as it describes how pre-existing networks are considered as a resource at hand for the entrepreneur (Baker, Miner, & Eesley, 2003, p. 265).

Socially embedded ties – such as family, friends and close personal contacts – based on trust, loyalty and commitment developed over time and through experience of dealing with others (Cropanzano & Mitchell, 2005; Elfring & Hulsink, 2007; Newbert, Tornikoski, & Quigley, 2013), are thought to be beneficial for entrepreneurs (Jack, 2005). Such ties provide emotional and practical support, connections and access to critical resources (Jack, 2010; Jack & Anderson, 2002; Uzzi, 1997).

Yet it has also been said that as organizations emerge and grow, socially embedded ties become constraining and inefficient (Baker & Nelson, 2005; Uzzi, 1997). Hence, entrepreneurs are encouraged to develop ties to others, often strangers, to grow organizations (Ruef, 2002). This is because such ties offer the opportunity for diversity in information and resources and connections to other social systems (Elfring & Hulsink, 2007). Indeed, the common assumption of the extensive benefits other ties can bring appears well grounded both theoretically and practically. However, this does not sit comfortably with the notion of network bricolage and the idea of using pre-existing/contacts. After all, the network bricolage construct emphasizes patterns of behaviour in which entrepreneurs depend on contacts as their primary means at hand (Baker et al., 2003). And while the practice of network bricolage has been said to offer a useful contrast with 'networking' and other behaviours in which entrepreneurs seek resources from strangers' (Baker et al., 2003, p. 270; McKague & Oliver, 2016), work to-date has been limited as to how this might work.

What the above shows is that the ideas of network bricolage and how they relate to collective entrepreneurship are yet to be fully exploited (Baker et al., 2003; Duymedjian & Ruling, 2010). We take the view that entrepreneurs are immersed in relationships that provide value for building and developing their organization. The way these individuals experienced the practice of bricolage in their past can shape their decisions in the present and their aspirations for the future, which in turn might influence the development of their organization.

3. Research Method

3.1. Historical Organization Study Approach

Our historical organization study of SEUR (Lippmann & Aldrich, 2015; Maclean et al., 2016) uses microhistory techniques (Ginzburg, Tedeschi, & Tedeschi, 1993; Peltonen, 2001) to understand how the organization SEUR came to be. Drawing on a hermeneutic understanding of social reality (Vaara & Lamberg, 2016), we use microhistory to identify larger socio-historical patterns and their characteristics, through the close analysis of specific events, actions and practices (Ginzburg et al., 1993; Peltonen, 2001). Our approach is inspired by Vaara and Lamberg (2016) and Wadhwani and Jones (2014) and their comments about the importance of understanding the historical embeddedness of an organization.

3.2. A History of SEUR

SEUR's story of entrepreneurship is entwined with the rise of a new industry in Spain: the 24-hour express delivery (Gil-López, San Román, Jack, & Zozimo, 2021; Gil-López & San Román, 2021). Fig. 2 provides a timeline with the milestones in SEUR's history.

SEUR was set up in a difficult historical period, the beginning of General Franco's dictatorship, under an economic context of isolation and scarcity of resources. In this adverse context, two young entrepreneurs, Justo Yúfera and Jorge Fernández,[1] saw an opportunity for the quick delivery of goods between Madrid and Barcelona and founded SEUR in 1942. They settled on two independent companies in partnership, one based in each city, with SEUR transporting packages between them.[2]

At the end of the 1950s, Spain began a process of international integration. Encouraged by economic growth during the 1960s, SEUR's founding entrepreneurs decided to expand the business. However, this decision took time to exploit, and in 1973, the Spanish economy's growth slowed sharply due to the petroleum shock and Spain's transition to democracy after Franco's death. That historical context of economic constraints and political uncertainty coincides with SEUR's expansion throughout Spain: between the mid-1970s and mid-1980s, founders' relatives, friends or former employees joined the business as new partners. Each established a new independent company (hereinafter referred to as affiliate) and became responsible for promoting SEUR's express transport in one or several Spanish provinces or cities (see Table 8). At the beginning, each new affiliate worked in partnership and cooperated with the others informally, relying on close ties of trust and commitment among partners. This process of growth led to the legal foundation of SEUR ESPAÑA in 1984. SEUR ESPAÑA acted as

---

[1]Justo Yúfera was born in Barcelona in 1920. He spent much of his youth in France, Cameroon and Guinea. All his education was limited to basic school and French proficiency due to his expatriate status. Jorge Fernández was also born in Barcelona. He also lacked any higher education or experience in the express business and belonged to a family without financial resources. Jorge Fernandez left SEUR in 1985. Yúfera remained as Honorary President of SEUR until his death in 2020. (Interview with Justo Yúfera, October 28, 2010; 'Al habla con Jorge Fernández', in *La Revista de SEUR, 2,* 1983, 14; 'Al habla con Justo Yúfera,' in *La revista SEUR,* 1, 1983, 14; Tàpies et al., 2012).
[2]'Al habla con Jorge Fernández' in *La Revista de SEUR, 2, May* 1983, 14–15.

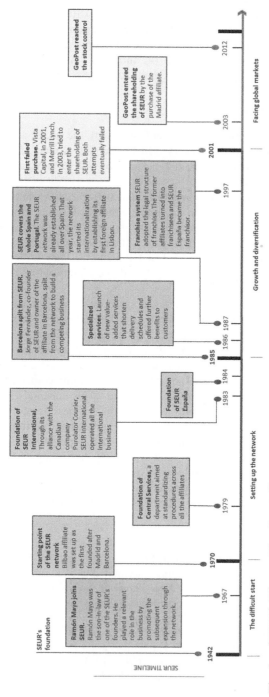

Fig. 2. SEUR's History Timeline: Milestones. *Source:* Own Elaboration.

Table 8. Participants.

Description of Participants								Description of Interviews		
Partners (43 Participants)										
Name	City	Year1	Year2	In/out	Age	G	Background	Kinship Tie	Type	Date	#
Justo Yúfera	Madrid	1942	2004	out	22	M	Self-Employed; Emigrant; No transport experience	Founder of SEUR	F	18/10/2010	1
Pepe Fuentes	Bilbao	1970	2005	out	26	M	Manager of a transport company	No previous tie	F	21/03/2011	1
Pedro Cortés	Valencia	1973		in	25	M	Self-Employed in the transport industry	No previous tie	T	07/07/2011	1
Roberto Ayuso	Mallorca	1974		in	30	M	Shop assistant	Friendship	F	07/03/2011	1
Rafael Cárabe	Sevilla	1975	2003	out	45	M	Self-Employed in the transport industry	No previous tie	T	19/07/2011	1
Gumersindo Andia	Zaragoza	1975	2005	out	25	M	Administrative officer	Family	T	14/07/2011	1
Dolores Fuentes	Murcia	1976		in	41	F	Administrative officer	Family	F	22/02/2011	1
Javier Velayos	San Sebastián	1976		in	20	M	Carpenter, Driver, Electrician	Former employee of SEUR Bilbao	F	21/03/2010	1
Teresa Debelius	La Coruña	1977		in	20	F	Student; Co-owner of the affiliate with her husband	Family	F	10/02/2011	1

(Continued)

Table 8. (*Continued*).

Description of Participants					Partners (43 Participants)				Description of Interviews		
Name	City	Year1	Year2	In/out	Age	G	Background	Kinship Tie	Type	Date	#
Anacleto Fernández	Valladolid	1977	2004	out	45	M	Truck Driver	Former employee of SEUR Valencia	F	28/03/2011	1
Alberto Puente	Asturias	1978		in	26	M	Shop assistant	Friendship	F	14/03/2011	1
Francisco Salcedo	Santander	1978	2007	out	18	M	Student	Friendship	F	14/02/2011	1
Jesús Bravo	Granada	1979		in	26	M	Bank employee	Family	F	07/03/2011	1
Julián Recuenco	Malaga	1979		in	25	M	Student: He became partner after his father died	Family	F	11/02/2011	1
Fernando Madrigal	Las Palmas	1979	1993	out	24	M	Worker in a firefighting equipment manufacturer	Former employee at Madrid affiliate	F	24/02/2011	1
Abel Salvador	Lerida	1980		in	30	M	Driver	Former employee of SEUR: truck driver	F	09/02/2011	1
Antonio Manuel Alba	Cádiz	1980		in	27	M	Agronomist; Unemployed	Friendship	F	17/02/2011	1

Name	Place	Year	Year		Age	Sex	Occupation	Relationship	F/T	Date	No.
Federico Reixa	Vitoria	1980		in	26	M	Deliveryman	Former employee of SEUR Bilbao	F	14/02/2011	1
José Ignacio Gabilondo	Pamplona	1980		in	24	M	Student; Deliveryman	Friendship	F	03/02/2011	2
Miguel Lazo	León	1980		in	30	M	Administrative officer; exiled from Chile	Friendship	F	10/02/2011	1
Fernando Carreira	Ferrol	1980	2010	out	25	M	Hospitality worker	Friendship	T	29/04/2011	1
José Andrés Estévez	Lugo	1980	2009	out	27	M	Administrative officer	Friendship	T	28/04/2011	1
José Civantos	Salamanca	1980	2003	out	25	M	Student	Family	F	08/03/2011	1
Javier Fernández	Valladolid / Baix Llobregat	1980 / 1998	2006	out	20	M	Student; He joined his father affiliate (Valladolid) in 1980	Family	F	28/03/2011	1
Antonio Rodríguez	Guadalajara	1981		in	30	M	Driver	Former employee of SEUR	F	02/02/2011	1
Francisco Álvarez	Huelva	1981		in	39	M	Worker in the military sector; Unemployed	Family	F	17/02/2011	1
José Santos	Logroño	1981		in	24	M	Deliveryman	Former employee of SEUR Bilbao	F	03/02/2011	1

(Continued)

Table 8. (*Continued*).

Description of Participants								Description of Interviews		
				Partners (43 Participants)						
Name	City	Year1	Year2	In/out	Age	G	Background	Kinship Tie	Type	Date	#
Juan Ramón Civantos	Cáceres	1981		in	39	M	Salesperson	Family; Former employee of SEUR	F	08/03/2011	1
Manuel Valle	Tenerife	1981		in	26	M	Administrative officer; unemployed	Friendship	F	10/03/2011 29/03/2011	2
Aniceto Guillén	Teruel	1981	2009	out	33	M	Truck Driver	Friendship	F	03/03/2011	1
Elías García	Albacete	1981	2009	out	38	M	Worker in an automotive company	Family	F	03/03/2011	1
Ignacio Sanz	Burgos	1981	2005	out	24	M	Deliveryman	Former employee at Valladolid affiliate	F	24/02/2011	1
Angel Sáiz	Algeciras and Ceuta	1982		in	39	M	Administrative officer in an automotive company	Family	F	07/02/2011	1
Antonio Fuentes	Lorca	1982		in	36	M	Worker in an auto parts company	Family	F	22/02/2011	1

Name	Place	Year		in/out	Age	Sex	Occupation	Relationship	Gender	Date	
Carlos Guerra	Mérida	1982		in	24	M	Student; Deliveryman	Family and former employee in SEUR Badajoz	F	02/03/2011	1
León Muñoz	Ávila	1982		in	40	M	Truck Driver	Former employee of SEUR	F	02/02/2011	1
Yolanda Salvador	Huesca	1982		in	20	F	Administrative officer	Family	F	09/02/2011	1
Yolanda Fernández	Palencia	1982	2009	out	21	F	Student: She collaborated in his father's affiliate (Valladolid)	Family	F	28/03/2011	1
Francisco Rubio	Don Benito	1983		in	23	M	Student	Friendship	F	02/03/2011	1
José Carlos Torres	Ciudad Real	1983		in	36	M	Unemployed. Formerly, worker in a manufacturing company	Family	F	08/02/2011	1
Antonio Civantos	Zamora	1983	2012	out	34	M	Self-employed in the insurance market	Family	F	08/03/2011	1
Manuel Cárabe	Tarragona	1986		in	35	M	Deliveryman	Family	F	22/02/2011	1
José Valle	Lanzarote	1987		in	34	M	Worker in a refurbishment company	Family	F	25/02/2011	1

(Continued)

Table 8. (Continued).

SEUR Managers (5 Participants)

Name	Entry Year	Position	Background	Kinship Tie	Type	Date	#
Ramón Mayo	1972	Former manager at Madrid affiliate; owner of the affiliate in Alicante; and President of SEUR foundation	Student	Family	F	21/10/2010	1
Juan Cueto	1981	Former director of SEUR Clearing House	n.a.	Friendship	F	06/06/2011	1
Fernando Rodríguez Sousa	1984	Former CEO of SEUR España	Bank employee	No previous tie	F	15/02/2011	1
Daniel Fernández De Lis	1991	Former director of the Corporate Legal Advice Department	Lawyer	No previous tie	F	24/04/2011	1
Pedro Gallego	1991	Director of Operations Department	n.a.	No previous tie	F	01/03/2011	1

Source: Own elaboration from Tàpies et al. (2012, pp. 49–54).

Notes: Y1 = year of partnership; Y2 = end of partnership; In/out = in or out of SEUR during data collection; Age = age of the partner when joining SEUR; G = gender; F = face-to-face; T = telephone; n.a. = data non available.

the parent company owned by all affiliates[3]. This led to increased professionalization and diversification of services from the mid-1980s, and the transformation of SEUR into a franchise system by 1997.[4] Nevertheless, legal and professional updates barely changed how SEUR operated, which remained very much based on social relationships, trust and commitment amongst partners.

At the beginning of the twenty-first century, SEUR held 17.8% of the Spanish courier.[5] Understanding the need for internationalization, the French organization GeoPost became in 2004 SEUR's international partner and began the process of acquiring some of SEUR's franchisees from its partners until reaching majority in 2012.[6]

The above historical narrative draws attention to how SEUR's founding members enacted socially embedded ties to form a network of independent partners all over Spain. This network of independent partners operated as a business group linked primarily by informal ties (San Román, Fernández, & Gil-López, 2014). Unlike hierarchical organizations, SEUR's network structure made it more dependent on mechanisms of social exchange, cooperation and reciprocity. In building the organization the way they did, SEUR also constitutes an example of the shared economy, being founded and developing on the sharing of both risks and benefits, which, in turn, constituted a powerful glue that held participants together for a long time.

As pointed out in the introduction, we focus on the period 1970–2000.

3.3. Data Collection and Source Reflection

Our study is based on an extensive collection of written and oral sources gathered through a business history project initiated with the celebration of SEUR's 70th anniversary.[7] Data collection took place between 2011 and 2012, from three main sources: (i) interviews with SEUR partners and top managers; (ii) archived internal company documents; and (iii) external reports, historic press and other secondary sources.

3.3.1. Interviews with SEUR Partners and Top Managers. Interviews were our primary source of data, allowing us to explore how participants made sense of their past experiences and the historical context, and how this in turn influenced practices. So, we considered SEUR members' testimonies and perceptions as the central source of information for our study (Kipping, Wadhwani, & Bucheli, 2014; Wadhwani, 2016).

A total of 48 interviews were carried out: 5 with top managers and 43 with partners. From the whole group of partners, 27 were still in the business at the

---

[3]Articles of SEUR España's incorporation (1987), SEUR's archive.
[4]Minutes of the Board of Directors of SEUR España, 24 September 1996.
[5]'Mensajería y Paquetería', DBK (2001).
[6]Minutes of General Meeting of Shareholders, 15th May 2004.
[7]The project was coordinated by the Chair of Family-Owned Business of IESE Business School.

time of data collection, in 2012, while 16 had already sold their affiliate and were out of SEUR.[8] Table 8 provides detailed information about interviews and participants.

Interviews mainly took place at the headquarters of SEUR or at SEUR's affiliated independent businesses across Spain. In five cases, telephone interviews were held because the partner was unable to participate face-to-face. Interviews lasted one to three hours and were guided by specific domains linked to our research. Interviews also focussed on tracing key events in SEUR's evolution, to appreciate how participants made sense of them, their decisions and reactions. We used techniques aligned with active interviewing (Holstein & Gubrium, 1995), allowing respondents to articulate their perceptions and experiences freely and spontaneously (Thompson & Bornat, 2017).

We addressed the issues of bias typically associated with interviewing by approaching numerous and highly knowledgeable informants who viewed the phenomena from diverse perspectives (Eisenhardt & Graebner, 2007). We interviewed three different types of informants: partners still in SEUR at the time of data collection, partners who had left SEUR, and top managers. Interviews with partners who had left SEUR allowed us to take into account Ritchie's (2011) suggestions about the reflective insights of the retired. Interviews with managers focussed on strategic and organizational issues of the business at different points in time. This allowed for a greater understanding of why events in SEUR occurred as they did and how they were dealt with. The combination of insider and outsiders' views and the plurality of testimonies from actors in different positions provided different perspectives to guide our interpretations and support the validity of our findings (Kipping et al., 2014).

3.3.2. Documentation.   In addition to interviews, we accessed internal company records and external documents for further triangulation, therefore avoiding the limitations associated with relying on single sources (Kipping et al., 2014).

We accessed a wealth of internal company records about the organization, its evolution and strategic actions. These included strategic reports, minutes from the Board of Directors and shareholders' meetings (since 1984), and other recorded documents from particular moments, such as the articles of SEUR's incorporation (1987) and franchise contracts (1997 and 2003). One document was especially important, *La Revista de* SEUR, an internal corporative magazine published monthly between February 1983 and November 1985. Throughout the 20 volumes published, many of the partners were interviewed about their work, their trajectory before entering SEUR, their connections to others and particular organizational role.

---

[8]In total, we interviewed 86% (43 out of 50) of the total number of partners involved with SEUR between 1970 and 2000. By the time of data collection, in 2012, 16 partners had left SEUR which by this time consisted of 34 partners, of whom 6 were unavailable for interview. Those unavailable were the owners of the affiliates in Almeria, Badajoz, Cuenca, Eibar, Ibiza and Plasencia. All of these are small affiliates.

Our third source of data was external documents. We consulted the historic press, legislative documents, industry and market reports, and the few articles and books published which linked to SEUR.

4. Findings

4.1. Socially Embedded Ties as a Network Resource

The presentation of our findings is based on three main sets of practices derived from our sources: identifying, activating and sustaining social ties. These practices illustrate core processes of bricolage and show how SEUR members actively use and leverage socially embedded ties as the resource *at hand* to create new growth opportunities for the organization.

4.2. Identifying the Social Ties at Hand

By the early 1970s, SEUR saw the opportunity to grow the business and achieve national coverage, but financial resources were limited[9]; 'We realized that demand for courier services existed in the whole of Spain (...) [but] we didn't have enough resources to expand the business independently' (owner of an affiliate). The only solution to face the constraining environment was to work with others: 'This was a view but also a necessity because it was impossible to build the business network independently' (owner of an affiliate).

They chose to expand their operation by identifying individuals with strong social connections to them, who became independent partners of SEUR.[10] We label these individuals as independent partners because each settled and developed their own affiliate, which became part of SEUR's national network. As shown in Table 8, most independent partners joined between 1970 and 1984, and their recruitment originated from three main sources: family members, friends and former employees. This search was an active process where founding entrepreneurs identified enterprising individuals within their immediate social circle.

Building on the contacts 'at hand', the most common was to identify partners through family ties.[11] One partner explained:

> My brother had started working with me. He was an engineering student (...) and decided to combine work and study. My father-in-law agreed and my brother started working with us in 1974–75.

When family relationships were not available, founding entrepreneurs described how they drew on personal links, mostly friendship, to identify further independent partners:

---

[9]'Cuarenta años al servicio del transporte urgente', in *la Revista de SEUR*, 0, February 1983, 3–4.
[10]'Al habla con Jorge Fernández', in *La Revista de SEUR*, 2, May 1983.
[11]'Al habla con Justo Yúfera', in *La Revista de SEUR*, 1, 1983.

> I had a friend (...) who in turn was a close friend of [another SEUR partner]. [He] had been working with [him] for a long time and we used to meet regularly. (Owner of an affiliate)

Former employees were the third source of partner identification. They had knowledge about the business, and ultimately, the community was aware of their performance and their commitment.[12] Several SEUR's partners explained: 'I worked one year and a half as a deliveryman in Bilbao'; 'I started working as assistant in Bilbao. I used to go with him to deliver parcels (...) [He] offered me the opportunity to establish an affiliate in San Sebastián'. What this shows is SEUR was built by the immediate contacts that each affiliate had available, a very homogeneous group of partners linked through informal ties. Homogeneity was evident in that partners were relatively young, of similar academic and personal background and had previous personal or professional links to SEUR's partners.[13]

Table 8 calls attention to how established partners tend to identify prospective partners 'at hand' irrespectively of their economic resources and sometimes even without prior knowledge or experience of transport services. Instead, 'at hand' meant they had to demonstrate commitment and work ethic to be identified as fit to join the network. Some informants explained: 'We were asked what we could offer SEUR. I told him: I can offer a pair of hands and a strong will to work' (owner of an affiliate); 'I was interested in people with commitment to work and necessity' (manager); 'The main factor was keen ambition' (owner of an affiliate). Through building on socially embedded relationships, SEUR offered partners a way to earn a living within the difficult economic climate in Spain between 1970 and 1984.

4.3. Activating and Combining Ties as a Social Resource

The process of embedding was essential to the way the business network operated and how socially embedded ties were activated as a resource. Because of the penurious context, peer-to-peer support was the key to welcoming a new partner. Some SEUR's partners explained: '[He] accompanied me when I was seeking the right premises to set up my business'; 'All of us used to learn from the experience and knowledge of other partners'; 'It was very usual to see partners helping each other'.

The ways of facing a constrained environment were purposefully shared with new partners that learnt alongside a veteran partner about the business and how it worked.[14] This helped strengthen each affiliate, but it also created cycles of bricolage practices at each location and cultivated and strengthened personal relationships throughout the network.

---

[12]'Por las rutas del norte', in *La Revista de SEUR*', 3, June 1983.
[13]'Dos caras para una moneda', in *La Revista de SEUR*, 4, July 1983
[14]'Al lomo de un tres ejes', in *La Revista de SEUR*, 0, February 1983.

A key element in the development of the network of ties was reciprocity (Larson & Starr, 1993). Partners acknowledged the need to rely on others to survive and make the business grow. Working together was especially important because the organization was financially constrained until the second half of the 1980s. In SEUR, profits were shared equally among partners in any transaction, and this strengthened integrity and loyalty of partners.

Relationships between partners were rewarded by creating multiple spaces for joint and innovative decision-making.[15] The bricolage approach at each affiliate meant that, from time to time, a more structured approach to their relationship with the network and the organization was needed:

> Every month we had meetings, in different places. They were very positive because they encouraged relationships between all people, and we could exchange information. We were always very supportive, we helped each other. (Owner of an affiliate)

These meetings represented a powerful mechanism through advanced friendship and cohesion among all involved in the network.[16] They established a space for 'fraternizing with everyone else' (Tàpies et al., 2012, p. 78), while discussing important strategic issues and taking joint business decisions.[17] They also created conditions for a more formalized approach described in the following period.

4.4. Sustaining Social Ties

Participants highlighted how the network formed through the social activation of resources was critical to SEUR's growth so that the whole business developed with a strong sense of membership: they all needed each other in order to make the business prosper and ensure their own venture was successful. Although the context started to change in 1985 and the Spanish economy achieved growth (and with it, the organization too), SEUR members purposely decided to sustain the social base of the business by continuing the collective practices associated with network bricolage.

Sustaining this social base was achieved by the reinforcement of principles, meaning that affiliates worked towards the same goals. These principles were regarded as the SEUR's DNA (Tàpies et al., 2012). The DNA was guided by four key principles. First was the notion of urgency: parcels had to be delivered within a maximum of 48 hours. 'We do not sell transportation, we sell time' (owner of an affiliate). Second, profits were shared equally among the partners involved in one delivery: 'No one commanded more than the other, and profits were shared equally' (manager). Third, affiliates had to offer a quality service, and deliveries had to be made irrespective of external conditions: 'In all our time, there was only

---

[15]'Mi entrevista con Justo Yúfera', in *Marcha. La Revista de SEUR*, 19, May 1985.
[16]'Programa de Festejos', in *Marcha. La Revista de SEUR*, 11, May–March 1984.
[17]*La Revista de SEUR*, 19, May 1985, 19.

once when we could not send a package and we were really upset... that night we could not sleep' (owner of an affiliate). Fourth, affiliates delivered all types of parcels, regardless of size or weight, in a time when the Postal Service had substantial restrictions: 'Refusal [to any kind of parcel] is unacceptable' (Tàpies et al., 2012, p. 79). Through participation and collaboration between partners, SEUR's DNA provided the 'rules of the game'. Interestingly, it was never formally written down.

Informal norms and values played a powerful role in imposing moral obligations and expectations for sustained cooperation over time. This worked to prevent the emergence of opportunistic behaviour within the network. This also alerted members of anomalies and called them to collective action. Interviewees agreed on a critical event that tested this assumption, shaking the organization and demonstrating how things worked across the SEUR network.

In 1985, Jorge Fernández, co-founder of SEUR and owner of the affiliate in Barcelona, split from the network to build a competing business. The impact of not covering a region like Barcelona was potentially very damaging for SEUR. On becoming aware of Jorge's intentions, SEUR's partners reacted immediately and collectively to address this situation. They ensured trucks going to Barcelona were stopped, so the affiliate of Barcelona did not receive any parcels. This was not easy as trucks were en-route and communications were not as fast as they are today. Partners and employees travelled from all corners of Spain to manage this situation. Working together they delivered parcels in Barcelona, reorganized operations, found new premises and rebuilt the operation from scratch 'It was a unanimous reaction' (Tàpies et al., 2012, p. 106).

We found that the bricolage practices associated with the social base remained unchanged even when the Spanish environment improved after joining the EU, leading the company to register a strong growth. Indeed, from 1985 SEUR's growth was faster and beyond the initial ambitions of the partners. In a few years, the network spread all over the country, and every partner's independent company expanded. Partners commented 'We were almost unable to manage this growth' (manager). This economic success did not erode the practices that held together the social base of the organization. Rather, this social base, underpinned by strong relationships between partners, was what sustained SEUR's growth and fulfilled its economic needs.

5. Interpretation and Analysis

Our findings describe three critical practices associated with the process of network bricolage within SEUR over time. In a typical bricolage fashion, founding partners adopted a purposeful approach when *identifying* network relations on hand utilizing them beyond the original purpose of the relationship. Social network ties turned into usable, key resources for the growth and expansion of SEUR. At the heart of this, we see resourcefulness, a resource-creation focus instead of a mere resource-seeking behaviour of bricoleurs (McKague & Oliver, 2016). Through mechanisms of trust building, reciprocity, commitment and interest alignment, socially embedded ties began to be *activated* and *maintained* while the organization developed. So, entrepreneurs capitalized on the embeddedness of social ties as a key resource and used this as a platform for organizational growth (Baker & Nelson, 2005). This enabled the entrepreneurs to build and extend the network in ways that produced new social and economic outcomes. In contrast to the arguments put forward by Baker and Nelson (2005), the case of SEUR shows that network bricolage can be applicable well beyond start-up.

As the SEUR network was established and developed over time, entrepreneurs became more socially embedded as they experienced reciprocity and cooperative resource sharing (Uzzi, 1997). Trust-based ties helped reduce perceived risks and increase expectation of value creation, thus enabling greater contributions and sharing of resources among network members (Reficco & Márquez, 2012). Our findings also show how, through time, partners in the network were involved in regular and purposeful exchanges allowing the social and the economic spheres of the organization to become increasingly equated (Jack, 2005; Kim & Aldrich, 2005). Knowledge, capital, clients and other economic resources arrived at SEUR through the combination and activation of socially embedded ties. However, what is interesting and very evident here is the way SEUR's bricoleurs recognized how the economic needs could only be fulfilled through social relationships. Partners felt themselves part of the same group, aligned in the perception that network bricolage offered the mechanism to sustain the economic activity of the firm.

While the case of SEUR extends our understanding on how shared and collective bricolage might emerge over time (Duymedjian & Ruling, 2010; Garud & Karnøe, 2003) it also demonstrates something more critical. Our data illustrate that the practice of network bricolage through the identification and activation of socially embedded ties was a necessity for SEUR to survive and grow in the constrained Spanish context of the 1970s and early 1980s. Yet, our data also show that during the prosperous period post-1985, after Spain joined the EU, this practice of network bricolage was sustained as the way to continue growing the business. The entrepreneurs perceived the changing, more prosperous context, but rather than seeing network bricolage as something that in this new context could be set aside, they saw it as a routine. In part, this happened because network bricolage had given them the flexibility and resources to face a past context of severe resource constraints.

So, what the case of SEUR shows is how network bricolage can become a mechanism that re-employs past experiences of entrepreneurs to shape an organization's future. Socially embedded ties combined with fruitful collaboration and the initial successful outcomes of network bricolage create an 'experience' that repurposes the practice of bricolage over time. This form of understanding bricolage, underpinned by socially embedded ties, creates a 'path' (Garud et al., 2010), a self-reinforcing mechanism (a routine) in which the entrepreneur is not passive but an active agent who purposely chooses to build the future of the organization on social ties. As an outcome of their past experiences, partners in SEUR reproduced and reinforced the bricolage way of doing things. The endurance of network bricolage over time in SEUR was, therefore, an outcome of social embeddedness combined with a particular understanding of past experience and an ambition to co-create their own future.

6. Conclusions

Our interest was in understanding, *how entrepreneurs draw on their past, on their experience of network bricolage, to build an organization for the future.* Through this study, we add theoretical and empirical nuance to network bricolage, as a form of collective entrepreneurship, in significant ways.

First, we address the lack of understanding about the practice of bricolage over time (Duymedjian & Ruling, 2010). Here, our contribution shows how the practice of network bricolage can evolve as a form of collective entrepreneurship, leading to a group of bricoleurs who, bound by strong bonds of trust and reciprocity, reinforce bricolage as the way to build and develop an organization over time.

Second, through our study, we contextualize and re-conceptualize network bricolage, its significance, and its endurance over time as an outcome of social embeddedness. We understand the development of SEUR as the outcome of the way its entrepreneurs understood their past experiences of using social ties and the consequences. So, socially embedded ties combined with an understanding of past experience can create a 'path' for bricoleurs. In light of our findings, we therefore argue that bricolage repurposes experience: memories of the past always linger, and so the future is never tabula rasa; it is always written in the present but built from the past in articulation with an imagined future.

Finally, our study also joins others in growing the domain of historical organization studies (Gil-López et al., 2016; Maclean et al., 2016). We demonstrate the usefulness of an historical approach to developing understanding about the practice of network bricolage and how it underpins the development of an organization. Following Kipping and Üsdiken (2014), we treated history as a key part of our theoretical understanding of entrepreneurship and moved away from letting it 'merely' serve as empirical evidence for context (Vaara & Lamberg, 2016).

Acknowledgements

Research has benefitted from public research project Spanish Project PGC201S8-093971-B-I00 granted by the Ministry of Science and Innovation Programme for Knowledge Generation, funded by MCIU/AEI/FEDER, UE

References

Baker, T., Miner, A. S., & Eesley, D. T. (2003). Improvising firms: Bricolage, account giving and improvisational competencies in the founding process. *Research Policy, 32*(2), 255–276.

Baker, T., & Nelson, R. E. (2005). Creating something from nothing: Resource construction through entrepreneurial bricolage. *Administrative Science Quarterly, 50*(3), 329–366.

Cropanzano, R., & Mitchell, M. S. (2005). Social exchange theory: An interdisciplinary review. *Journal of Management, 31*(6), 874–900.

Desa, G., & Basu, S. (2013). Optimization or Bricolage? Overcoming resource constraints in global social entrepreneurship: Optimization versus bricolage in global social entrepreneurship. *Strategic Entrepreneurship Journal, 7*(1), 26–49.

Dodd, S., Anderson, A., & Jack, S. (2013). Being in time and the family-owned firm. *Scandinavian Journal of Management, 29*(1), 35–47.

Duymedjian, R., & Ruling, C. C. (2010). Towards a foundation of bricolage in organization and management theory. *Organization Studies, 31*(2), 133–151.

Eisenhardt, K. M., & Graebner, M. E. (2007). Theory building from cases: Opportunities and challenges. *Academy of Management Journal, 50*(1), 25.

Elfring, T., & Hulsink, W. (2007). Networking by entrepreneurs: Patterns of tie formation in emerging organizations. *Organization Studies, 28*(12), 1849–1872.

Fisher, G. (2012). Effectuation, causation, and bricolage: A behavioral comparison of emerging theories in entrepreneurship research. *Entrepreneurship Theory and Practice, 36*(5), 1019–1051.

Garud, R., & Karnøe, P. (2003). Bricolage versus breakthrough: Distributed and embedded agency in technology entrepreneurship. *Research Policy, 32*(2), 277–300.

Garud, R., Kumaraswamy, A., & Karnøe, P. (2010). Path dependence or path creation? *Journal of Management Studies, 47*(4), 760–774.

Gil-López, Á. (2015). *Desde la encrucijada: historia empresarial y emprendimiento en el transporte urgente.* PhD thesis. Universidad Complutense de Madrid.

Gil-López, Á., & San Román, E. (2021). Emprendimiento público y privado en la configuración del transporte urgente español. *Investigaciones de Historia Económica, 17*(1), 1–14.

Gil-López, Á., San Román, E., Jack, S., & Zozimo, R. (2016). At the crossroads. Management and business history in entrepreneurship research. *Journal of Evolutionary Studies in Business, 1*(2), 156–200.

Gil-López, Á., San Román, E., Jack, S., & Zozimo, R. (2021). Driving through change at speed. Opportunity conditions and entrepreneurial responses in the history of the express industry. *Revista de Historia Industrial,* (81), 21–53.

Ginzburg, C., Tedeschi, J., & Tedeschi, A. C. (1993). Microhistory: Two or three things that I know about it. *Critical Inquiry, 20*(1), 10–35.

Hernández-Barahona, J., San Román, E., & Gil-López, Á. (2022). Bricolage and innovation in the emergence and development of the Spanish Tourism Industry. *Enterprise & Society,* 1–43.

Holstein, J. A., & Gubrium, J. F. (1995). *The active interview.* California, USA: SAGE.

Jack, S. L. (2005). The role, use and activation of strong and weak network ties: A qualitative analysis. *Journal of Management Studies, 42*(6), 1233–1259.

Jack, S. L. (2010). Approaches to studying networks: Implications and outcomes. *Journal of Business Venturing, 25*(1), 120–137.

Jack, S. L, & Anderson, A. R. (2002). The effects of embeddedness on the entrepreneurial process. *Journal of Business Venturing, 17*(5), 467–487.

Janssen, F., Fayolle, A., & Wuilaume, A. (2018). Researching bricolage in social entrepreneurship. *Entrepreneurship and Regional Development, 30*(3–4), 450–470.

Kim, P. H., & Aldrich, H. E. (2005). *Social capital and entrepreneurship.* Hanover: Now Publishers Inc.

Kipping, M., & Üsdiken, B. (2014). History in organization and management theory: More than meets the eye. *The Academy of Management Annals, 8*(1), 535–588.

Kipping, M., Wadhwani, R. D., & Bucheli, M. (2014). Analyzing and interpreting historical sources. In M. Bucheli & R. D. Wadhwani (Eds.), *Organizations in time: History, theory, methods* (pp. 305–395). Oxford: Oxford University Press.

Kwong, C. B., Cheung, C., Mauzoor, H., & Rashid, M. U. (2019). Entrepreneurship through Bricolage: A study of displaced entrepreneurs at times of war and conflict. *Entrepreneurship and Regional Development, 31*, 435–455.

Larson, A., & Starr, J. A. (1993). A network model of organization formation. *Entrepreneurship: Theory and Practice, 17*(2), 5–15.

Levi-Strauss, C. (1966). *The savage mind. The nature of human society series.* Chicago, IL: Univ. of Chicago Press.

Lippmann, S., & Aldrich, H. (2015). A rolling stone gathers momentum: Generational units, collective memory, and entrepreneurship. *Academy of Management Review, 41*(4), 658–675.

Maclean, M., Harvey, C., & Clegg, S. R. (2016). Conceptualizing historical organization studies. *Academy of Management Review, 41*(4), 609–632.

McKague, K., & Oliver, C. (2016). Network bricolage as the reconciliation of indigenous and transplanted institutions in Africa. *Africa Journal of Management, 2*(3), 300–329.

McKeever, E., Anderson, A., & Jack, S. L. (2014). Entrepreneurship and mutuality: Social capital in processes and practices. *Entrepreneurship and Regional Development,26*(5–6), 453–477.

McMullen, J. S., & Dimov, D. (2013). Time and the entrepreneurial journey: The problems and promise of studying entrepreneurship as a process. *Journal of Management Studies, 50*(8), 1481–1512.

Newbert, S. L., Tornikoski, E. T., & Quigley, N. R. (2013). Exploring the evolution of supporter networks in the creation of new organizations. *Journal of Business Venturing, 28*(2), 281–298.

Peltonen, M. (2001). Clues, margins, and monads: The micro-macro link in historical research. *History and Theory, 40*(3), 347–359.

Reficco, E., & Márquez, P. (2012). Inclusive networks for building BOP markets. *Business & Society, 51*(3), 512–556.

Ritchie, D. A. (Eds.) (2011). *The Oxford handbook of oral history.* Oxford handbooks series. New York, NY: Oxford University Press.

Ruef, M. (2002). Strong ties, weak ties and islands: Structural and cultural predictors of organizational innovation. *Industrial and Corporate Change, 11*(3), 427–449.

San Román, E., Fernández, P., & Gil-López, Á. (2014). As old as history: Family-controlled business groups in transport services: the case of SEUR. *Business History, 56*(8), 1–22.

Senyard, J., Baker, T., Steffens, P., & Davidsson, P. (2014). Bricolage as a path to innovativeness for resource-constrained new firms: Bricolage as a path to innovativeness. *Journal of Product Innovation Management, 31*(2), 211–230.

Stinchfield, B. T., Nelson, R. E., & Wood, M. S. (2013). Learning from Levi-Strauss' Legacy: Art, craft, engineering, bricolage, and brokerage in entrepreneurship. *Entrepreneurship Theory and Practice, 37*(4), 889–921.

Tàpies, J., San Román, E., & Gil-López, Á. (2012). *SEUR. 70 años de entrega.* Madrid: Ediciones Universidad de Navarra.

Tasavori, M., Kwong, C., & Pruthi, S. (2018). Resource bricolage and growth of product and market scope in social enterprises. *Entrepreneurship & Regional Development, 30*(3–4), 336–361.

Thompson, P., & Bornat, J. (2017). *The voice of the past: Oral history* (4th ed.). Oxford oral history series. New York, NY: Oxford University Press.

Uzzi, B. (1997). Social structure and competition in interfirm networks: The paradox of embeddedness. *Administrative Science Quarterly, 42*(1), 35–67.

Vaara, E., & Lamberg, J. A. (2016). Taking historical embeddedness seriously: Three historical approaches to advance strategy process and practice research. *Academy of Management Review, 41*(4), 633–657.

Wadhwani, R. D. (2016). Entrepreneurship in historical context: Using history to develop theory and understand process. In F. Welter & W. B. Gartner (Eds.), *A research agenda for entrepreneurship and context* (pp. 65–78). Cheltenham: Edward Elgar Publishing.

Wadhwani, R. D., & Bucheli, M. (2014). The future of the past in management and organization studies. In M. Bucheli & R. D. Wadhwani (Eds.), *Organizations in time: History, theory, methods* (pp. 3–30). Oxford: Oxford University Press.

Wadhwani, R. D., & Jones, G. (2014). Schumpeter's Plea: Historical reasoning in entrepreneurship theory and research. In M. Bucheli & R. D. Wadhwani (Eds.), *Organizations in time: History, theory, methods* (pp. 192–216). Oxford: Oxford University Press.

Chapter 8

The Asymmetry of Expectations on the Outcomes of Strategic Alliances Between Biotechnology Start-Ups and Pharmaceutical Corporations

Felix Barahona Márquez, Susana Domingo Pérez and Ernest Solé Udina

Abstract

This chapter focuses on the relationship between biotechnology start-ups and larger pharmaceutical corporations when they work as partners in innovation strategic alliances. For three decades, these companies have become major players in innovation in the health sector. This means that the development of many products is a result of the cooperation they carry out. However, due to the great differences between these companies, certain problems can often arise. More specifically, our analysis explores the perceptions of the achievement expected by each partner. This is an important aspect to determine the satisfaction of these firms among strategic alliance. The authors follow qualitative methods to address the topic, conducting personal interviews with managers of these companies. Our findings reveal the concrete facts that can prevent reaching the proposed goals of these partners as well as stress the crucial importance of the human aspect to mitigate potential problems.

Keywords: Biotechnology start-ups; expectations; strategic alliances; pharmaceutical corporations; innovation; conflict management

Collective Entrepreneurship in the Contemporary European Services Industries:
A Long Term Approach, 117–133
Copyright © 2023 by Emerald Publishing Limited
All rights of reproduction in any form reserved
doi:10.1108/978-1-80117-950-820231008

1. Introduction

The way in which companies innovate has dramatically changed over the past three decades, from the in-house development projects to cooperative agreements with other companies or institutions. The main protagonists of this change are the high technology industries and, within these, the biotechnological and pharmaceutical sectors. The former is a young sector with a large number of small companies, including many start-ups (ASEBIO, 2021). These firms aim to develop projects based on new knowledge that emerged from discoveries of the last 40 years on Genomics, Proteomics, Pharmacogenomics and Sequencing/Synthesis/Engineering of proteins and other molecules, among others. Biotechnology start-ups often lack financial and material resources, as well as business management skills, as they are frequently managed by scientists (Arqué-Castells, 2012; Baum & Silverman, 2004). Due to their innovative technology, companies, face a high degree of uncertainty about the results of their R&D projects, which end up having a high failure rate (Baum & Silverman, 2004; Schoonmaker, Solomon & Rau, 2017). Considering that these R&D projects are very expensive, the financial risk associated with this activity is extremely high and, therefore, start-ups lack the resources needed to pursue their development projects. Meanwhile, the long existing pharmaceutical corporations have been, and still are, more structured organizations. These companies not only have a long history of developing new or improved drugs but also of protecting the intellectual property, obtaining governmental authorization, even at the international level or manufacturing and successfully bringing them to the market. However, in the last decades, the drug development activity, especially in regard to its first stage, has moved from mainly being an in-house process to a more open scheme, with projects often based on the biotechnological developments by those small biotechnology start-ups (Yagüe-Perales, Niosi & March-Chorda, 2015). By skipping these earlier stages of development and their very high level of uncertainty and failure, the pharmaceutical corporations tap the opportunities that the biotechnology start-ups offer when they have a development project that has successfully passed these early stages and becomes a promising product. That way, pharmaceutical corporations avoid high levels of financial and reputational risk and, at the same time, they can innovate more and in a more diversified way. As many scholars have stated, the novelty brought by the biotechnology start-ups combined with the well-established pharmaceutical corporations resulted in a higher level of innovation (Beers & Zand, 2014; Deeds & Hill, 1996; Quintana & Benavides, 2007).

In this way, our research focuses on the establishment of strategic alliances between the biotechnology start-ups and the pharmaceutical corporations as an important way to foster innovation, as this alliance can strongly mitigate the high-level risk in the start-up's development projects. Developed countries have evolved differently in the growth of their biotechnological industry and vary the pace at which start-ups and pharmaceutical corporations establish cooperative agreements. Spain is not a leading country in any of these industries, and its biotechnological sector has suffered, since its irruption, from a low level of governmental support, and venture capital investment. As a result, the biotechnology start-ups were reluctant to establish strategic alliances with the pharmaceutical corporations, until the first years of this century. However, this reluctance has gradually been decreasing, as the remarkably growing number of deals comes up (ASEBIO, 2021; March-Chordà, Yagüe-Perales & Seoane-Trigo, 2009). Our study has been carried out on Spanish biotechnology start-ups and pharmaceutical corporations where we had the opportunity to verify that both parties have had long experience in establishing various strategic alliances.

Many studies have explored the establishment of strategic alliances among biotechnology start-ups and pharmaceutical corporations (most of them from the strategic or the financial view), observing their effects on Technological Innovation and financial performance of the companies involved (Durand, Bruyaka & Mangematin, 2008; Hoenig & Henkel, 2015; Mohr, Garnsey & Theyel, 2013). But a strategic alliance established by a biotechnology start-up and a pharmaceutical corporation is more than just a contract between them (Aalbers, 2010). These firms have workers, scientists, and managers, with different experiences, work protocols, orientations, and goals. Moreover, the outcome of the strategic alliance is something that is still uncertain, possibly a challenge for which both firms have a lot of coordinated work to do. Besides, these are different firms in terms of their business strategy, internal organization and available resources. All these aspects seem to point to a critical issue: the human factor. More specifically, the human factor is involved in the processes and situations such as, the difficulties faced in the search for the right partner, the level of trust in each other, the conflicts that can arise and the ways to face them, the internal changes required by the cooperative deal in one or both firms, and the differences in the organizational culture – and background culture, in some cases. Last, but not the least, the aspect of special interest in this work: the level of expectations' fulfilment of both partners. On the one hand, the biotechnology start-up partner, is a small company oriented to the development of new drugs that often come from basic research, a very early stage. These types of start-ups usually lack financial and human resources. On the other hand, the pharmaceutical corporation is a large company devoted to the development of drugs at a later stage, manufacture, and commercialization with clear organizational protocols and vast resources available.

These differences amongst partners generate different expectations. Few studies to date have analyzed these issues. From a quantitative perspective, Cabello-Medina, Carmona-Lavado & Cuevas-Rodriguez (2020) analyzed the effectiveness of various management capabilities in the innovation alliances formed by the Spanish biotechnology firms. Albeers (2010) studied the importance of trust on each part of the alliances, whereas Elia, Petruzzelli and Piscitello (2019) investigated the impact of cultural diversity among participants in the strategic alliances. Farazi, Gopalakrishnan and Perez-Luño (2019) addressed the potential changes in equity ownership of biotech start-ups when they established alliances with larger pharmaceutical companies. Likewise, but from a qualitative perspective, Harada, Huayi Wang and Shintaro (2021) studied the types of alliances between the Japanese biotechnology start-ups and large pharmaceutical corporations leading to more sustainable practices, while He, Von Krogh, Sirén and Gersdorf (2021) analyzed the asymmetries between a large pharmaceutical and its academic partners on the orientations and perceptions of conflict. Ariño (2003) analyzed the fulfilment of the alliance strategic goals, but solely from the perspective of one of the parties involved.

Our study narrows the gap by explaining the relationship between the biotechnology start-ups and the larger pharmaceutical corporations with emphasis on the perceptions of the expectations' achievement by each partner. To address the research question, we used qualitative methods, using a semi-structured interview with managers of the Spanish biotechnology start-ups and pharmaceutical corporations, who perceived the fulfilment of expectations of each managerial team, as well as the factors that have had the greatest impact.

This chapter proceeds as follows: The next section contains the theoretical framework for cooperative technological development, describing this type of agreement between companies. The third section details the qualitative methodology applied, while section four includes the results of the analysis from the interviews. Finally, the conclusions are presented in Section 5.

2. Theoretical Framework

Technological Innovation is the application of science's results but, at the same time, it is a counter-concept to the idea of basic research. The concept of Technological Innovation emerged in the twentieth century as an explanation of economic progress as something caused by the actions of many specialists, not only scientists, and the activities that went beyond the basic research and led companies and countries to achieve competitive advantages and wealth (Godin, 2016). Companies have traditionally carried out innovations by themselves without considering external agents as crucial partners in these processes. However, since the last decade of the twentieth century, this vision has evolved into the paradigm of the Open Innovation (Chesbrough, 2003). This approach starts from the assumption that companies can and should use both internal and external ideas to innovate and internal and external ways to commercialize these innovations, so that external ideas and external ways of commercialization can be as important as the internal ones (Chesbrough, 2003). According to this paradigm, Open Innovation[1] is defined *from the outside in* (*inbound*) and *from the inside out* (*outbound*): Inbound consists on taking advantage of the technologies and discoveries from others. Outbound consists of establishing relationships with third-party organizations, to which one's own technologies are transferred for commercial exploitation (He & Wong, 2004).

There are some industries for which innovation is their most essential characteristic such as the biotechnological and pharmaceutical industries. The biotechnology sector has numerous start-ups created as spin-offs from academia, research centres and hospitals, among other start-ups from other origins. Some start-ups are mainly dedicated to the biotechnological research and development (R&D). The risk level of development projects for this type of company is very

---

[1]Opposed to the Closed Innovation Paradigm, which is inwardly focussed.

high, as they face uncertainty about the results, often ending in failure, generating a significant financial loss for the firm (Solé, Domingo, & Amat, 2022). Besides, when these start-ups emerged within the University, Hospital or Research Institutions' spin-offs, the level of uncertainty was greater when the managerial team came from the scientific field rather than the business administration's (Arqué-Castells, 2012; Baum & Silverman, 2004). For the above reasons, undertaking joint projects is one way to mitigate the risk and to increase the possibilities of innovation' success. Hence, it is a standard practice/accepted/common to establish these relationships with other organizations through strategic alliance.

A strategic alliance is a cooperative agreement between firms that involves exchanging, sharing or co-developing, and it can include contributions by partners of capital, technology, or firm-specific assets (Gulati, 1999). On the pharmaceutical corporations' side (where the resources and skills biotech start-ups lack can be easily found), the willingness to take part in such agreement responds to their need for knowledge and for disruptive insights in their development projects. Biotechnology emerged in the 1970s of the twentieth century as a technological discontinuity that broke down barriers to entry in the pharmaceutical industry (Tushman & Anderson, 1986), but without having triggered a Schumpeterian process of creative destruction (Schumpeter, 1949), as the pre-existing pharmaceutical companies were enjoying a good competitive position and interest in adapting themselves to the technological change (Christensen & Rosenbloom, 1995). As a result, collaboration with the emerging biotechnology firms became a new way to maintain their competitive position (Gopalakrishnan, Scillitoe & Santoro, 2008; Greis, Dibner & Bean, 1995). Besides, due to the highly formal business structure of corporations, they are slow in their decision-making processes, their managers are risk averse and often reluctant to undertake development projects from their starting point (McCutchen & Swamidass, 2004). Throughout these strategic alliances with biotechnology start-ups, pharmaceutical corporations could avoid the riskiest stages of a development process, invest smaller amounts, and diversify their pipelines, thus managing their financial and reputational risks. As Pisano and Verganti (2008, p. 5) state, 'The new leaders in innovation will be those who can understand how to design collaboration networks and how to tap their potential'. According to these authors, the ability to choose the right partners to start a collaborative partnership, is crucial for successful innovation. Furthermore, strategic alliances can foster innovation, but its dynamic is usually complex, and therefore managers of the companies involved should be aware that is time and resource consuming. This idea emphasizes the need to choose the partners, terms, and expectations very carefully when starting a strategic alliance (Hoffmann & Scholsser, 2001). Once a start-up finds the right partner, its performance improves as it gets involved in more strategic alliances, with the limits imposed by its capacity to manage them (Moghaddam, Bosse & Provance, 2016).

There are some different kinds of strategic alliances, depending on their goals. Some are devoted to basic research, which are unlikely in the biotechnology start-up and pharma corporation's environment, because it will take many years to deliver a new treatment to the market (Baum & Silverman, 2004). The most common strategic alliances between these two kinds of firms are the R&D and the marketing strategic alliances.

R&D alliances are established for completing the development projects of biotech start-ups as they usually cannot go beyond the preclinical stage or the very first clinical stages, they need the resources that a pharma corporation provides for clinical tests, governmental authorization, among others (Durand et al., 2008; Hoenig & Henkel, 2015; Janney & Folta, 2003; Mohr et al., 2013; Nicholson, Danzon & McCullough, 2005; Rothaermel, 2001; Wang, Wuebker, Han & Ensley, 2012). The goal of a Marketing alliance is to bring a product or service developed by the biotech start-up, or in alliance with another firm, to the market, using the resources from a pharma corporation, like its manufacturing capacity, domestic and international distribution channels, and some fourth clinical stage procedures, amongst others (Hu, McNamara & McLoughlin, 2015). Coherently, in this work, we focus on these two latter kinds of strategic alliances between biotech start-ups and pharma corporations.

Several authors have conducted research works on these collaborative combinations. Some have analyzed the reasons for establishing strategic alliances among firms (Baum & Silverman, 2004; Bianchi, Cavaliere, Chiaroni, Frattini & Chiesa, 2011), whilst others have analyzed the effects of this cooperation in terms of the successful development of new products (Rothaermel, 2001), as well as in terms of funding received, in business performance (Durand et al., 2008; Mohr et al., 2013), and in some other financial measures (Hoenig & Henkel, 2015). But not so many authors have analyzed aspects related to the difficulties arising when firms get involved in these innovation alliances (Christoffersen, 2013).

Starting from the analysis of the complementarity of the potential partners, that is crucial for the success of the deal, Colombo, Grilli, and Piva (2016) stated that one partner possesses some distinctive technological competences, meanwhile the other possesses other specialized assets for generating economic returns on the technological developments of the former. Lee, Park, Ryu and Baik (2010) stated that these companies are looking for synergies in these cooperative agreements. Hence, it is crucial that all parts involved are able to properly identify and assess these competences, assets and synergies for the future success of the alliance and its alignment with the strategy of the companies involved (Hoffmann & Scholsser, 2001). The establishment of a strategic alliance is made throughout formal contracts, but, as Aalbers (2010) pointed, trust is a very important factor for a successful development of a collaboration agreement, as it reduces the costs of transaction, mainly by decreasing the frequency of the interaction between partners. Besides, according to Aalbers (2010), trust is never a substitute, but a complement of the contracts. Once a strategic alliance has been established, there is often inescapable organizational adaptation alongside emergence of conflicts and the way conflicts are handled can determine the future success or failure of the deal (Merchant, 2002). According to Jehn and Mannix (2001), good levels of trust, respect and, open discussion among the firms' teams, can help to solve these conflicts. Moreover, the cultural differences within firms' teams can negatively affect trust and cooperation and increase conflict (Kim & Parkhe, 2009; Merchant, 2002). A final essential aspect that strongly influences the decision-making processes for future deals is the level of fulfilment of expectations by the managers of all counterparties involved in a strategic alliance and the reasons for that fulfilment or lack of it (Ariño, 2003). As it has been said, some start-ups' management teams are formed by scientists with lacking business skills, so it can be hard to determine, in advance, their appropriate expectations from a strategic alliance regarding a specific objective within a specific corporation. Moreover, a biotech start-up under financial stress, or impatient to find a company' support to complete a development and/or bring it to the market, can easily make a poor decision about the right partner in a strategic alliance. As a result, the start-up will face frustration regarding its objectives. He et al. (2021) stated that the differences in objectives and expectations of the counterparts caused by different perceptions of reality, seriously hinder this collaboration by producing more potential conflicts between the companies' managerial teams. Ariño (2003) distinguished between the fulfilment of the partners' expectations in terms of the strategic goals. In terms of process performance – so, the interaction between – being the first one the most important for the managers involved. In other words, if the strategic alliance met the initial expectations, some other aspects, such as the personal experience in the interactions between partners, will not be as important as the first one, in the decision-making process about the establishment of future strategic alliances. As Hoffmann and Scholsser (2001) pointed out, expectations about the pace at which a strategic alliance is established, as well as the different perceptions of the reality among partners, can lead to unfulfilled expectations. This analysis of the level of achievement of the alliance goals was conducted on one of the partners, which is common in the literature (Ariño, 2003). But in a strategic alliance involving a start-up and a pharma corporation that does not meet the expectations set by each partner, this misalignment may be perceived differently by each part, due to the situation of asymmetric orientation (Ariño, 2003).

3. Methodology

The eight cases were chosen for their relevance and expected contribution to the objectives of the research (Eisenhardt, 1989). Specifically, the guiding criteria were: (1) participation in at least 3 alliances in the last 10 years; (2) biotech start-ups (BS_i) and pharmaceutical corporations (PC_i) had to be proportionally represented; (3) BS and PC located in a similar geographical area, ensuring parallelism in terms of organizational culture, political and legal framework, homogenous innovative and entrepreneurial environment; and (4) registration of, at least, 5 patents (or software applications, in the case of bioinformatics start-ups) in the last 10 years, as a measure of their innovation capacity. Table 9 provides an overview of these companies and their main characteristics.

Data were collected through in-depth semi-structured interviews, conducted between July and September 2022, of approximately 90 minutes. Meetings were held with managers of the organizations (see Table 9) selected due to their direct involvement in the alliance processes alongside first-hand knowledge of the biotechnology sector. The interviews were structured in three blocks in accordance with a predetermined script based on a review of the literature: the objective of the

Table 9.   Information of the Eight Companies Analyzed.

Organization	Activity	Location	Interviewees
BS$_1$	Biomedical development from academic sources.	Barcelona	Innovation manager
BS$_2$	Bioinformatics development and services.	Barcelona	CEO
BS$_3$	Development of biotechnological immunotherapies.	Barcelona	CEO
BS$_4$	Development of treatments for organ failure.	A Coruña	CEO
PC$_1$	Development, manufacture and distribution of drugs and nutritional supplements.	Barcelona	Innovation manager
PC$_2$	Development, manufacture and distribution of drugs and nutritional supplements.	Barcelona	CEO
PC$_3$	Development, manufacture and distribution of prescription drugs.	Barcelona (Subsidiary)	Innovation manager
PC$_4$	Development, manufacture and distribution of drugs.	Barcelona	Innovation manager

first block was to obtain an overview of the organization and the development of its business. In the second block, respondents were asked to describe the formation process of the alliances established, the effects of these alliances on the innovation, and the structure of their companies. The third block explored the perception of the fulfilment of expectations in the alliances, as well as, details about the cultural and relational aspects among their participants. Data analysis started by processing all the information and filtering out any irrelevant content. The interviews were recorded when permitted, transcribed, and coded to structure the data, thereby ensuring further reassessment. Any subsequent doubts about specific explanations were resolved through mail exchanges and additional conversations (Yin, 2003).

4. Results

Due to its relevance to human health, the biopharmaceutical industry is pressured to continuously innovate. In this sense, advances in knowledge and the emergence of new technologies have made it possible to developing new products. Thus, for a couple of decades, companies in the biotechnological sector, mainly start-ups, and medium and large pharmaceutical corporations have been intensely collaborating. According to the innovation manager of PC$_1$: '*Apart from very core issues, we make alliances in almost all developments*'. Likewise, the innovation manager of BS$_1$ noted:

> Now innovation always works through alliances…in other words, innovation is due to alliances, it is not that they manage to improve it, but that it is the way it works. The big pharmaceutical companies are very focused on identifying start-up biotechs that developed interesting things.

And they add:

> Also, many professionals, who were in R&D departments in big firms, have left for start-ups. All this allows for more innovation, more different ideas, and everything flows faster and faster.

It could be said that the protagonists of the main innovations in the industry are the start-ups and large corporations. Put simply, innovation is a result of the alliances established between these partners. Their connections are explained mainly by two motives. First, the R&D departments of the PC often lose track of the most innovative research. In this sense, cutting-edge innovations come from academia, and start-ups – often spin-offs from universities – have a closer relationship with the academic world and then pick up much more of this radical innovation. Second, large PC with their research departments have great and often unused costs, resulting in problems. Coherently, both parties have clear reasons to cooperate, whereas start-ups get mainly financial and managerial support, larger pharmaceutical corporations access innovation through start-ups without the need to make very large investments of their own. Therefore, establishing these alliances is of great interest to both parties, although there is evidence of the specific types of alliances that are, usually, the most fruitful in terms of innovation. In the words of PC_1 innovation manager: '*Both R&D and market alliances have led to more innovation, basic research not so much*'. This is entirely consistent with the literature, so for a pharmaceutical corporation is less risky to invest and cooperate with start-ups in the later stages of product development (Baum & Silverman, 2004). Moreover, these bigger companies usually have many projects to choose from which means that they do not have a great need to venture into early stage projects. In this respect, the innovation manager of BS_1 reported:

> The start-ups always take the initiative because they have a greater need to find a partner. In fact, I know that some pharmaceutical companies receive about 8,000 proposals a year.

It would be difficult to determine precisely which type of alliance is more effective, R&D or commercial, both seem equally important and in fact complement each other. Indeed, the PC_4 innovation manager reported,

> R&D alliances and commercialization alliances are both important and highly interconnected. For example, in a commercialization alliance you get a presence in the market and this finances and feeds back into the R&D activity. Obviously, all the knowledge

and resources provided by the partner to develop projects are key
to create a product.

Due to the expected complexity of developing joint projects, involving great investment, the analysis process of the complementarity between partners is onerous/
time consuming. In fact, sometimes this process can be easily extended for two
years because great care must be taken in some details. However, frequently this
period of time tends to be shortened, as the PC_4 innovation manager explained,

> This depends a lot on the interest of the pharmaceutical company;
> if there is a lot of interest because the product is very new, the
> process speeds up a lot, it goes much faster.

Interestingly, many managers agreed that complementarity is easier when both
parties develop the same product, as there will be more guarantees of obtaining
a powerful version, that is, one of the two versions will be the best. This makes
the alliance's terms and conditions to be concluded more quickly. All interviewees agreed that this process is equally crucial, both for the start-ups and for the
large corporations. For example, for the start-ups, despite taking the initiative and
being the financially weakest partner, they try to be careful not to be rejected in
future collaborations. As the innovation manager of BS_1 mentioned, '*There is a
lot of thinking about taking the step to have conversations to close alliances, the reason is clear, not to lose credibility*'. On the other hand, PC ensure the right choice
of the partner since they will invest large financial resources and a resounding
failure could mean their loss of reputation in the industry. As the PC_3 innovation manger pointed out: '*You also need to make sure that the potential partner
will be able to work at a pace similar to yours*'. Once the compatibility has been
analyzed, the starting point of this collaboration involves that both parts should
have to mutually adapt to change. It is also true that the biggest effort is made by
start-ups since they are the weakest structural part, very often, with few resources.
For example, the pharmaceutical corporations become shareholders of the start-
ups and implement in their partners greater standardization (protocols), sophisticated computer programs, extra steps to prepare budgets, among others. There
is a fusion of ideas regarding the sustainability actions and a powerful human
resources area is shared. The BS_2 CEO mentioned: '*Yes, alliances cause changes in
the company, for example, merging and restructuring research departments and even
the relocation of laboratory, moving it to another city*'.

All these changes and efforts are made based on expectations, that is, thinking
about the expected objectives. In this regard, the clear objective shared between
start-ups and large corporations is that innovation becomes effective, i.e. the
product finally reaches the market. However, despite this shared main goal, the
particular expectations of each partner may not be met at the expected levels. In
the course of the strategic alliances, the differences in the participants' expectations are manifested. The origin of these disparities is centred on the business
dimension, which determines the objectives set, the urgency to achieve results,

the daily operational decisions, to name a few. As the BS_1 innovation manager pointed out:

> I feel that problems and clashes arise, for example start-ups have far fewer protocols, everything is faster. On the other hand, large companies present many more procedures, decision-making is slower... in our eyes they seem a 'ministry'.

Generally, the start-ups' expectations of time and financial resources are frustrated, because larger corporations want to speed up. It must be considered that these innovation alliances are usually established when start-ups have been researching for a long time. Thus, when they start to cooperate in the final stages of development and these are especially cautious, this can generate some despair on the other counterpart. The financial aspect concerns start-ups and generates pressure. They pursue eagerly to reach the end of a development, improving the chances of survival and above all, improving the results of the firm. As start-ups they had the original idea of the development, they excessively believed in the potential of the product. The innovation manager of PC_1 explained:

> I think there is always more frustration on the part of the start-up because very often they have expectations that the market is easier than it is, they think everything will be smooth sailing because the product is very good, they are very excited about their technology and the partner (big company) is the one who 'queer the pitch'.

The issue of royalties is also controversial. At the time of negotiating the royalties, pharmaceutical corporations are more realistic than start-ups because of their greater experience in the market. Subsequently, market estimations do not usually meet the initial expectations of start-ups. For its part, pharmaceutical corporations seek interesting and competitive projects to grow, and ultimately, to be aligned with the latest technology. Consequently, their expectations do not meet the expected requirements. The corporate managers interviewed agreed that they always wanted to obtain a better product than the market standard, and when this cannot be achieved, the disappointment is great. In the words of PC_4 innovation manager, '*When that happens, you bury the product...the start-up wants to try again, but the big company usually shuts down because it feels cheated*'.

Another relevant aspect lies in the decision-making process, since particular interests should be aligned with different opinions that have to be integrated. In that regard, it is crucial that partners involve teams of specialized lawyers to prevent these circumstances. Start-ups and corporations have to establish control mechanisms, for instance, to what extent one partner can veto a project or hold certain decisions. Overall, the agreed terms are respected, and partners try to make the negotiation process as smooth as possible. In this sense, pharmaceutical corporations look forward to innovative projects and are not usually abusive; they need start-ups. In turn, the latter, being smaller in size, needs support at the final stages of the development.

Geographical and cultural proximity also play a significant role in the relationship between the alliance participants. In these collaborations, it is important that partners understand each other properly, recognize the subtle nuances and interpretations. Often, working with individual participants from other places becomes complicated because misunderstandings tend to arise, i.e. communication is not entirely effective. In this regard, the innovation manager of BS$_3$ explained:

> Yes, I think it is essential to be able to physically meet the other party. Culturally speaking it is also quite necessary to be close, for example, it has been difficult for us to work with the Japanese, I think they are brilliant but they are very strict, very rigid and in this aspect we have collided, we are more flexible and with much more ability to improvise.

And they added:

> The cultural thing always matters…you seem to have understood and then they send you something else. It is very important, in the end, the projects are thought up and executed by people, therefore it is very important to understand each other well.

In a similar vein, the PC$_4$ innovation manager explained that

> *Cultural proximity is very important, you get along faster. In my case, we have worked with Japanese and Chinese people and the cultural differences weigh heavily. For example, they respect hierarchies too much and this often causes decision-making to be slow and, in general, communication is not easy at all.* Then if you are not talking to a person who has enough power in the company, they tell you yes to everything and then they have to consult with the superiors, taking longer. *With the Americans, for example, you don't have many problems, except that the business culture is very different.*

Besides, it is true that, as companies accumulate experience in forming alliances, this problem is reduced. As the CEO of BS$_2$ reported:

> I think it is relatively important, if the company has experience in alliances, cultural distance does not play an important role. However, if we talk about the first experiences, they seek the partner that is closest from cultural and geographical proximity.

Mitigating these challenges is possible and, with effort, is achievable.
The innovation manager of PC$_4$ said:

> The most important thing is that the working teams are well coordinated, so great care is taken in managing people. We had

> communication problems with partners and had to agree on a specific way to report documentation, even establishing rules on how to respond to an email.

And added:

> Also holding online meetings and sharing the screen helps a lot to better visualize certain topics, because otherwise it is a constant source of misunderstanding and the interpretation of nuances is very important.

In sum, the importance of co-developed projects and in itself the great need to understand each other in order to reach a successful conclusion make the partners strive for it. There is some evidence of the aspects that contribute to strengthening the relationship between the participants in the alliances. Moreover, managers agree on emphasizing the emotional aspect, and more specifically values such as transparency and honesty. Accordingly, the PC_2 CEO said: '*When you realize that one partner is not transparent and the real objective is not the initial one, mistrust is generated*'. The CEO of BS_2 also agreed that frankness is essential to improve the partners' relationship. They added:

> Feeling that the other partner helps and understands you. I believe that empathy is something very important, and in this sense, I think that it is better to deal with an SME entrepreneur than with a manager from a large corporation... the connection is close and you can talk about common things.

The latter idea adds an interesting nuance – that the one-to-one relationship sometimes does not happen between managers of start-ups and their counterparts at pharmaceutical companies. It seems that leaving a certain degree of freedom influences and smooths the process, as BS_1 innovation manager mentioned:

> We fought to have greater autonomy to make expenses, because authorizations take a long time and, finally they got it. It is a matter of talking about it and then arriving at the most practical solution. This is achieved over time.

Thus, due to the efforts of both partners, these innovation alliances enable new products to reach the market. Developing products takes a lot of financial resources, experience, and knowledge which is, precisely, what this kind of alliances brings. In addition, the last phases of product development are challenging, but the alliances support the process so that everything moves forward. Managers of both partners agreed that if some problems arose in the working relationships but everything had gone well at the business level, they would repeat the process because it is not easy to open these paths.

5. Conclusions

In this study, we analyzed the relationship between the biotech start-ups and the larger pharmaceutical corporations, emphasizing the perceptions of the expectations' achieved by each partner. The managers of the biotechnology start-ups and the pharmaceutical companies involved in a strategic alliance are looking for a common objective by complementing their resources. However, their expectations can be different in terms of timing, market size, and strategic priorities.

In light of these results, this study offers several insights for academics and practitioners. On the one hand, these expectations are different for each partner, because of the disparities in the available resources, business skills, size, experience, organizational culture, development stages, and market orientation of each partner. Moreover, in some cases, strategic alliances contribute greatly to enhancing the start-up's survival, then these firms can be hasty when choosing a partner (Chang, 2004). At the same time, pharmaceutical corporations should ensure that their potential partners have proper capabilities and keep real expectations of the product's novelty. Furthermore, both parties should/are advised to take their time to carry out an appropriate analysis of their complementarity, with an emphasis on their goal's alignment. Thus, it is essential to prioritize projects, because it will provide better outcomes (Kim & Parkhe, 2009; Merchant, 2002).

On the other hand, drawing on these findings, we can point out that the contractual aspects such as the agreed terms are relevant, but the human part is of crucial importance for continuing alliances. Start-ups generally have very high expectations, often considering over-optimistic market forecasts. A new biotechnological discovery is an exciting successful event for the scientific team involved, so it can produce some euphoria about its medical and commercial potential. It is their partners, the large companies, who keep them down-to-earth, considerably lowering their estimated level of sales. At this point, the start-ups' expectations start decreasing, and the establishment of effective and honest communication channels arises, through which both managerial teams can understand each other well and fix all the misunderstandings. Thus, it is necessary a good balance between the achievements of both partners. Empathy is even more necessary when the partners belong to different national cultures, so they should consider their cultural traits and manage the situation respectfully, striving to find a way to mutual understanding.

Lastly, our study revealed that regardless of the initial plans in the strategic alliance, the outcomes are uncertain. For instance, low effectiveness of a new drug or its eventual unwanted serious side effects would lead to the fall of the development project. Or, even when the technological outcome is satisfactory, it has yet to face the last crucial test: the market. Internal or external events from the corporation side, can speed up, or slow down the pace of the project during the last stages of development and its commercialization. In these situations, conflicts can arise, and the mentioned values of transparency, honesty, and empathy are crucial to overcome them and progress with the deal. The size, skills, resources, and level of formalism of the corporation can become overwhelming for the start-up, especially in these situations, but the corporation should admit that it is not the start-up that must bear the burden derived from deviations from what was initially agreed.

We recognize certain limitations in this study, which in all circumstances provides clear indications for future research. First, our qualitative analysis is based on interviews with representatives from four biotechnology start-ups and four pharmaceutical corporations, and they are few in number. Thus, it is necessary to expand the current sample to make it more representative. Also, it would be interesting to extend the number of the European countries observed and determine potential disparities with the Spanish case. Finally, the study has been focussed on the biotechnology start-ups and the pharmaceutical corporations forming a strategic alliance, which are a subset of a wider kind of strategic alliances. There are some cooperative agreements between this subset and other companies and organizations such as small pharmaceutical companies, chemical companies of all sizes, Hospitals, Research Centres, and Universities. These additional perspectives would add to a more complete vision of the innovation context through strategic alliances.

References

Albeers, R. (2010). The role of contracts and trust in R&D alliances in the Dutch biotech sector. *Innovation, 12,* 311–329. doi:10.5172/impp.12.3.311

Ariño, A. (2003). Measures of strategic alliance performance: An analysis of construct validity. *Journal of International Business Studies, 34,* 66–79. doi:10.1057/palgrave. jibs.8400005

Arqué-Castells, P. (2012). How venture capitalists spur invention in Spain: Evidence from patent trajectories. *Research Policy, 41,* 897–912. doi:10.1016/j.respol.2012.01.0008

ASEBIO. (2021). Asociación Española de Bioempresas. *ASEBIO Annual Report.* Madrid, Spain.

Baum, J. A. C., & Silverman, B. S. (2004). Picking winners or building them? Alliance, intellectual, and human capital as selection criteria in venture financing and performance of biotechnology startups. *Journal of Business Venturing, 19,* 411–436. doi:10.1016/S0883-9026(03)00038-7

Beers, C., & Zand, F. (2014). R&D Cooperation, partner diversity, and innovation performance: An empirical analysis. *Journal of Product Innovation Management, 31*(2), 292–312. doi: 10.1111/jpim.12096

Bianchi, M., Cavaliere, A., Chiaroni, D., Frattini, F., & Chiesa, V. (2011). Organisational modes for Open Innovation in the bio-pharmaceutical industry: An exploratory analysis. *Technovation, 31,* 22–33. doi: 10.1016/j.technovation.2010.03.002

Cabello-Medina, C., Carmona-Lavado, A., & Cuevas-Rodriguez, G. (2020). A contingency view of alliance management capabilities for innovation in the biotech industry. *Business Research Quarterly 23,* 1–17. Doi: 10.1177/2340944420901050.

Chang, S. (2004). Venture capital financing, strategic alliances, and the initial public offerings of Internet startups. *Journal of Business Venturing, 19*(5), 721–741. doi: 10.1016/j.jbusvent.2003.03.002

Chesbrough, H. (2003). *Open innovation: The new imperative for creating and profiting from technology.* Boston, MA: Harvard Business School Press.

Christensen, C. M., & Rosenbloom, R. S. (1995). Explaining the attacker's advantage: Technological paradigms, organizational dynamics, and the value network. *Research Policy, 24,* 233–257. doi:10.1016/0048-7333(93)00764-K

Christoffersen, J. (2013). A review of antecedents of international strategic alliance performance: Synthesized evidence and new directions for core constructs. *International Journal of Management Reviews*, *15*(1), 66–85. doi: 10.1111/j.1468-2370.2012.00335.x

Colombo, M. G., Grilli, L., & Piva, E. (2006). In search of complementary assets: The determinants of alliance formation of high-tech start-ups. *Research Policy*, *35*(8), 1166–1199. doi: 10.1016/j.respol.2006.09.002

Deeds, D. L., & Hill, W. L. (1996). Strategic alliances and the rate of new product development: An empirical study of entrepreneurial biotechnology firms. *Journal of Business Venturing*, *11*, 41–55. doi:10.1016/0883-9026(95)00087-9

Durand, R., Bruyaka, O., & Mangematin, V. (2008). Do science and money go together? The case of the french biotech industry. *Strategic Management Journal*, *29*, 1281–1299. doi:10.1002/smj.707

Eisenhardt, K. M. (1989). Building theories from case study research. *The Academy of Management Review*, *14*(4), 532–550. doi:10.2307/258557

Elia, S., Petruzzelli, A. M., & Piscitello, L. (2019). The impact of cultural diversity on innovation performance of MNC subsidiaries in strategic alliances. *Journal of Business Research*, *98*, 204–213. doi:10.1016/j.jbusres.2019.01.062

Farazi, M. S., Gopalakrishnan, S., & Perez-Luño, A. (2019). Depth and breadth of knowledge and the governance of technology alliances. *Journal of Engineering and Technology Management*, *54*, 28–40. doi:10.1016/j.jengtecman.2019.08.002.

Godin, B. (2016). Technological innovation: On the origins and development of an inclusive concept. *Technology and Culture*, *57*(3), 527–566. doi:10.1353/tech.2016.0070

Gopalakrishnan, S., Scillitoe, J. L., & Santoro, M. D. (2008). Tapping deep pockets: The role of resources and social capital on financial capital acquisition by biotechnology firms in biotech-pharma alliances. *Journal of Management Studies*, *45*(8), 1354–1376. doi:10.1111/j.1467-6486.2008.00777.x

Greis, N. P., Dibner, M. D., & Bean, A. S. (1995). External partnering as a response to innovation barriers and global competition in biotechnology. *Research Policy*, *24*, 609–630. doi:10.1016/S0048-7333(94)00789-6

Gulati, R. (1999). Network location and learning: The influence of network resources and firm capabilities on alliance formation. *Strategic Management Journal*, *20*, 397–420. https://doi.org/10.1002/(SICI)1097-0266(199905)20:5<397::AID-SMJ35>3.0.CO;2-K

Harada, Y., Huayi Wang, K. K., & Shintaro, S. (2021). Drug discovery firms and business alliances for sustainable innovation. *Sustainability*, *13*(7), 3599. doi:10.3390/su13073599

He, S. L., & Wong, P. K. (2004). Exploration vs. exploitation: An empirical test of ambidexterity hypothesis. *Organization Science*, *15*, 481–494. doi:10.1287/orsc.1040.0078

He, V. F., Von Krogh, G., Sirén, C., & Gersdorf, T. (2021). Asymmetries between partners and the success of university-industry research collaborations. *Research Policy*, *50*(10), 104356. doi:10.1016/j.respol.2021.104356

Hoenig, D., & Henkel, J. (2015). Quality signals? The role of patents, alliances, and team experience in venture capital financing. *Research Policy*, *44*, 1049–1064. doi:10.1016/j.respol.2014.11.011

Hoffmann, W. H., & Scholsser, R. (2001). Success factors of strategic alliances in small and medium-sized enterprises – An empirical survey. *Long Range Planning*, *34*, 357–381. doi:10.1016/S0024-6301(01)00041-3

Hu, Y. H., McNamara, P., & McLoughlin, D. (2015). Outbound open innovation in biopharmaceutical out-licensing. *Technovation*, *35*, 46–58. doi:10.1016/j.technovation.2014.07.004

Janney, J. J., & Folta, T. B. (2003). Signaling through private equity placements and its impact on the valutation of biotechnology firms. *Journal of Business Venturing*, *18*, 361–380. doi:10.1016/S0883-9026(02)00100-3

Jehn, K. A., & Mannix, E. A. (2001). The dynamic nature of conflict: A longitudinal study of intregroup conflict and group performance. *Academy of Management Journal, 44,* 238–251. doi:10.2307/3069453

Kim, J., & Parkhe, A. (2009). Competing and cooperating similarity in global strategic alliances: An exploratory examination. *British Journal of Management, 20,* 363–376. doi:10.1111/j.1467-8551.2008.00580.x

Lee, J., Park, S. H., Ryu, Y., & Baik, Y.-S. (2010). A hidden cost of strategic alliances under Schumpeterian dynamics. *Research Policy, 39*(2), 229–238. doi:10.1016/j.respol.2009.12.004

March-Chordà, I., Yagüe-Perales, R. M., & Seoane-Trigo, R. (2009). Asymmetric behaviour of biotechnology business patterns in Spain. *Technology Analysis & Strategic Management, 21*(6), 765–782. doi:10.1080/09537320903052780

McCutchen, J. R., & Swamidass, P. M. (2004). Motivations for strategic alliances in the pharmaceutical/biotech industry: Some new findings. *Journal of High Technology Management Research, 15,* 197–214. doi:10.1016/j.hitech.2004.03.003

Merchant, H. (2002). Shareholder value creation via international joint ventures: Some additional explanations. *Management International Review (MIR), 42,* 49–69. http://www.jstor.org/stable/40835907

Moghaddam, K., Bosse, D. A., & Provance, M. (2016). Strategic alliances of entrepreneurial firms: Value enhancing then value destroying. *Strategic Entrepreneurship Journal, 10*(2), 153–168. doi:10.1002/sej.1221

Mohr, V., Garnsey, E., & Theyel, G. (2013). The role of alliances in the early development of high-growth firms. *Industrial and Corporate Change, 23*(1), 233–259. doi:10.1093/icc/dtt056

Nicholson, N., Danzon, P. M., & McCullough, J. (2005). Biotech-pharmaceutical alliances as a signal of asset and firm quality. *The Journal of Business, 78*(4), 1433–1464. doi:10.1086/430865

Pisano, G., & Verganti, R. (2008). Which kind of collaboration is right for you? *Harvard Business Review, 86*(12), 78–86.

Quintana, C., & Benavides, C. A. (2007). Concentraciones territoriales, alianzas estratégicas e innovación. Un enfoque de capacidades dinámicas. *Cuadernos de Economia y Dirección de la Empresa, 30,* 5–38. doi:10.1016/S1138-5758(07)70072-5

Rothaermel, F. T. (2001). Complementary assets, strategic alliances, and the incumbent's advantage: An empirical study of industry and firm effects in the biopharmaceutical industry. *Research Policy, 30,* 1235–1251. doi:10.1016/S0048-7333(00)00142-6

Schoonmaker, M. G., Solomon, G. T., & Rau, P. A. (2017). Early-stage of innovations: Selection system criteria for funding U.S. Biotech SME. *Journal of Small Business Management, 55*(S1), 60–75. doi:10.1111/jsbm.12332

Schumpeter, J. A. (1949). Economic theory and entrepreneurial history. In R. R. Wohl (Ed.), *Change and the entrepreneur: Postulates and patterns for entrepreneurial history* (pp. 131–142). Cambridge, USA: Harvard University Press.

Solé, E., Domingo, S., & Amat, O. (2022). Biotechnology firms, signals, and venture capital investment. *Intangible Capital, 18*(3), 350–369. doi:10.3926/ic.1978

Tushman, M. L., & Anderson, P. (1986). Technological discontinuities and organizational environments. *Administrative Science Quarterly, 31*(3), 439–465. doi:10.2307/2392832

Wang, H., Wuebker, R. B., Han, S., & Ensley, M. D. (2012). Strategic alliances by venture capital backed firms: An empirical examination. *Small Business Economics, 38,* 179–196. doi:10.1007/s11187-009-9247-x

Yagüe-Perales, R. M., Niosi, J., & March-Chorda, I. (2015). Benchmarking biotechnology industries: A comparative perspective. *International Entrepreneurship and Management Journal, 11,* 19–38. doi:10.1007/s11365-013-0272-5

Yin, R. K. (2003). *Case study research: Design and methods.* London: Sage Publications.

Chapter 9

Effects of the Subsidiaries' Networks on the Service Multinationals Innovation Activity

Paloma Miravitlles, Fariza Achcaoucaou and Tim Laurin Spieth

Abstract

This research explores how subsidiary embeddedness in different networks, both internal and external to the firm, contributes to the innovation of the service multinational corporation (MNC). Specifically, the authors analyze the different effects of networks on MNC's subsidiaries performing competence-creating or competence-exploiting innovation activities, in the context of the service industry. The present study analyzes the data of 178 foreign-owned subsidiaries in the service sector performing innovation in Spain. The results of data analysis at two points in time show that external and internal embeddedness have a positive impact on the subsidiary innovation. Moreover, external embeddedness has a major positive influence on the competence-creating rather than on the competence-exploiting activities, while the internal embeddedness is equally important for both types of innovation. Therefore, this study contributes to further our understanding of how subsidiaries' linkages affect innovation of the service MNC.

Keywords: Embeddedness; networks; service multinationals; subsidiaries; innovation

1. Introduction

Accessing geographically dispersed knowledge around the world is becoming a central source of competitive advantage for the MNCs (Rugman & Verbeke,

Collective Entrepreneurship in the Contemporary European Services Industries:
A Long Term Approach, 135–151
doi:10.1108/978-1-80117-950-820231009

2001) resulting in the increasing importance and participation of the subsidiaries in the innovation activities of the MNCs (Almeida & Phene, 2004). As a consequence, foreign-owned subsidiaries play a more active role within the MNC as sources of new ideas, products discoveries, and innovative capabilities that inspire new business opportunities (Frost, 2001).

This phenomenon is especially relevant in the context of the service MNCs. Due to differential characteristics of the service business – such as intangibility, perishability, customization, simultaneity of production and consumption and consumer participation in production (Boddewyn, Halbrich, & Perry, 1986), much of the innovation is developed in the host countries and then transferred to the rest of the corporation beyond national borders (Forsgren, 2008). Hence, the specific nature of the service business makes the foreign subsidiaries an essential piece of the service MNC strategy. Because of the service inseparability, service MNCs compete either through centralized innovation, or on the contrary, through high national responsiveness (Campbell & Verbeke, 1994). As a result, an increasing number of subsidiaries in the service industry, are generating new knowledge for the entire MNC, mainly from local relationships with the clients, suppliers, R&D institutions, as well as from the internal relationships with other peer units within the MNC network. Subsidiaries in the service MNCs are embedded in two environmental contexts: the external environment (host country), and the internal environment (the global corporation) (Kostova & Roth, 2002); so, both types of relationships acquire crucial importance for exchanging information, knowledge, and know-how with the goal of global innovation (Dellestrand, 2011).

The influence of foreign subsidiary embeddedness in the external and internal MNC networks has been deeply studied in the literature (see for example, Andersson, Forsgren, & Holm, 2002; Almeida & Phene, 2004; Ciabuschi, Holm, & Martín, 2014). However, little is known specifically about the relationships of the foreign subsidiaries in the service industry. Some exceptions were Frenz, Girardone, and Ietto-Gillies (2005) and Alam (2011) that analyzed MNC innovation in the financial service industry; and, Najafi-Tavani, Giroud, and Sinkovics (2012) that examined the influence of networks on knowledge development within the knowledge-intensive business services (KIBS) MNCs. The specificity and unique features of the service MNCs can make the subsidiaries behave differently in terms of their contributions to global innovation. Therefore, we want to close this gap, by fully understanding how these, internal and external, networks come together and influence the subsidiary's capability of innovation in the service MNCs. In particular, this study analyzes innovation activities regarding the subsidiary's ability of gathering information, supporting innovation, and thus in helping the corporation to achieve global competitive advantage in the service industry. Subsidiaries can develop different types of innovation activities related to a role of competence-creating or competence-exploiting (Cantwell & Mudambi, 2005). While the latter implies performing demand-driven activities that consist of adapting and adjusting services and processes developed elsewhere in the MNC to the local market needs, the former is linked to supply-driven activities that imply the development and creation of a relevant service innovations to the MNC as a whole (Cantwell & Mudambi, 2005).

We use an empirical methodology based on data from the Spanish Technological Innovation Panel (PITEC), that gathers information from the Survey on Innovation in Spanish Companies and Statistics on R&D activities, to analyze how internal and external networks influence subsidiary competence-creating and exploiting innovation activities in the context of service MNCs. We apply a partial least square (PLS) approach to structural equation modelling (SEM) on a sample of 178 foreign service subsidiaries on the Spanish market with data at two points in time (2008 and 2014). The results show that external embeddedness has major positive influence on competence-creating activities, while the internal embeddedness is equally important for both the competence-creating and competence-exploiting activities. Furthermore, the influence of external embeddedness on subsidiary innovation, through internal embeddedness, was confirmed. The results obtained contribute to explain how innovation can be increased and supported in the subsidiaries, and in the international corporate networks.

2. Theoretical Framework

The network-based view considers the MNC as an interorganizational network that helps to explain how headquarters and their subsidiaries are linked together and interconnected with each other (Ghoshal & Bartlett, 1990). Due to the possibility of exchanging information and know-how different units, in the network, manage to transfer innovation, grow, and obtain a better market position (Hosseini & Dadfar, 2012). The subsidiary participation in the surrounding networks through interorganizational relationships is called embeddedness (Gulati, Nohria, & Zaheer, 2000), and it could be external or internal. The external embeddedness explains how subsidiaries interact with other local market actors such as, customers, consumers, authorities, development partners, R&D institutions, suppliers, competitors, and companies from other industries among others (Andersson et al., 2002). Regarding the external embeddedness, the subsidiary can contribute greatly to the innovation process due to their knowledge of the market and their experience with the local customers and consumers (Cowden & Alhorr, 2013). With regards to the internal embeddedness, the subsidiary interacts with other peer units and the headquarters of the MNC, working together with the help of communication and an extensive 'exchange of information' and knowledge (Ciabuschi et al., 2014, p. 4). In fact, internal embeddedness is part of the MNC innovation process itself, since it is done in the subsidiary or in collaboration with other subsidiaries to export to the headquarters. Here, knowledge can be used either for the home market, or to be distributed and accessed by other foreign markets (Liang & Xu, 2011). Therefore, it is well established that internal as well as the external embeddedness are relevant and important drivers for innovation of MNCs (Achcaoucaou, Miravitlles, & León-Darder, 2017; Collinson & Wang, 2012).

The purpose of connecting, communicating, and exchanging information could be diverse from one corporate network to another, and dependent on the type of innovation performed by the different subsidiaries. The innovation activities can vary greatly and depend on the role of the subsidiary within the company. For instance, a subsidiary could just do activities related exclusively to the adoption of services to the local needs, mainly playing an executor, passive or competence-exploiting role (Cantwell & Mudambi, 2005). This means that the subsidiary uses the given infrastructure, knowledge, resources, and processes developed in the parent company to adapt and exploit them at the host country. For example, the global fast-food chains often apply successful strategies, from one market to another, and most of the subsidiaries repeat it practically in the same way in their local countries. Instead, other subsidiaries can generate innovation for the rest of the MNC, through getting a better understanding of each market and helping the MNC to build up common know-how about the customer's behaviour, alongside offering new services to keep their satisfaction and loyalty. These subsidiaries are called competence-creating (Cantwell & Mudambi, 2005), and play a more active role, creating valuable knowledge for the whole MNC. This was the case, for example, of the Australian subsidiary of the North American McDonalds. As the financial success was crumbling, the local subsidiary in Australia decided to open a coffee shop to offer a wider range of products to their customers (RusHolts, 2017). This new business soon turned out to be a major success in the country, where McCafé soon was amongst the leading brands for coffees and hot beverages (RusHolts, 2017; Schmid & Gombert, 2018). As the new service contributed to a higher revenue for McDonalds in Australia, the new business model was transferred and implemented across other foreign countries where, the MNC operated (RusHolts, 2017; Schmid & Gombert, 2018). Therefore, the combination of the new knowledge accessed in the host country, with the internal knowledge available in the MNC (Almeida & Phene, 2004; Kogut & Zander, 1993; Phene & Almeida, 2008) was useful to develop and create relevant innovation for the rest of the MNC (Almeida & Phene, 2004; Kogut & Zander, 1993; Phene & Almeida, 2008).

3. Development of Hypotheses

Services by nature are significantly locally oriented, which means that most types of services require a high proximity of suppliers and consumers and, even, their active participation in the production process (Boddewyn et al., 1986). Therefore, subsidiary local agents, in the host countries, where the service activity actually occurs play a crucial role in the innovation activities of the MNC. Foreign subsidiaries absorb new knowledge from the environment through external embedded relationships with the individual actors in the host country (Andersson et al., 2002). As a result of their knowledge of the market and experience with the local customers, they can greatly contribute to the MNC innovation process (Cowden & Alhorr, 2013). Due to the proximity, time of the processes, language barriers and other regional circumstances, the information is usually first received by the subsidiaries. This gives them the time, and the possibility, to first elaborate innovative solutions and improvements, to then suggest and report them to the headquarters (Cowden & Alhorr, 2013). Therefore, gaining new knowledge to develop innovations comes initially from the relationships with the local agents in the host country.

Moreover, if external knowledge sourcing proves to be successful, this might be shared within the internal network and thus with the other foreign subsidiaries of the group. The knowledge generated is transferred and used internally, not only in the focal subsidiary, but also in the other parts of the MNC (i.e. the sister subsidiaries and headquarters) to innovate, improve and develop new and better services and products for the whole MNC (Ciabuschi et al., 2014). Given the combination of knowledge and experience from all parties (internal and external), the product and the processes might be optimized, so less mistakes in development process might occur. In that sense, the external network is essential for innovation, while the internal network is more important for exchanging the gained knowledge (Ciabuschi et al., 2014). Hence, this supports the argument that the subsidiary generates new knowledge for the whole MNC, through combining the new knowledge directly accessed externally in their own host country, with the internal knowledge available in the MNC (Almeida & Phene, 2004; Kogut & Zander, 1993; Phene & Almeida, 2008). Therefore, the following hypothesis is posed:

> *H1:* External embeddedness influences directly the service subsidiaries innovation activities and indirectly through internal embeddedness.

The external embeddedness has been described as a major driver for innovation (Johnston & Paladino, 2007). According to Hallin, Holm, and Deo Sharma (2010), the greater the embeddedness of the relationships in the subsidiary's external business network, the greater the innovation's contribution to the subsidiary business performance. Indeed, this positive relationship is expected to be higher for the competence-creating subsidiaries in the service MNCs, since they are the ones that make more radical or disruptive innovation comparing to the competence-exploiting activities. Due to the personal interaction and difficulties in separating production and the consumption of the service activities, close relationships with consumers and other local agents (suppliers, competitors, universities, etc.) are the main source of inspiration in the service MNCs. Because many services are location-bound, the competence-creating subsidiaries embed themselves in external networks to access tacit, sticky and context-specific knowledge (Narula, 2014; Rugman & Verbeke, 2001). According to Najafi-Tavani, Giroud, & Sinkovics (2012) tacit knowledge plays a pivotal role in the services, so it constitutes the raw material of innovation. To achieve local responsiveness, the foreign subsidiaries have to develop close relations with local counterparts to access and absorb knowledge embodied in the local context (Almeida & Phene, 2004) in order to innovate and increase the service experience to costumers (Miozzo & Yamin, 2012). In fact, costumers of the KIBS companies are considered to be 'co-producers' and 'co-creators' of the new knowledge (den Hertog, 2000; Najafi-Tavani et al., 2011). Hence, it is reasonable to expect that the subsidiaries that perform the competence-creating activities in the service MNCs have higher levels of external embeddedness and a greater positive impact on innovation. Thus, we propose the following hypothesis:

> *H2:* External embeddedness has more positive effect on the competence-creating activities than on the competence-exploiting activities in MNC service subsidiaries.

At the same time, the subsidiaries that perform more competence-exploiting activities that are more connected to service incremental innovation, can benefit to a greater extent from internal embeddedness, if the received knowledge matches the needs of their local market (Hallin et al., 2010). The type of knowledge shared within the internal network is replicated in nature and, thus, leads to more incremental innovation. The competence-exploiting subsidiaries usually act with foreign-tradable services (Boddewyn et al., 1986), where innovations can be transportable across national boundaries from the site of production (normally at the parent company) to the location of the consumer's receipt or used in the foreign market. Accordingly, internal embeddedness is the channel that allows knowledge to be transferred, as well as the means by which the subsidiary can access and use that knowledge within the international corporate (Astley & Sachdeva, 1984). Although foreign markets might be different and, therefore, the customer needs could vary, the subsidiaries often have similar, tasks or processes, through which they could work on, improve and innovate. Internal embeddedness is the main source of innovation for the competence-exploiting subsidiaries in service MNCs compared to the competence-creating subsidiaries. Hence, we posit the following hypothesis:

> *H3:* Internal embeddedness has more positive effect on the competence-exploiting activities than on the competence-creating activities in MNC service subsidiaries.

Fig. 3 shows the theoretical model that illustrates how service subsidiaries interact with external and internal networks to develop different innovation activities within the MNC.

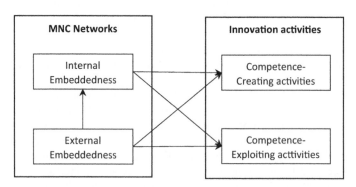

Fig. 3.   Theoretical Model.

4. Methods

4.1. Questionnaire and Data

The data were extracted from the Spanish Technological Innovation Panel (PITEC), which is collected by the national statistical office of Spain in the framework of the Community Innovation Survey. PITEC provides direct information over time on the innovation process of the Spanish resident companies from a wide range of industries. This research focusses on the indicators referred to the subsidiaries of the foreign MNC in the service sector.

The current chapter reports on quantitative research, at two points in time, to assure no changes in perception of companies surveyed. The years 2008 and 2014 were used as the two more separate survey waves with less modifications in the questionnaire design. Dataset from these two years contains valid information for the study variables of 4,520 enterprises, of which 658 are MNC subsidiaries, with at least 50% of the shares owned by the foreign shareholders. After filtering by service sector, the final sample was narrowed down to 178 foreign subsidiaries. The composition of the sample by service industry is illustrated in Table 10.

Table 10.　Main Economic Activity of the Subsidiaries in the Sample.

Service Activities	NACE-2009[a]	Frequency	Percentage
Trade	45; 46; 47	46	25.8
Transportation and storage	49; 50; 51; 52; 53	11	6.2
Hospitality	55; 56	4	2.2
Telecommunications	61	6	3.4
Programming, consulting and other information activities	62	29	16.3
Other information and communication services	58; 59; 60; 63	12	6.7
Financial and insurance activities	64; 65; 66	23	12.9
R&D services	72	8	4.5
Other activities	69; 70; 71; 73; 74; 75	24	13.5
Administrative activities and auxiliary services	77; 78; 79; 80; 81; 82	9	5.1
Health and social service activities	86; 87; 88	3	1.7
Other services	95; 96	3	1.7
Total		178	100.0

[a]Correspondence of the service activities identified in the PITEC database to the CNAE-2009 classification system.

4.2. Constructs and Measures

4.2.1. Measures of Subsidiary R&D Activities. The orientation towards the competence-creating or competence-exploiting activities is measured based on the objectives of innovation of the subsidiaries. Following similar operationalizations (e.g. Knudsen & Lien, 2015; Sofka, Shehu, & de Faria, 2014), we use the information in PITEC questionnaire that gathers the degree of importance of a wide range of objectives (on a four-point Likert scale ranging from 'not relevant' to 'highly important'). On the one hand, the objectives of innovation of the subsidiaries related to radical innovation, namely linked to a broader range of services, substitution of services or processes, as well as penetrating new markets, and expanding the market quota, are used for measuring the competence-creating related activities. On the other hand, the objectives targeted at more incremental innovation, such as greater flexibility and the capacity of provision of services, as well as lower labour, material and energy costs, are used to operationalize the competence-exploiting activities.

4.2.2. Measures of Network Embeddedness. Network embeddedness is captured based on the strength of the subsidiaries' linkages for innovation. Following Achcaoucaou and Miravitlles (2021), two questions of the PITEC survey are combined in order to construct embeddedness measures. That means, the responses that grade the importance of the information sourced from different partners (on a four-point Likert scale ranging from 'not used' to 'high importance') with the answers that point out the cooperation with those partners (that take the value of 1, if collaboration exists, and 0, if otherwise). To construct external embeddedness, the importance of information sources is added to the collaboration in the host-country immediate environment, which results in a five-point Likert scale measurement. The variable is modelled as a second-order construct where market agents (i.e. suppliers, clients and competitors) are distinguished from R&D agents (i.e. consultants, universities and research centres).

Internal embeddedness, instead, operationalizes network ties within the corporation (i.e. headquarters and sister subsidiaries) worldwide, so the sum of collaborations with corporate units located in other European countries, United States, and other countries is considered. Subsequently, an average of the importance of the corporate units as a source of information with their collaboration worldwide is calculated. This turned out into a single item on seven-point Likert scale. Table 11 displays a summary of the constructs used. All constructs in the model are estimated as composites in Mode A.

4.2.3. Control Variables. Three control variables are introduced in the model. First, the subsidiary size is included as the number of employees in natural logarithms. Second, there is a dummy variable that collapses service activities according to knowledge intensity classification of Eurostat (1 = knowledge-intensive services; 0 = less knowledge-intensive services). Finally, a dummy variable to control for the home region of the MNC is applied (the latter takes the value of 1, if headquarters are located in an European country, and 0, if otherwise).

Table 11. Constructs and Measures.

Construct/dimension/ indicator	Definition	Mean 2008	SD 2008	Standardized Loadings 2008	Mean 2014	SD 2014	Standardized Loadings 2014
INTERNAL EMBEDDEDNESS	*Strength of the linkages with corporate partners worldwide*						
IE1	Headquarters and sister subsidiaries jointly (no broken-down information available)	1.857	0.553	s.i.	1.919	0.585	s.i.
EXTERNAL EMBEDDEDNESS	*Strength of the linkages with external host-country partners*						
Market linkages							
EE2	Suppliers	2.685	1.194	0.369	2.803	1.271	0.494
EE3	Private/public clients	2.612	1.245	0.704	2.708	1.325	0.740
EE4	Competitors	2.225	1.117	0.707	2.169	1.122	0.759
R&D linkages							
EE5	Consultants or commercial laboratories	1.961	1.096	0.761	2.253	1.292	0.721
EE6	Universities	2.022	1.306	0.774	2.034	1.336	0.755
EE7	Public/private research centres	1.736	1.059	0.761	1.848	1.214	0.778

(Continued)

Table 11. (Continued)

Construct/dimension/indicator	Definition	Mean 2008	SD 2008	Standardized Loadings 2008	Mean 2014	SD 2014	Standardized Loadings 2014
COMPETENCE-CREATING ACTIVITIES	*Objectives directed towards competence-creating activities*						
Objet1	Broader range of goods/services	2.517	0.768	0.832	2.472	0.804	0.834
Objet2	Substitution of products/processes	2.264	0.898	0.730	2.365	0.841	0.724
Objet3	Penetration in new markets	2.382	0.857	0.894	2.253	0.895	0.839
Objet4	Greater market quota	2.421	0.821	0.904	2.360	0.886	0.880
COMPETENCE-EXPLOITING ACTIVITIES	*Objectives directed towards competence-exploiting activities*						
Objet5	Better quality of goods/services	2.596	0.762	0.607	2.551	0.788	0.528
Objet6	Greater flexibility in provision of services	2.438	0.773	0.663	2.416	0.854	0.783
Objet7	Greater capacity for provision of services	2.388	0.824	0.769	2.404	0.866	0.762
Objet8	Lower labour costs	2.096	0.881	0.839	2.101	0.890	0.812
Objet9	Fewer materials	1.691	0.817	0.794	1.646	0.805	0.772
Objet10	Less energy	1.652	0.818	0.801	1.736	0.866	0.764
CONTROL VARIABLES							
Size	Number of employees (ln)	-	-	-	5.247	1.824	s.i.
Knowledge intensity	High vs less knowledge intensity (dummy)	-	-	-	0.326	0.470	s.i.
Home region	European home region (dummy)	-	-	-	0.840	0.367	s.i.

Note: SD = standard deviation; s.i. = single item; n.a. = not applicable.

4.3. Data Analysis Technique

Since the research model includes latent variables measured with multi-item scales and intertwined hypotheses, we use a SEM. This technique allows one to simultaneously deal with the psychometric properties of the measurement model, and with the prediction of the structural relationships between the latent constructs (Chin, 1998). Specifically, we adopt a partial least square (PLS-SEM) approach because it is preferable to other methods for estimating models with high-order constructs (Dijkstra & Henseler, 2015) in situation of non-normal (Fornell & Larcker, 1981), unknown distribution (Falk & Miller, 1992), and small sample size (Chin & Newsted, 1999; Reinartz, Haenlein, & Henseler, 2009). The analysis is performed with the SmartPLS 3.3.9 software (Ringle, Wende, & Becker, 2015).

4.4. Analyses and Results

4.4.1. Measurement Model. As external embeddedness is modelled, as a second-order latent variable with the same number of indicators loading on each dimension, the repeated indicator approach is used to estimate the model (Wetzels, Odekerken-Schroder, & van Oppen, 2009). This implies reusing the first-order latent variable items as indicators for the higher order construct in the estimation (Becker, Klein, & Wetzels, 2012). Thus, the psychometric properties of the measurement model are assessed, considering the whole nomological network at once, and in terms of the reliability and the validity of the variables used (Hair, Sarstedt, Ringle, & Mena, 2012). In the first stage, as per individual reliability, only items EE2, from the External Embeddedness scale, and objet5 and objet6, from the competence-exploiting scales, present standardized factor loadings below the threshold of 0.707, recommended by Carmines and Zeller (1979). As shown in Table 11, we decide to retain these items in the model, since they prove to be different from zero (significant at the 0.01 level, based on a Student (4999) distribution, two-tailed test).

In Table 12 (page overleaf), the construct reliability assessment brings values for composite reliability (from 0.786 to 0.907) above the benchmark of 0.7, suggested by Nunnally and Bernstein (1994). All the constructs have the average variance extracted (AVE) above the minimum 0.50 value for convergent validity (from 0.552 to 0.741). Discriminant validity is also met by achieving the more restrictive criterion of heterotrait – monotrait ratio of correlations below 0.9 in the lower order constructs (Henseler, Ringle, & Sarstedt, 2015), which guarantees that all latent measures differ sufficiently from each other. Taken together, these results provide sufficient confidence that the measurement model used is reliable and valid.

4.4.2. Structural Model and Results of Hypothesis Testing. Fig. 4 summarizes the results derived from the structural model. The R-square values for the endogenous variables, and the positive values of the Stone-Geisser Q2, suggest that the model has predictive capacity (Falk & Miller, 1992) and relevance (Geisser, 1974; Stone, 1974), respectively. The algebraic sign of the structural path coefficients and its significance, determined by means of the bootstrap procedure

Table 12.   Measurement Model Assessment.

	Composite Reliability	AVE	1	2	3	4	5	6	7	8	9	10	11	12	13	14	15
1. IE$_{2008}$	s.i.	s.i.	s.i.														
2. IE$_{2014}$	s.i.	s.i.	0.213														
3. EE$_{2008}$	h.c.	h.c.	0.500	0.167													
4. EE$_{2014}$	h.c.	h.c.	0.120	0.476	0.548												
5. EEmarket$_{2008}$	0.786	0.560	0.544	0.163	n.a.	0.491											
6. EEmarket$_{2014}$	0.834	0.629	0.082	0.473	0.384	n.a.	0.525										
7. EEr&d$_{2008}$	0.896	0.741	0.363	0.135	n.a.	0.476	0.622	0.199									
8. EEr&d$_{2014}$	0.884	0.719	0.130	0.384	0.584	n.a.	0.364	0.668	0.626								
9. CC$_{2008}$	0.907	0.710	0.386	0.185	0.523	0.248	0.649	0.233	0.320	0.213							
10. CC$_{2014}$	0.892	0.675	0.071	0.488	0.268	0.474	0.285	0.486	0.199	0.370	0.392						
11. CE$_{2008}$	0.884	0.563	0.376	0.171	0.455	0.234	0.515	0.199	0.315	0.219	0.608	0.205					
12. CE$_{2014}$	0.879	0.552	0.079	0.447	0.170	0.395	0.174	0.527	0.131	0.199	0.170	0.528	0.422				
13. Size	s.i.	s.i.	0.050	0.093	0.205	0.198	0.231	0.233	0.143	0.128	0.244	0.099	0.128	0.119			
14. Knowledge intensity	s.i.	s.i.	0.170	0.138	0.207	0.285	0.193	0.263	0.174	0.248	0.172	0.194	0.110	0.088	0.023		
15. Home region	s.i.	s.i.	0.138	0.027	0.128	0.100	0.065	0.114	0.148	0.068	0.054	0.077	0.048	0.076	0.146	0.046	

Note: s.i. = single item; n.a. = not applicable; h.c. = hierarchical component; IE = internal embeddedness; EE = external embeddedness; CC = competence-creating; CE = competence-exploiting.

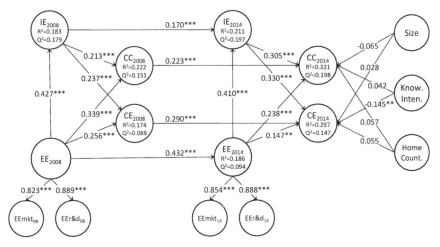

Fig. 4. Structural Model Assessment.
Note: ***$p < 0.01$; **$p < 0.05$; *$p < 0.1$ (based on a Student t(4999) distribution, one-tailed test); IE = internal embeddedness; EE = external embeddedness; CC = competence-creating; CE = competence-exploiting.

(5,000 resamples) to generate standard errors and t-statistics (Chin, 1998), brings support to the appropriateness of the theoretical model.

These results confirm *H1*, which suggests that external embeddedness impacts innovation activities of the service subsidiaries, directly and indirectly, through internal embeddedness. In fact, as displayed in Fig. 4, all relationships in the model for two years, 2008 and 2014, are significant at 0.01. However, in 2014, the direct relationship of external embeddedness on the competence-exploiting activities is, somewhat, weak but, significant at the 0.05 level ($\beta = 0.147$, t-Value = 1.910**) as the path that determines the indirect relationship through internal embeddedness is always significant at the 0.01 level. Indeed, this amounts for a total effect on the competence-creating ($\beta_{2008} = 0.430$, t-Value = 6.046***; $\beta_{2014} = 0.363$, t-Value = 4.874***) and on the competence-exploiting activities ($\beta_{2008} = 0.358$, t-Value = 4.676***; $\beta_{2014} = 0.282$, t-Value = 3.512***) significant at the 0.01 level. Hence, we can state that *H1* is supported.

There is a strong support for *H2*, which confirms that the direct effect of external embeddedness is higher on the competence-creating activities ($\beta_{2008} = 0.339$, t-Value = 4.097***; $\beta_{2014} = 0.238$, t-Value = 3.109***) than on the competence-exploiting activities ($\beta_{2008} = 0.256$, t-Value = 3.061***; $\beta_{2014} = 0.147$, t-Value = 1.910**), which, as mentioned above, in the year 2014 is only significant at 0.05. In other words, although it has been proved to have a positive impact on both types of innovative activities, close relationships with market agents (suppliers, customers, competitors), and R&D partners (laboratories, universities and research centres) seem to be of greater importance for the competence-creating activities.

Finally, with regards to *H3*, that posits a greater effect of internal embeddedness on the competence-exploiting than on the competence-creating activities, inconclusive results have been found. Although the effect on the competence-exploiting activities is slightly higher (β_{2008} = 0.237, t-Value = 2.784***; β_{2014} = 0.330, t-Value = 3.945***) than on the competence-creating activities (β_{2008} = 0.213, t-Value = 2.475***; β_{2014} = 0.305, t-Value = 4.140***), the difference does not indicate that any of both types of innovation activities is conclusively more favoured over the other by the internal embeddedness.

Regarding the control variables, only the knowledge intensity of the service industry appears significant for the competence-exploiting activities, although with a small size effect (only significant at 0.05 level). The negative sign of the effect suggests that the more knowledge-intensive is the service, the less likely it is that the subsidiary will carry out the competence-exploiting activities. This brings the idea that the competence-exploiting activities are not in the priorities of the subsidiaries operating in the knowledge-intensive services in Spain. The rest of the controls are not found to be significant, either when affecting the competence-creating or the competence-exploiting activities.

5. Discussion and Conclusions

Building on the network perspective of the MNC, the present chapter has analyzed the effects of embeddedness on the innovation activities of the subsidiaries in the context of service industry. The findings have shown that both external and internal embeddedness have positive direct and indirect impacts on the innovation of the subsidiary in the service MNC. However, different embeddedness effects according to the type of innovation activity carried out by the subsidiary were detected. Specifically, we have found evidence that embedding in the external networks has more positive effect in the subsidiary competence-creating innovation activities, while a high degree of embeddedness in internal networks has shown a very similar positive relationship to both types of embeddedness.

These results have contributed to extant literature by adding to our understanding of how networks influence subsidiary innovation in the context of service MNCs. The very nature of the activities of service companies is substantially different from manufacturing firms and little effort, so far, has been done to understand this phenomenon. Additionally, the international business literature has well documented the influence of external and internal embeddedness on the innovation of manufacturing subsidiaries (Achcaoucaou et al., 2017; Almeida & Phene, 2004; Andersson et al., 2002; Ciabuschi et al., 2014), though in the service context this is not so clear. In that sense, the results from our study confirm the findings from Najafati-Tavani et al. (2011), in showing that to develop embedded relations with the local environment and the internal corporate network increases the ability of the subsidiary to generate new knowledge in the service industry. Moreover, we advance one step forward, by distinguishing the different levels of influence of the external and internal networks according to the type of innovation activity performed by the subsidiary. Close relationships with the local actors boost the subsidiary competence-creating activity, while nearby relations with the headquarters and peer subsidiaries within the internal network, similarly, improve both innovation activities. This means that the competence-exploiting activities, that usually generate more incremental types of innovation outputs, can be sustained mostly with the knowledge coming from the internal networks. In contrast, the competence-creating activities call for embedding in the external and internal networks in order to gather new knowledge and combine it with the company's resident knowledge. This might be explained by the idiosyncratic nature of the service firms such as, the inseparability of production and consumption, as well as their customizability to clients where the proximity to and contact with the market acquires special relevance, making external embeddedness strategically important for radical innovation.

Despite its contribution, this research is not exempt of limitations. The complex nature of service offerings is in itself part of the main limitation. Service characteristics are specific and diverse and although some aspects of services seem to be universal, others present differential traits that can bias the analysis. Regardless of the truly relevance of our results for the services in general, there is the possibility that, depending on the specific type of service offered, the effects found may not be applied or may be partially applied. Future research can analyze whether these research findings are valid across other types of industries and the extent of the difference regarding the results from the service sector.

Acknowledgements

Research has benefitted from public research project Spanish Project PGC201S8-093971-B-I00 granted by the Ministry of Science and Innovation Programme for Knowledge Generation, funded by MCIU/AEI/FEDER, UE.

References

Achcaoucaou, F., & Miravitlles, P. (2021). Dual Embeddedness as a determinant of competence-creating subsidiaries: A dynamic reinforcing spiral. EIBA conference, Madrid, Spain.

Achcaoucaou, F., Miravitlles, P., & León-Darder, F. (2017). Do we really know the predictors of competence-creating R&D subsidiaries? Uncovering the mediation of dual network embeddedness. *Technological Forecasting and Social Change*, *116*, 181–195.

Alam, I. (2011). Process of customer interaction during new service development in an emerging country. *The Service Industries Journal*, *31*(16), 2741–2756.

Almeida, P., & Phene, A. (2004). Subsidiaries and knowledge creation: The influence of the MNC and host country on innovation. *Strategic Management Journal*, *25*, 847–864.

Andersson, U., Forsgren, M., & Holm, U. (2002). The strategic impact of external networks: Subsidiary performance and competence development in the multinational corporation. *Strategic Management Journal*, *23*, 979–996.

Astley, W. G., & Sachdeva, P. S. (1984). Structural sources of intraorganizational: Power: A theoretical synthesis. *Academy of Management Review*, *9*(1), 104–113.

Becker, J. M., Klein, K., & Wetzels, M. (2012). Hierarchical latent variable models in PLS-SEM: Guidelines for using reflective-formative type models. *Long Range Planning*, *45*(5–6), 359–394.

Boddewyn, J. J., Halbrich, M. B., & Perry, A.C. (1986). Service Multinationals: Conceptualization, measurement and theory. *Journal of International Business Studies,* 17 (3), Fall 1986, 41–53.

Campbell, A., & Verbeke, A. (1994). The globalization of service multinationals. *Long Range Planning,* 27(2), 95–102.

Cantwell, J., & Mudambi, R. (2005). MNE competence creating subsidiary mandates. *Strategic Management Journal,* 26(12), 1109–1128.

Carmines, E. G., & Zeller, R. A. (1979). *Reliability and validity assessment.* California: Sage Publications.

Chin, W. W. (1998). The partial least squares approach to structural equation modelling. In A. Marcoulides (Ed.), *Modern methods for business research* (pp. 295–336). New Jersey: Lawrence Erlbaum Associates Publisher.

Chin, W. W., & Newsted, P. R. (1999). Structural equation modeling analysis with small samples using partial least squares. In R. H. Hoyle (Ed.), *Statistical strategies for small sample research* (pp. 307–341). California: Sage Publications.

Ciabuschi, F., Holm, U., & Martín, O. M. (2014). Dual embeddedness, influence and performance of innovating subsidiaries in the multinational corporation. *International Business Review,* 23(5), 897–909.

Collinson, S. C., & Wang, R. (2012). The evolution of innovation capability in multinational enterprise subsidiaries: Dual network embeddedness and the divergence of subsidiary specialisation in Taiwan. *Research Policy,* 41, 1501–1518.

Cowden, B. J., & Alhorr, H. S. (2013, August 9th). Disruptive innovation in multinational entreprises. *Multinational Business Review,* 21(4), 358–371.

Dellestrand, H. (2011). Subsidiary embeddedness as a determinant of divisional headquarters involvement in innovation transfer processes. *Journal of International Management,* 17, 229–242.

den Hertog, P. (2000). Knowledge-intensive business services as co-producers of innovation. *International Journal of Innovation Management,* 4(4), 491–528.

Dijkstra, T., & Henseler, J. (2015). Consistent partial least squares path modeling. *MIS Quarterly,* 39(2), 297–316.

Falk, R. F., & Miller, N. B. (1992). *A primer for soft modelling.* Ohio: University of Akron Press.

Fornell, C., & Larcker, D. F. (1981). Evaluating structural equation models with unobservable variables and measurement error. *Journal of Marketing Research,* 18(1), 39–50.

Forsgren, M. (2008). *Theories of the multinational firm.* Uppsala: Edward Elgar Publishing.

Frenz, M. Girardone, C., & Ietto-Gillies, G. (2005). Multinationality matters in innovation: The case of the UK financial services. *Industry and Innovation,* 12(1), 65–92.

Frost, T. S. (2001). The geographic sources of foreign subsidiaries' innovations. *Strategic Management Journal,* 22(2), 101–123.

Geisser, S. (1974). A predictive approach to the random effects model. *Biometrika,* 61(1), 101–107.

Ghoshal, S., & Bartlett, C. A. (1990). The multinational corporation as an interorganizational network. *The Academy of Management Review,* 15(4), 603–625.

Gulati, R., Nohria, N., & Zaheer, A. (2000). Strategic networks. *Strategic Management Journal,* 21(3), 203–215.

Hair, J. F., Sarstedt, M., Ringle, C. M., & Mena, J. A. (2012). An assessment of the use of partial least squares structural equation modeling in marketing research. *Journal of the Academy of Marketing Science,* 40, 414–433.

Hallin, C., Holm, U., & Deo Sharma, D. (2010). Embeddedness of innovation receivers in the multinational corporation: Effects on business performance. *International Business Review,* 20, 362–373.

Henseler, J., Ringle, C., & Sarstedt, M. (2015). A new criterion for assessing discriminant validity in variance-based structural equation modeling. *Journal of the Academy of Marketing Science,* 43, 115–135.

Hosseini, M., & Dadfar, H. (2012). Network-based theories and internationalization of firms: Applications to empirical studies. *The Business and Management Review*, *3*(1), 182–191.

Johnston, S., & Paladino, A. (2007). Knowledge management and involvement in innovations in MNC subsidiaries. *Management International Review*, *47*(2), 281–302.

Knudsen, E., & Lien, L. (2015). Hire, fire, or train: Innovation and human capital responses to recessions. *Strategic Management Journal*, *9*(4), 313–330.

Kogut, B., & Zander, U. (1993). Knowledge of the firm and the evolutionary theory of the multinational corporation. *Journal of International Business Studies*, *24*(4), 625–645.

Kostova, T., & Roth, K. (2002). Adoption of an organizational practice by subsidiaries of multinational corporations: Institutional and relational effects. *Academy of Management Journal*, *45*(1), 215–233.

Liang, F. H., & Xu, D. (2011). Knowledge network and innovation activities by MNC subsidiaries: The effects of internal and external knowledge resources. In *IEEE Int'l Technology Management Conference* (pp. 388–394). New Jersey: Rutgers Business School.

Miozzo, M., & Yamin, M. (2012). Institutional and sectoral determinants of headquarters subsidiary relationships: A Study of UK Service Multinationals in China, Korea, Brazil and Argentina. *Long Range Planning*, *45*, 16–40.

Najafi-Tavani, Z., Giroud, A., & Sinkovics, R. R. (2012). Knowledge-intensive business services: Does dual embeddedness matter? *The Service Industries Journal*, *32*(10), 1691–1705.

Narula, R. (2014). Exploring the paradox of competence-creating subsidiaries: Balancing bandwidth and dispersion in MNEs. *Long Range Planning*, *47*(1–2), 4–15.

Nunnally, J. C., & Bernstein, I. H. (1994). *Psychometric theory*. New York, NY: McGraw-Hill.

Phene, A., & Almeida, P. (2008). Innovation in multinational subsidiaries: The role of knowledge assimilation and subsidiary capabilities. *Journal of International Business Studies*, *39*(5), 901–919.

Reinartz, W., Haenlein, M., & Henseler, J. (2009). An empirical comparison of the efficacy of covariance-based and variance-based SEM. *International Journal of Research in Marketing*, *26*(4), 332–344.

Ringle, C. M., Wende, S., & Becker, J.-M. (2015). "SmartPLS 3." Boenningstedt: SmartPLS GmbH. *Journal of Service Science and Management*, *10*(3), 32–49.

Rugman, A. M., & Verbeke, A. (2001). Subsidiary-specific advantages in multinational enterprises. *Strategic Management Journal*, *22*(3), 237–250.

RusHolts. (2017). McDonald's McCafe History – The Story of Success. Retrieved from https://retailhoreca.net/mccafe-mcdonalds-history

Schmid, S., & Gombert, A. (2018). McDonald's: Is the fast food icon reaching the limits of growth? In S. Schmid (Ed.), *Internationalization of business* (pp. 155–171). Cham: Springer International Publishing AG.

Sofka, W., Shehu, E., & de Faria, P. (2014). Multinational subsidiary knowledge protection – Do mandates and clusters matter? *Research Policy*, *43*(8), 1320–1333.

Stone, M. (1974). Cross-validatory choice and assessment of statistical predictions. *Journal of the Royal Statistical Society*, *36*(2), 111–147.

Wetzels, M., Odekerken-Schroder, G. and Van Oppen, C. (2009) Using PLS Path Modeling for Assessing Hierarchical Construct Models: Guidelines and Empirical Illustration. *MIS Quarterly*, *33*, 177–195.

Chapter 10

The Collective Entrepreneurial Process: From Public Entrepreneurship to Collective Action for the Common Good

Lizbeth Arroyo and Jaume Valls-Pasola

Abstract

In this chapter, the authors explore collective entrepreneurship through the lens of how public entrepreneurship boosts collective action towards a common good. The role of public entrepreneurs and the collaborative nature of innovation community members evidence a collective action that pursues a socio-political change. Through a case study contextualized during the COVID-19 pandemic crisis in Spain, the authors explore how a public entrepreneur triggered a collective action that led to the creation of the innovation community: The Coronavirus makers. This collaborative network groups more than 20,000 researchers, developers, and engineers. They altruistically put their knowledge and resources at the service of the community to provide solutions for one of the healthcare system's main problems at that time – the shortage of medical supplies to cope with the increasing number of COVID-19 cases. The collective action of the Coronavirus makers has impacted the health and well-being fields, the community and the values that should define social change and allow the construction of a more open, equitable and sustainable society. Potentially, our findings confirm that collective entrepreneurship derives from a function of collective action.

Keywords: Collective entrepreneurship; public entrepreneurship; collective action; innovation community; collaborative networks; wellbeing

Collective Entrepreneurship in the Contemporary European Services Industries:
A Long Term Approach, 153–168
Copyright © 2023 by Emerald Publishing Limited
All rights of reproduction in any form reserved
doi:10.1108/978-1-80117-950-820231010

1. Introduction

In early March 2020, the media in Spain initiated discussions regarding a potential healthcare system collapse due to the accelerated rise in hospital admissions of COVID-19 patients requiring admission to Intensive Care Units (ICUs). This situation resulted in a lack of available resources within the healthcare system, with particular concern over the scarcity of ventilators. Concern among the medical community, scientists and public institutions was growing. By March 12, the process had accelerated, 84 people had died, and almost 3,000 were infected. In that second week of March, a group of doctors, engineers, entrepreneurs and makers began to organize themselves through social networks and to develop one of the largest collective innovation projects in Spain, the Coronavirus Makers community.

With the support of foundations, institutions and companies, the collaborative network Coronavirus Makers integrated more than 20,000 researchers, developers and engineers, who altruistically put their knowledge and resources at the service of the community to provide a solution to one of the main problems faced by the healthcare system at that time, the shortage of medical supplies due to the increase in cases of COVID-19. The aim was to provide a certain type of equipment that was feasible for 'maker' manufacturing: visors, masks, electro valves or respirators were some of the designs and prototypes that the members of the network were able to generate in a brief period.

In this context, the entrepreneurial phenomena go beyond wealth creation; it is more about advancing social aims. The pandemic triggered actions by social agents and organizations to address the situation. Although the established pieces of literature on collective action (Kuhnert, 2001; Olson, 1971), entrepreneurship (Montgomery, Dacin, & Dacin, 2012; Roberts, 1992, 2006; Schoonhoven & Romanelli, 2001), and the maker movement as an innovation community (Camarinha-Matos, 2007; Harhoff & Lakhani, 2016) address them as a mechanism for social progress, it is worth asking how the collective entrepreneurial process involved multiple groups in pursuing the common good?

This chapter explores collective entrepreneurship through the lens of how public entrepreneurship boosts collective action towards a common good. The role of public entrepreneurs and the collaborative nature of innovation community members evidence a collective action that pursues a socio-political change. To this end, a case study has been designed (Einsenhardt, 1989; Einsenhardt & Graebner, 2007; Yin, 2013). A single case has been selected to examine this phenomenon in greater depth: the Coronavirus Makers community. A unique programme that arose from the maker community in Spain was set up to respond to the specific needs of the health system in the context of the COVID-19 health emergency. This research was based on analyzing, on one side, an in-depth interview with one of the founders of the network; on the other side, a total of 6 original tweets, including 419 answers.

The main findings offer insights framed in a health crisis about the convergence between collective entrepreneurship, the public entrepreneurship and collective action. Moreover, it describes an overview of the collective entrepreneurial process and the role of public entrepreneurs as makers. The chapter is organized to offer a synthesis of the theoretical framework concerning public entrepreneurship, collective entrepreneurship and innovation communities. The methodology follows this section, results and discussion are presented, and the analysis closes with some concluding remarks.

2. Theoretical Framework

This section presents a basic overview of the literature on public entrepreneurship and collective action to extend our view of collective entrepreneurship. Thus, these topics are relevant for analyzing the Coronavirus Makers network presented in Section 3.

2.1. Collective Action and Entrepreneurship

The new wave of entrepreneurship researchers is increasingly exploring a myriad of emerging directions that explore the idea that entrepreneurship derives as a function of collective action (Schoonhoven & Romanelli, 2001). Based on the Olsons' dilemma of collective action:

> Unless the number of individuals is quite small, or unless there is coercion or some other special device to make individuals act in their common interest, rational, self-interested individuals will not act to achieve their common or group interests. (Olson, 1971 [1965], p. 2)

Authors refer to entrepreneurship as the collective initiatives to affect change concerning regional and local development, public policy, and social or cultural norms (Burress & Cook, 2009). Collective action engaged by groups can create commons to respond to economic, socio-cultural and environmental stress through creating organizational forms for providing goods and services (Meyer, 2020).

Accordingly to Roberts (2006), collective entrepreneurship draws on the process in which multiple people get involved and shape an idea through initiation, design, and implementation into a full-blown innovation. In the same line, Silva and Rodrigues (2005) highlight that the collective nature of this type of entrepreneurship is connected to the fact that these actions concern sets or clusters of firms with similar productive interests and public and semi-public agents.

Following both conceptualizations, collective action is essential for acquiring and deploying resources from multiple actors through various activities and strategies to share ideas, mobilize supporters, bring together diverse viewpoints, and collaborate to drive change (Meyer, 2020; Montgomery et al., 2012). Successful change also relies heavily on collaboration, partnerships, coalitions, alliances, and other forms of collective action (Maguire, Hardy, & Lawrence, 2004).

2.2. Public Entrepreneurship

In her work, Roberts (1992, pp. 57–58) defines public entrepreneurship 'as the generation, design, and implementation of an innovative idea into public sector practices acknowledges three general phases or sub-processes to the overall process: creation, design, and implementation' (Fig. 5).

Creation involves the generation of an innovative idea and associating that new idea with some need, problem, or concern. Design begins the developmental activities to transform the idea into reality. Implementation begins the reality testing of the innovative idea as it has emerged from the design process (Roberts, 1992).

Public entrepreneurs are representatives of government agencies at various levels of government. These entrepreneurs are generally characterized by being charismatic innovators, possessing good networking skills and being motivated by their willingness to invest their resources (time, reputation, and/or knowledge) (Meijerink & Huitema, 2010).

2.3. Innovation Communities and Makers Community

According to Lakhani (2016), the innovation community emerges from groups of people united through a common technology or used condition. They connect either online or physically to share willingly and freely their problems and solutions to the various use conditions of that technology. When specific results are obtained, the community is committed to sharing and achieving a collective outcome that leads to an operational solution.

In this line, a maker community describes a broad community built on an individual's ability to be a creator of new technologies and practices (Morreale, Moro, Chamberlain, Benford, & McPherson, 2017; Papavlasopoulou, Giannakos, & Jaccheri, 2017), primarily 3D (Dufva, 2017; Papavlasopoulou et al., 2017), that are developed working collaboratively depending on community members (Morreale et al., 2017).

Communities democratize innovation by aggregating inputs from different participants to address a given problem in a shared way. With technological progress, innovation communities have found means for self-organization. Virtual organizations are defined as a set of individuals or groups that are geographically dispersed, agile, temporarily or permanently associated, that pursue a common goal, and that communicate, coordinate and produce through the use of technologies (Ahuja & Carley, 1999; Camarinha-Matos, 2007; Meléndez, Obra, & Rosa, 2003; Serrano & Fischer, 2007).

They are characterized by informal communication through information technologies, such as virtual meetings, e-mail or messaging services; the absence of shared physical space among members; no organizational routines or non-routine activities and challenges in resource management (Ahuja & Carley, 1999).

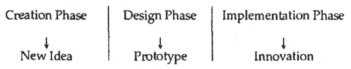

Fig. 5.   Phases of the Entrepreneurial Process Based on Roberts (1992).

3. Methodology

This chapter aims to explore collective entrepreneurship as a mechanism for social change. Specifically, it draws on to identify how collective action drives innovation to pursue the common good. To this end, a case study has been designed (Einsenhardt, 1989; Einsenhardt & Graebner, 2007; Yin, 2013). A single case has been selected to examine this phenomenon in greater depth: the Coronavirus Makers community.

The Coronavirus Makers collaborative network was selected because it groups more than 20,000 researchers, developers, and engineers. They altruistically put their knowledge and resources at the service of the community to provide solutions for one of the healthcare system's main problems at that time – the shortage of medical supplies to cope with the increasing number of COVID-19 cases. The idea was to design and manufacture a type of personal protection equipment (PPE) feasible for the maker network: mainly visors, masks and ear guards. But there were other remarkable products, especially a ventilator designed in a record time of fifteen days.

The primary source of data for this chapter was the open-ended interview. The people interviewed were one of the Coronavirus Makers movement's leading promoters, Esther Borao. The first interview was held on 24 July 2020, at the site of ITAINNOVA, Aragon's Technological Institute, belonging to the Government of Aragon,[1] and lasted 105 minutes. The interviews were structured around four theoretical categories, emphasizing the emergence of the Coronavirus makers in Spain.

However, once the data analysis stage started emerging, the need to include more information. In this case, it was identified that a critical milestone in the Coronavirus makers foundation took place on Twitter. This platform is emerging as a relevant channel for communication. Tweet content can be analyzed to understand conversation topics, individual or organization tweeting characteristics, and public beliefs and opinions about a specific topic (Kim et al., 2013).

A total of six original tweets of Jorge Barrero, Director of Fundación Cotec, were analyzed, including 419 answers (Table 13). It also used secondary sources (news in national newspapers, podcasts, web pages, etc.) to contextualize the case. These sources enabled us to triangulate to build more robust interpretations (Yin, 1984).

Data analysis included narrative analysis and first-order and second-order constructs (Gioia, Corley, & Hamilton, 2013). It was a narrative analysis to identify the main elements of the interviewees' narratives related to the emergence of the innovation communities and how collective entrepreneurship is related to public entrepreneurship and collective action. The following section will report and discuss the findings (Table 13).

---

[1] During this interview, all safety measures derived from the pandemic were followed, such as social distancing and the use of masks.

Table 13.   Tweets Associated with the Coronavirus Maker Foundation.

Name	Username	Retweets	Comments	Favourites	Date	Tweet Text
Jorge Barrero	Jorge_ barrero_f	7,001	355	13,117	12/03/20 20:25:21	Esta mañana 25 médicos, ingenieros, emprendedores, makers hemos creado un grupo de WhatsApp para pensar posibles soluciones baratas y rápidas de ventilación de pacientes. Ahora descubro no estamos solos... nos sumamos a Open Source Ventilator Project! #cheapVentilators
Jorge Barrero	Jorge_ barrero_f	132	15	538	12/03/20 20:46:20	Desde mañana @Cotec_Innova se echa a un lado para que ceder liderazgo "ingenieril" a @tecnalia. Gracias @Inaki_Sanse @amcliment @elsatch @MTurrado y resto de voluntarios. Ha sido un placer provocar y catalizar vuestra maravillosa reacción. En sólo 12 horas habéis hecho magia. ⊙
Jorge Barrero	Jorge_ barrero_f	154	11	535	12/03/20 22:43:58	Todo surge de leer posibles problemas de suministros en respiradores de alta tecnología. Ojalá no pase, pero si pasara, queremos ofrecer planos "open source" de dispositivos más sencillos que pudieran fabricarse rápido y de forma distribuida usando - por ejemplo- impresión 3D.

Jorge Barrero	Jorge_barrero_f	144	7	625	12/03/20 22:47:39	Lo que empezó como un simple chat a tres bandas hace 10 horas es ahora un grupo que suma know how de neumología, electromedicina, impresión 3D, enfermería, electrónica. Entre sus miembros gente que hoy está atendiendo enfermos en la UCI y diseñadores e ingenieros lejos de allí.
Jorge Barrero	Jorge_barrero_f	84	3	476	12/03/20 22:52:15	En tiempo real se transmiten necesidades y propuestas de la trinchera a la retaguardia y a partir de mañana tomará forma el proyecto. No sé lo que saldrá de todo ésto, pero estoy realmente desbordado, emocionado y orgulloso. Cosas parecidas pasan en otros sitios: venceremos.
Jorge Barrero	Jorge_barrero_f	198	28	327	13/03/20 11:46:28	Gracias a todos los que habéis compartido esta iniciativa. Es increíble sentir esta energía sobre todo en días como hoy. El colectivo ya tiene nombre "Ayuda Innovadora a la Respiración". Podéis seguir @AIRE_Covid19 si queréis participar o estar informados. #cheapventilators

4. Findings

After a process of iterative data analysis, it identified that collective entrepreneurship draws on the leadership of public entrepreneurs that trigger the collective action of multiple people concerned to innovate to tackle common social problems. The structure of the findings section illustrates the common ground among collective entrepreneurship, public entrepreneurship, and collective action, which allows understanding of the collective entrepreneurial process.

4.1. Collective Entrepreneurship, Public Entrepreneurship and Collective Action

The foundation of the Coronavirus makers community is evidence of the close relationship between collective entrepreneurship, public entrepreneurship, and collective action. This convergence depicted in Fig. 6 shows that collective entrepreneurship is strongly related to public entrepreneurship (Schoonhoven & Romanelli, 2001).

Firstly, as Silva and Rodrigues (2005) propose, collective entrepreneurship involves different groups with similar productive interests, including public agents. Given the nature of the contextual factors, the COVID-19 health crisis of 2020, from the public sphere, different public servers (mainly executive positions in research institutes and NGOs) began to seek solutions to attack the lack of health materials, especially artificial respirators and personal protective equipment.

The first identified call to the maker community was launched by Jorge Barrero, Director of the COTEC Foundation (Fig. 7). By his profile, Jorge represents a public entrepreneur manifesting similar characteristics found in innovators in economic sectors (Roberts, 1992). He generated innovative ideas (administrative and technical) to bring solutions to the health crisis (Meijerink & Huitema, 2010; Roberts, 1992).

As Meyer (2020) observed in their study, entrepreneurs mobilize community members. Jorge evidences the public entrepreneur's leadership role in the collaborative initiative's foundation in this tweet. He initiated a collective action, taking the role of professional organizer leading the organization of the first WhatApp

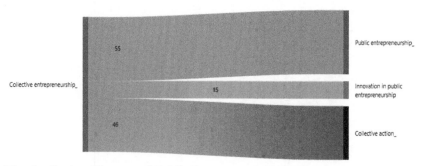

Fig. 6.   Sankey Diagram of Public Entrepreneurship, Collective Entrepreneurship, and Collective Action.

Jorge Barrero
@Jorge_barrero_f

Esta mañana 25 médicos, ingenieros, emprendedores, makers hemos creado un grupo de WhatsApp para pensar posibles soluciones baratas y rápidas de ventilación de pacientes. Ahora descubro no estamos solos... nos sumamos a Open Source Ventilator Project! #cheapVentilators
twitter.com/ColinJ_Keogh/s...

Este Tweet fue eliminado por su autor. Más información

9:25 p. m. · 12 mar. 2020 · Twitter for Android

7.001 Retweets   **597** Tweets citados   **13,1 mil** Me gusta

Fig. 7.   First Tweet to Call on the Maker Community.

group of makers to develop cheap and fast patient ventilation solutions. These findings support the idea that collective entrepreneurship derives from a function of collective action (Meyer, 2020; Schoonhoven & Romanelli, 2001).

In the thread triggered by this tweet, other profiles of public servers were identified, such as Esther Borao, recognized as one of the founders of Coronavirus makers. Esther Borao, Director of ITAINNOVA, declared herself a 'maker' and passionate about technology, innovation, and education. At the same time, she has an entrepreneurial background (Borao interview, 24 July 2020).

Esther reported that, from her position, on 12 March 2020, she discussed with Raul Oliván, Director General of Open Government and Social Innovation of the Government of Aragon, the possibility of generating a sort of 'Wallapop' platform to connect people with resources and people in need (Borao interview, 24 July 2020). Finally, Esther created a Telegram group that reached in the next 48 hours more than 900 participants (Figure 8); supporting the relevance of public entrepreneurs' innovations to propose new organizational forms and technical solutions and their capacity to mobilize resources and innovation (Roberts, 1992).

Esther Borao @EstherBorao · 12 mar. 2020
En respuesta a @Jorge_barrero_f
Hola Jorge!! Justo había creado un grupo de telegram para aportar lo que pudiéramos como centro tecnológico en Aragon y comunidad maker, cómo podemos ayudar?

t.me
Join group chat on Telegram

Fig. 8.   Twitter as a Platform for Collective Action for Self-Organization.

Both initiatives, the WhatsApp group, created by Jorge and the Telegram group created by Esther, converged on the same communication channel, Twitter, that for a first moment, worked as the organizational platforms used by these public entrepreneurs to call to action and promote the self-organization of the maker community.

During all that 12 March 2020, makers responded to the call. Multiple experts, NGOs, and public institutions are involved in the emerging initiative (Fig. 9). A cross-sector partnership to create, what will shortly be called Coronavirus makers, was consolidated (Harting, Kunst, Kwan, & Stronks, 2011; Maguire et al., 2004). The partnership's success could be thanks to Jorge and Esther's network capacity building (Meijerink & Huitema, 2010).

Also, the foundation of Coronavirus makers evidences a similar path. The pattern is like the one described by Roberts (1992) for public entrepreneurship. In the next section, we develop the process of what we assume to be the collective entrepreneurial process.

4.2. The Collective Entrepreneurial Process: From Public Entrepreneurship to Collective Action for the Common Good

In her work, Roberts (1992, 2006) proposed that collective and public entrepreneurship follow a similar process to deliver an innovative idea: initiation, design, and implementation (Table 14). Coronavirus makers' lifecycle analysis is intrinsically related to outside events, the public entrepreneurs' leadership, and community members' actions (Arroyo, Sanchez-Asin, Valls-Pasola, & Hormiga, 2021).

The creation phase initiates when contextual factors force the collective action. On 12 March 2020, a group of public entrepreneurs sought to address the global health crisis, which put health systems at risk. Innovative ideas emerged to tackle the lack of health equipment in Spain.

Public entrepreneurs opened the full-blown innovation and took the role of professional organizers. New administrative ideas, such as technical and

Jorge Barrero @Jorge_barrero_f · 12 mar. 2020
Esta mañana 25 médicos, ingenieros, emprendedores, makers hemos creado un grupo de WhatsApp para pensar posibles soluciones baratas y rápidas de ventilación de pacientes. Ahora descubro no estamos solos... nos sumamos a Open Source Ventilator Project! #cheapVentilators
twitter.com/ColinJ_Keogh/s...

Este Tweet fue eliminado por su autor. Más información

○ 355   ⟲ 7.591   ♡ 13,1 mil   ↥

camcar_soft
@camcar_soft

En respuesta a @Jorge_barrero_f y @Obijuan_cube

Contad con mi Impresora 3D. Llamamiento a
@OSHWDem @CloneWarsRepRap

10:13 a. m. · 13 mar. 2020 · Twitter for Android

Fig. 9.   Call to Action and Networking Capacity Building.

organizational forms, emerged. Public entrepreneurs mobilized the Makers community using different digital platforms, such as Twitter, WhatsApp and Telegram. Participation in maker forums was fundamental to setting up and centralizing communication channels for common-good resource management.

Once the call to action was published on Twitter, the design phases began. Makers were encouraged to self-organize the nascent network. During this phase, plans were formulated to move the innovative ideas offered by the community to something tangible. The common resources were put in common. The community members were willing to contribute with time, knowledge, and material resources (e.g. 3D printers).

Finally, on 13 March 2020, CoronavirusMaker was structured as a collaborative network (Camarinha-Matos, 2007), consolidated by the implementation phase AIRE emerged as the unified platform to manage the designs based on the shared knowledge and continuing with the maker community management.

Table 14.   Data Structure.

1st Order	2nd Order	Aggregate Dimensions
* Covid19 health crisis as a global societal challenge * Innovative ideas needed to solve the lack of health equipment in Spain	Contextual factors as an external force driving collective entrepreneurship	*Creation*
* Initiating collective action * Innovation origination * Mobilization of Makers community	Professional organizers	
* Setting up and centralizing communication channels for common-goods resources management	New administrative idea-organizational forms	
* Makers community autonomy * Bottom-up actions * Organizational challenges * Computer-based commons * Adoption of innovative solutions all around the world	Self-organization	*Design*
* New technological idea designs based on shared knowledge * Consolidation of a unified platform	Delivering prototypes for the common good	*Implementation*

4.3. Public Entrepreneur and Maker: A Shared Motivation to Act

As observed, as public entrepreneurs, Jorge and Esther demonstrate a common ground with the maker community. Arroyo et al. (2021) identified this link, describing the existence of different makers' profiles and roles. Their study observed a maker that plays the role of a 'strategic facilitator' characterized by their capacity to mobilize the community and count on institutional support.

Additionally, the findings show that both public entrepreneurs and makers share their common willingness to invest their resources (time, reputation, and/ or knowledge) (Meijerink & Huitema, 2010) to contribute to solving and having an impact on common problems (Meyer, 2020; Montgomery et al., 2012). This motivation, as observed, is driven by a sense of solidarity and altruism (Meyer, 2020) and executed under principles of flexibility, adaptability and highly entrepreneurial orientation (Arroyo et al., 2021) (Table 15).

Table 15.   Commonalities Between Public Entrepreneurs and Makers.

Common Ground Between Public Entrepreneurs and Makers	Excerpt
Contributing to solving and having an impact on common problems	*[42:20 ¶ 323 en 200731 ESTHER BORAO]* "The main benefit that stands out is having been part of a collective experience in which, in an altruistic way, they contributed their grain of sand to the solution of a humanitarian crisis of great dimensions, which was unfolding at home, threatening everyone, family, friends, loved ones?"
Altruism and solidarity as a basis for the collective action	*[42:33 ¶ 330 en 200731 ESTHER BORAO]* "The main attraction of the initiative lies in the sense of belonging to a collective that is working for the common good, in a disinterested way and facing a problem that exceeds the possibilities of solution through the usual mechanisms (market, administration, public and private services, etc.)."
Willingness to share their resources: time, knowledge, material resources, reputation, network	*[42:27 ¶ 326 en 200731 ESTHER BORAO]* "The community has reached an enormous size and involves both people who can contribute their knowledge (doctors, psychologists, engineers, scientists) and people who, having heard about the initiative, have wanted to contribute what they had: time, materials, equipment, etc.

Table 15. (*Continued*)

Common Ground Between Public Entrepreneurs and Makers	Excerpt
	[44:6 ¶ 18 en tweets6 *320ab7864a3b-Jorge_barrero* *_f-1238199423403950080]* @Jorge_barrero_f Hola Jorge!! Justo había creado un grupo de telegram para aportar lo que pudiéramos como centro tecnológico en Aragón y comunidad maker, cómo podemos ayudar? https://t.co/eGOZpeOxns
	[44:14 ¶ 42 en tweets *6320ab7864a3b-Jorge_barrero* *_f-1238199423403950080]* @Jorge_barrero_f @adrianibanez Si necesitáis un entorno web para descargas o bases de datos. Os monto uno rápido.

Note: Original data is in Spanish; excerpts were translated, assuring language accuracy.

5. Discussion

The main goal of this chapter was to explore collective entrepreneurship, identifying how collection action drives innovation to pursue the common good. Analyzing the foundation of the Coronavirus makers case, it identified the leadership role of public entrepreneurs, the collective entrepreneurial process and the common ground between public entrepreneurs and makers.

The founding of Coronavirus makers illustrated Olson's dilemma of collective action. The COVID-19 health crisis in 2020 cracked the national sanitary systems and pushed societies to act; the public entrepreneurs and makers community demonstrated their interest in the common good, collective responsibility and social change. Consequently, collective entrepreneurship relies on actions based on the values of altruism, solidarity, and collaboration.

This collective entrepreneurial process, in particular, is created from public entrepreneurs' leadership and institutional legitimacy. Although several individuals designed their initiatives, the 'magic' happened thanks to the call to action made by public servants that mobilized more than +900 people during the first 48 hours.

Fundamentally, the success of Coronavirus makers as the result of a collective entrepreneurial process was to count on public entrepreneurs with a maker background. Their individual ability to be a creator of new technologies and practices, the networks capacity building and the willingness of the members to contribute their resources to provide a solution to the crisis.

Despite the complexity of the context in Spain in March 2020: health restrictions and home confinement, public entrepreneurs found in virtual platforms such as Twitter, WhatsApp, or Telegram became the best communication channel to coordinate the transformation of innovative ideas into reality and to manage the common shared knowledge.

The advantage of the community approach is that not all community members have to solve all the problems posed by a given technology; instead, they share tasks. Different members solve micro problems or local problems and then share them with the rest of the community. In short, communities serve to address innovation problems in which individuals (members) focus on specializing in specific areas and in which value is generated by aggregating collective work.

6. Conclusions

This chapter has analyzed a unique network: the Coronavirus Makers network, which was created to respond to the health system's needs in the context of the COVID-19 health emergency. This network has become a successful initiative thanks to its flexibility and capacity to respond to the slower pace associated with the inertia of large organizations or government entities.

It evidenced a relationship between collective entrepreneurship, the public entrepreneurship and collective action. In particular, collective entrepreneurship is strongly related to public entrepreneurs. Contrasting with the individualistic narratives associated with being an entrepreneur, collective entrepreneurship is a mechanism to tackle social challenges. Public entrepreneurs, as makers, demonstrated an active role in the foundation of innovation communities. In addition, makers can take on one or more functions depending on their roles within an innovation community and their versatile profiles.

The implications of this study are practical. The analysis highlights the importance of public administrations in identifying maker profiles within their organizations. It is suggested that encouraging the maker profile within organizations would entail potential benefits due to their relational capital. At the same time, they can also impact open innovation, institutional visibility and the encouragement of intrapreneurs.

As shown, a public entrepreneur with a maker profile can lead changes through collective innovative processes. It recommends fostering innovation capacity building based on training programs based on learning by experience, and learning by doing is recommended. In this sense, it is suggested that innovation communities, as strategic allies for public institutions, could help to maximize the social impact of policy making.

Acknowledgements

Research has benefitted from public research project Spanish Project PGC201S8-093971-B-I00 granted by the Ministry of Science and Innovation Programme for Knowledge Generation, funded by MCIU/AEI/FEDER, UE.

References

Ahuja, M. K., & Carley, K. M. (1999). Network structure in virtual organizations. *Organization Science, 10*(6), 741–757. doi:10.1287/orsc.10.6.741

Arroyo, L., Sanchez-Asin, J. J., Valls-Pasola, J., & Hormiga, E. (2021). The coronavirus makers network. Understanding the success of an innovation community facing COVID-19 in Spain. *Palgrave Studies in Governance, Leadership and Responsibility*, 15–36. doi:10.1007/978-3-030-73847-1_2/COVER

Burress, M. J., & Cook, M. L. (2009). A primer on collective entrepreneurship: A preliminary taxonomy. In *Aewp 2009-4* (Vol. 4, Issue 573). Retrieved from http://age consearch.umn.edu/bitstream/92628/2/aewp2009-4.pdf

Camarinha-Matos, L. M. (2007). Collaborative networked organizations in manufacturing. *IFAC Proceedings Volumes (IFAC-PapersOnline), 1*(PART 1), 187–198.

Dufva, T. S. (2017). Maker Movement creating knowledge through basic intention. *Techne Series – Research in Sloyd Education and Craft Science A, 24*(2), 129–141.

Eisenhardt, K. M. (1989). Building theories from case study research. *Academy of Management Review, 14*, 532–550.

Eisenhardt, K. M., & Graebner, M. E. (2007). Theory building from cases: Opportunities and challenges. *Academy of Management Journal, 50*(1), 25–32. https://doi.org/10.5465/AMJ.2007.24160888

Gioia, D. A., Corley, K. G., & Hamilton, A. L. (2013). Seeking qualitative rigor in inductive research: Notes on the Gioia methodology. *Organizational Research Methods, 16*(1), 15–31.

Harhoff, D., & Lakhani, K. (2016). *Revolutionizing innovation: Users, communities, and open innovation* (p. 577). Cambridge: The MIT Press.

Harting, J., Kunst, A. E., Kwan, A., & Stronks, K. (2011). A "health broker" role as a catalyst of change to promote health: An experiment in deprived Dutch neighbourhoods. *Health Promotion International, 26*(1), 65–81. doi:10.1093/heapro/daq069

Kim, A. E., Hansen, H. M., Murphy, J., Richards, A. K., Duke, J., & Allen, J. A. (2013). Methodological considerations in analyzing Twitter Data. *Journal of the National Cancer Institute Monographs, 47*(47), 140–146. doi:10.1093/jncimonographs/lgt026

Kuhnert, S. (2001). An evolutionary theory of collective action: Schumpeterian entrepreneurship for the common good. *Constitutional Political Economy, 12*, 13–29.

Maguire, S., Hardy, C., & Lawrence, T. B. (2004). Institutional entrepreneurship in emerging fields: Hiv/Aids treatment advocacy in Canada. *Academy of Management Journal, 47*(5), 657–679. doi:10.2307/20159610

Meijerink, S., & Huitema, D. (2010). Policy entrepreneurs and change strategies: Lessons from sixteen case studies of water transitions around the globe. *Ecology and Society, 15*(2), 17. doi:10.5751/ES-03509-150221

Meléndez, P., Obra, Á., & Rosa, A. (2003). La Evolución de las formas organizativas de la estructura simple a la organización en red y virtual. *Investigaciones Europeas de Dirección y Economía de La Empresa, 9*(1994), 69–94.

Meyer, C. (2020). The commons: A model for understanding collective action and entrepreneurship in communities. *Journal of Business Venturing, 35*(5), 106034. doi:10.1016/j.jbusvent.2020.106034

Montgomery, A. W., Dacin, P. A., & Dacin, M. T. (2012). Collective social entrepreneurship: Collaboratively shaping social good. *Journal of Business Ethics, 111*(3), 375–388. doi:10.1007/s10551-012-1501-5

Morreale, F., Moro, G., Chamberlain, A., Benford, S., & McPherson, A. P. (2017). Building a maker community around an open hardware platform. In CHI 2017: ACM CHI Conference on Human Factors in Computing Systems, 6-11

May 2017, Denver, Colorado, USA, 2017-May (pp. 6948–6959). https://doi.org/10.1145/3025453.3026056

Olson, M. (1971). *The logic of collective action: Public goods and the theory of groups, second printing with new preface and appendix (Harvard Economic Studies)*. Working Paper, 186. https://www.hup.harvard.edu/catalog.php?isbn=9780674537514

Papavlasopoulou, S., Giannakos, M. N., & Jaccheri, L. (2017). Empirical studies on the Maker Movement, a promising approach to learning: A literature review. *Undefined, 18*, 57–78. doi:10.1016/J.ENTCOM.2016.09.002

Roberts, N. C. (1992). Roberts: Public entrepreneurship and innovation. *Review of Policy Research, 11*(1), 55–74. doi:10.1111/j.1541-1338.1992.tb00332.x

Roberts, N. C. (2006). Public entrepreneurship as social creativity. *World Futures, 62*(8), 595–609. doi:10.1080/02604020600948909

Schoonhoven, C. B., & Romanelli, E. (2001). *The entrepreneurship dynamic: Origins of entrepreneurship and the evolution of industries*. Stanford, CA: Stanford Business Books.

Serrano, V., & Fischer, T. (2007). Collaborative innovation in ubiquitous systems. *Journal of Intelligent Manufacturing, 18*(5), 599–615. doi:10.1007/s10845-007-0064-2

Silva, M., Rodrigues, H. (2005). Public-Private Partnerships and the Promotion of Collective Entrepreneurship. FEP Working Papers, 172.

Yin, R. K. (2013). *Case Study Research: Design and Methods*. Sage Publications, Thousand Oaks.

Index